AN UTTERLY EXASPERATED HISTORY OF MODERN BRITAIN

or 60 Years of Making the Same Stupid Mistakes as Always

AN UTTERLY EXASPERATED HISTORY OF MODERN BRITAIN

or 60 Years of Making the
Same Stupid Mistakes as Always

John O'Farrell

Doubleday

LONDON · TORONTO · SYDNEY · AUCKLAND · JOHANNESBURG

TRANSWORLD PUBLISHERS
61–63 Uxbridge Road, London W5 5SA
A Random House Group Company
www.rbooks.co.uk

First published in Great Britain
in 2009 by Doubleday
an imprint of Transworld Publishers

A CIP catalogue record for this book
is available from the British Library.

ISBNs 9780385616225 (cased)
9780385616232 (tpb)

Addresses for Random House Group Ltd companies outside the UK
can be found at: www.randomhouse.co.uk
The Random House Group Ltd Reg. No. 954009

The Random House Group Ltd makes every effort to ensure that the papers used in its books are
made from trees that have been legally sourced from well-managed and credibly certified forests.
Our paper procurement policy can be found at: www.randomhouse.co.uk/paper.htm

Typeset in 12/15.25pt Ehrhardt by
Falcon Oast Graphic Art Ltd.
Printed and bound in Great Britain by
CPI Mackays, Chatham, ME5 8TD

2 4 6 8 10 9 7 5 3 1

Mixed Sources
Product group from well-managed
forests and other controlled sources
www.fsc.org Cert no. TT-COC-2139
© 1996 Forest Stewardship Council
FSC

For Mark Burton

Contents

Introduction

Why write a funny history book? ~~Well the last one sold quite well and my accountant said~~ It's not simply a question of making difficult historical facts easier to digest; of producing a *Horrible History for Grown-ups* because humour is more fun than scholarly study. I believe that comedy is an appropriate prism through which to view the past because the British sense of humour has actually helped shape our island story.

As well as cheering people up through centuries of suffering and exploitation, irreverence, sarcasm and humour have been a distinctive feature of the British mindset down the centuries. Millions of Italians thought Mussolini was their national saviour. Millions of Germans were prepared to kill or be killed for Adolf Hitler. But how did the British people react to their own would-be führer Oswald Mosley? They laughed at him. They took the piss. They thought he was a joke. And it's hard to give the fascist salute to your 'master race' when lots of them are shouting, 'Oi, Oswald? Show us your sweaty armpits again!!' before falling about laughing. Whether it's the religious zealots of the Reformation or the Socialist Workers shouting outside the Arndale Centre, our instinct has always been to chuckle at their certainty, to be amused rather than angered. You'd never get a British kamikaze pilot. They'd just go, 'Absolutely, mate, I'm definitely going to deliberately crash my plane into that big ship . . .' and an hour later all the members of the Suicide Squad Union would be in the canteen having a cup of tea and saying, 'He's having a bloody laugh, he is. I'm not flying my plane into an enemy warship. It's against Health and Safety for a start.'

This book follows directly on from my epic bodice-ripper, *An Utterly Impartial History of Britain (or 2000 Years of Upper Class Idiots in Charge)*, although you don't have to have read that book to enjoy this one. Like that irreverent history, this account is, of course, anything but impartial. However, I won't give any hints as to my political leanings, though readers may pick up little clues along the way, such as when I write 'Mrs Thatcher! Boo!' or 'Nye Bevan! Hooray!'

The story begins with the end of the Second World War, with Britain bankrupt and massively in debt, and ends in 2008 with Britain . . . well, you get the general idea. For that extra sense of authenticity I decided to write and research this book in the appropriate manner for each decade. So the chapter on the late 1940s was painstakingly researched in a dusty old library with the assistance of a shy but beautiful librarian who wore glasses and consequently had never married. To write about the 1960s I just dropped a huge tab of LSD and bashed out a stream of consciousness on a portable typewriter. And for the twenty-first century with my deadline looming – well, I just found an undergraduate essay on the internet and cut and pasted the whole lot.

J O'F – Summer 2009

1

1945–1951

How a Labour government fundamentally changed Britain and the world for the better, but it was all rather spoiled by the absence of chocolate

April 1945. Much of Europe lay in ruins. Whole cities were reduced to rubble; roads, railway lines and bridges had been destroyed. Millions had lost their lives, the old world order had been shattered and Adolf Hitler, chief architect of this utter catastrophe, was now considering suicide. So it was a pretty tough call for the trainee counsellor manning the phones at the Samaritans that evening.

'You mustn't blame yourself for everything. Try and look on the positive side . . .'

'*There is no positive side*. I am personally responsible for the death of thirty million people; I have destroyed an entire continent and brought disaster and shame upon my own country . . .'

'Yes, but . . . it's better than bottling it all up.'

'And now everyone's against me: Russia, Britain, America; they all think I'm like, a *really bad* person . . .'

'Well, we all do bad things sometimes. But at least you were trying to make a difference, that's the main thing . . . What was that bang?'

'I've just shot my Alsatian. And now I am going to shoot myself through the mouth.'

'Er, hang on . . . I'll just see if my supervisor is free at the moment; I'm going to put you on hold; you'll hear some light classical music, hello? Hello?'

Britain 'wins' Second World War

Great Britain had, of course, played a central role in the titanic conflict whose outcome had so depressed Adolf Hitler. The Russians may have sacrificed more lives, the Americans may have spent more money, but by refusing to surrender in 1940, Britain crucially provided *the time* for the world to gather itself and eventually turn the tide against fascism. Thus it was that the British emerged from the war with an enormous sense of pride at the lone stand made against the Nazis and Britain's huge contribution to the eventual defeat of Germany. Fascism was discredited as a political creed; democracy was virtuous and triumphant. Henceforth middle-aged men at medal fairs would only be interested in the emblems of the victorious Allied forces; Nazi insignia and the badge caps of the Waffen-SS would have no titillating appeal whatsoever.

The war had been in the papers a lot over the previous six years but unlike so many of the headlines today – *Lottery winner had ASBO, Kid 13 is a dad* and *Person who is on the telly once did something bad* – the national front pages* really mattered. The

---

* Although the front page of *The Times* was still notices and small ads. So to our eye, the most important event of VE Day appears to be the announcement by the Polytechnic, Regent St W1, that 'the Governors invite applications for the post of ASSISTANT LIBRARIAN', on a starting salary of £248 per annum.

news was directly experienced by the nation. The outcome of the Battle of Britain determined the future for everyone. Information about the Blitz was a matter of life or death. You can't help feeling that if we were living through the Blitz today, ITV would do a cheery Bomb Forecast, followed by the Bombing Forecast for Your Local Area sponsored by Powergen.

But that's not to say the people fully grasped what had just happened, and on 8 May 1945, a misleadingly positive bit of government spin was sold to the British people. They were told they had won the Second World War. The government dared to tell them that after six years of crippling conflict, the destruction of homes, factories, the loss of the merchant shipping fleet and the gold reserves, Great Britain was somehow one of the winners. 'But they just have to look out the window at the rubble everywhere . . .' said a worried Winston Churchill, '. . . or count the casualties, or look at the national bank balance to see that by any measure, we are completely and utterly stuffed . . .'

But the exhausted British people were more than happy to believe the whole 'total victory' story, despite the obvious absence of tons of looted gold treasure or whole new swathes of wealth-creating territory. The crowds thronged around Buckingham Palace, cheering the King and Queen and the Prime Minister; they sang 'Rule Britannia' and 'God Save the King' and climbed up lamp posts waving the Union Jack, as complete strangers hugged one another, shared bottles of beer and had drunken euphoric sex in shop doorways. Nineteen-year-old Princess Elizabeth and her sister Princess Margaret had been permitted to mingle anonymously in the crowd, though whether the future Queen snogged any drunken squaddies is not recorded. Everyone was swept along with jubilation and pride and relief that invincible Britain had finally emerged victorious.* And that is where the problems really began.

Now let's lose the peace!

Germany knew it had cocked up in quite a big way. Japan knew it had to totally rethink how it came up with blue-sky ideas like 'Let's go to war with America'. Even the French had witnessed the total failure of its pre-war systems and the disastrous consequences of its complacency and deep internal divisions. But Britain's institutions seem to have been completely vindicated by the outcome of the war; after all, hadn't this experience been the nation's 'finest hour'? The civil service weren't hanging their heads in shame in 1945 and saying, 'What an utter disaster! How did we let things come to this?' The Foreign Office weren't asking, 'Why did our chaps trust this Hitler fellow for so long? Why were we so unprepared for war?' The army weren't asking why it didn't win a single victory until after Russia and America came into the war; the newspapers weren't being asked how so many of them had supported Hitler in the 1930s; the public schools weren't facing up to their failures and admitting, 'We are responsible for generations of leaders who have been imbued with a disastrous combination of supreme arrogance and utter ignorance about life in Britain. Clearly we owe it to the nation to abolish ourselves.' And so the decades after the war saw Britain being overtaken by countries that had started from an

* Our idea of VE Day is shaped by the photographs that made the best images and stories: Humphrey Lyttelton playing his trumpet down Piccadilly, or the throng of patriots outside Buckingham Palace. In fact, outside of Central London the day passed off rather quietly; few places could muster big enough crowds for there to be much sense of occasion. Across most of the country, people glanced out from behind their curtains and asked, 'What's that noise down in the square?' 'Oh, something to do with the war ending.' 'Honestly, any excuse . . .'

even more desperate position in 1945 but were at least aware of it.

The support that had brought victory to Britain in wartime would not be there in peace. Much as they might have wished it, the British motorcycle industry could not rely on the Americans to bomb the Japanese moped factories. The German football team would not have to face eleven Russians attacking them from the other direction. In 1940 Britain had stood alone militarily. Now it had to stand alone economically, and nobody quite appreciated that this was going to be even harder.

It was decided that no post-war reparations would be required of Germany because the crippling compensation demanded after the First World War had been seen as a contributory factor to the rise of Hitler. However, given how well the German economy has done since the 1950s in relation to the British, one can't help wondering if it is not too late to change our mind about this. It might cause a bit of an awkward atmosphere in Brussels, but considering that Britain has never quite recovered the economic dominance of Europe that it enjoyed prior to 1939, a late invoice for, say, a trillion trillion euros as compensation for the Second World War has got to be worth a shot.

Future perfect

The history of post-war Britain really starts with an ageing former civil servant sitting down at his desk in 1941 having been instructed to write a very long and boring report. 'Social Insurance and Allied Services' it said at the top of his note from the Ministry of Labour. 'Hmmm,' pondered the academic. 'Social insurance . . . ? Social insurance . . . ?' And then he coloured in all the vowels on the memo and decided to make another cup of tea before he got started.

'It's just not fair,' he mused, staring out of the window of his poky office in Pimlico. 'Buffy is over in Crete fighting German paratroopers. Todge is in North Africa, pushing the Italians out of Libya. Fred is captain of a cruiser in the North Atlantic. And I'm stuck here trying to think of something interesting to say about the bloody anomalies of the various social insurance schemes . . .' At dinner parties friends would ask him what he was working on, and then their heads would fall into the soup out of utter boredom. His office staff would pretend to be German spies to get arrested rather than have to listen to him reporting how seven different government departments currently administered welfare provision.

So mind-numbingly boring was his task that he put it off for a whole year. And when he came back to it in 1942, when the Russians were pinning down the German Sixth Army in Stalingrad and the Japanese were losing the Battle of Midway in the Pacific, the only solution for this frustrated pen-pusher was to completely ignore his original remit and write something much more exciting instead.

Thus it was that the publication of the Beveridge Report in December 1942 utterly transformed the mood in wartime Britain, paving the way for a radical post-war Labour government and establishing the template for the modern welfare state. For Sir William Beveridge had used the opportunity of this dull internal government review to pen a radical proposal for a fairer, more compassionate society. Warming to his theme, he set out carefully costed proposals for a national insurance scheme, universal entitlement to old-age pensions, a family allowance and a 'national health service' available to all. He explained how Britain would be stronger and more prosperous if her people were set free from the five giant evils of 'Want, Ignorance, Disease, Squalor and Idleness'. Sadly no mention was made of 'Having too many remote controls for the DVD, telly and everything'.

So total was his failure to write the report that had been

commissioned that the other members of the committee had their names taken off the final draft. Winston Churchill and the rather alarmed Conservative Chancellor Sir Kingsley Wood made it plain that their government had no intention of implementing any of these extravagant and expensive recommendations. But in a classic example of one government department being unaware of what the other is thinking, the report was seized upon by the Ministry of Information, who saw its potential to boost morale during the dark days of 1942. The Beveridge Report became an immediate bestseller. A special pocket edition was produced for members of the armed services; it was translated into seven languages and shared among resistance fighters in occupied Europe. The timing had been particularly fortunate: it was published just after Britain's first victory at El Alamein, when at last it seemed possible that Germany might be defeated.* The debate about post-war Britain could begin, and the idealists had their manifesto already set out in detail by this elderly upper-class revolutionary. Social observers noted a marked shift to the left in British public opinion between 1942 and 1943; soldiers debated life after the war, determined that their sacrifices should not be rewarded with the post-war unemployment experienced by their fathers. The seeds were sown for the greatest electoral shock in British political history, the transformation of British society and, as had been requested, a tidying up of the haphazard social insurance system. That's the bit the accountants were really excited about.

---

* A copy of Beveridge's radical document was found in Hitler's bunker with a note stating that the plans were superior to any system of social insurance dreamt up by the Germans. 'Maybe we could bring in something like this after we've won the war,' the Führer had suggested to embarrassed coughs around the bunker.

Election very special

On 5 July 1945, the British people went to the polls for the first time in a decade. Both Winston Churchill and Clement Attlee had wanted the wartime coalition to continue until the defeat of Japan, but Labour's governing body ruled that the coalition should now end, and who was Winston Churchill in 1945 to argue with Labour's National Executive Committee?

The Labour Party was fighting from a very low base (a mere 154 Labour MPs had been elected in 1935); it had a particularly uncharismatic leader in the quietly spoken Clement Attlee, who was up against the hugely popular war leader Winston Churchill at his moment of triumph. No one gave Labour a hope.

Winston Churchill began the campaign with a crass misjudgement as he declared that Labour's socialist programme would need some sort of Gestapo to implement it. It was such a momentous gaffe that the deeply offended socialists resolved there and then never to call the Tories 'fascists' or compare any future Conservative leaders to 'Hitler' ever again; 'until, say, May 1979'. The next evening Clement Attlee went on the radio and thanked the Conservative leader for reminding everyone of the difference between Churchill the war leader and Churchill the party leader in peacetime.

But the election campaign continued with everyone still expecting Churchill to be returned with a large majority – the newspapers, foreign ambassadors, even the Labour leadership themselves were about to get a huge surprise. What they had all underestimated was the overwhelming feeling that the great sacrifices of the previous six years must be for something positive – that people could not have endured the suffering, the Blitz and the exaggerated cockney accents just to go back to things as they had been before. In 1918, the British had been promised a land fit for heroes, but the reward for veterans of the trenches had been years of unemployment and poverty. And now another terrible war had been endured, a conflict many blamed the Conservatives for allowing to develop, and servicemen and civilians had passed many long hours in barracks and air-raid shelters, mixing with strangers from all walks of life, reflecting and fantasizing about what might come after all this.

'What I hope is that all them scientists and boffins and whatnot get together and invent an iPod.'

'A what?'

'A little music player smaller than a packet of fags, but one you can keep all yer favourite hits on. Only digitally like.'

'Oh yeah, well, we was hoping for one of them after the last war but it'll never happen. Just give me a portable phone with a little camera in it; that's all I ask for.'

The omens on election day were not good for Churchill when it turned out that the great man himself did not appear on the electoral register and therefore could not vote. Maybe he was still undecided anyway. After the polls closed, the commentators on BBC's *Election Special* team began to speculate about what might be inferred from the rumours from the polling stations. 'Well, it's too early to say. Let's wait for the first actual results to come in – that's the only poll that really counts . . .'

'OK, well, it's always a race to see which constituency will declare first, and I have just heard that we can expect the very first result in – er – three weeks' time.'

'Three weeks??'

'Yes, they have to wait until all the forces' votes are in from overseas, so the election result won't be declared until July twenty-sixth. But don't go away because we'll be broadcasting live until then. So, Peter, what do you think the early signs suggest?'

'Er, well, it's really too early to say . . .'

Mr Churchill has secured his working majority, declared the *News of the World* the following weekend, and nobody had any reason to think their guess might be catastrophically wrong. In the meantime, 'the Prime Minister Unelect' had a minor bit of admin to get out of the way: meeting up with the presidents of America and Russia to redraw the map of Europe, and various parts of Europe were sacrificed to Stalin as long as the West could keep Greece. Being a public schoolboy and Classics swot, Churchill had always clung to some romantic notion about Greece as the cradle of civilization. 'Sorry, Bulgaria, but we never studied Bulgarian at Harrow.'

When the general election results were due to be declared, Churchill popped back from the Potsdam conference not even bothering to pack properly, so confident was he that he would be returning as the re-elected British Prime Minister in a few days' time. The leaders of America and Russia couldn't quite comprehend it when Clement Attlee returned in his place.

Labour had won just under 50 per cent of the vote, winning 393 seats to the Conservatives' 197; the perceived saviour of the nation was out and utterly humiliated. Churchill and the Conservatives were devastated by the shock defeat, although he was philosophical enough to tell one of his outraged aides: 'This is democracy, this is what we have been fighting for.' Stalin couldn't quite believe that the government had had the ballot boxes under their care for three weeks and still not got the result they had wanted.

'A modest man, with much to be modest about'

The new Prime Minister was an unlikely leader of a socialist revolution. Perhaps that's why there wasn't one. Like the only other Labour leader to win a landslide, he was a public schoolboy who had held conservative views in his youth and gone on to study law. He had been chosen as deputy leader of the Labour Party after virtually all the senior figures in the parliamentary party lost their seats in the electoral wipe-out of 1931. When George Lansbury stood down in 1935, Attlee succeeded him as leader, and so ten years later when Labour won its historic landslide, the former Mayor of Stepney was surprised to find greatness suddenly thrust upon him.

Attlee was not a man with enormous charisma or much ability as a public speaker; in addition to the alleged 'modest man' jibe, Churchill called him 'a sheep in sheep's clothing', but the former Gallipoli veteran* was a skilful consensus leader of a cabinet of huge and conflicting egos, who was prepared to listen, delegate and compromise but would assert his authority when it was required. On realizing they had received an unprecedented mandate for a radical socialist manifesto, Attlee's deputy, Herbert Morrison, thought this might be his moment to seize the leadership of the Labour Party. After a tense meeting between the two of them, Attlee slipped away and went straight to Buckingham Palace to be asked by the King to form the next government and Morrison's chance was suddenly gone.

The famously shy King George VI was so flabbergasted to be confronted by this socialist that the two of them stood in silence for what seemed like an age while the King tried to think of something to say. Eventually the embarrassed silence was broken by Attlee, who said, 'I've won the election.'

'I know,' replied the King. 'I heard it on the six o'clock news.' In fact, behind his awkward demeanour, the King was not-very-privately appalled at what had just happened. Perhaps the stunned

---

* Captain Attlee was the last man but one out of Suvla Bay in 1915. He possibly would not have survived the military disaster that was Gallipoli had he not caught dysentery and been hospitalized during the Battle of Sari Bair when many of his comrades were killed. The Gallipoli offensive had of course been masterminded by Winston Churchill, so Attlee got his own back by evicting him from Downing Street thirty years later.

reaction of the upper classes was best summed up by a well-to-do lady overheard in the Ritz: 'They've gone and elected a Labour government. The country won't stand for it!'

'How did you find your steak?' 'I just moved a chip and there it was.'

Such was the shock of the 1945 election result that it might be imagined that the conservative middle classes were now consumed with fear for their uncertain future, that on 26 July 1945 they suddenly became focused upon this assault on their freedoms, wealth and power. In fact, the day the results came in, the well-to-do British opinion formers were not thinking about increased tax burdens, or restrictions on their businesses, or the position of a socialist Britain between communist Russia and capitalist America. They were not thinking about domestic or global politics at all: they were thinking about cheese sandwiches. And steak and kidney pies, and pork sausages, and roast beef and Yorkshire pudding, and egg and bacon, and apple pie and custard and all the other delicious foodstuffs that had been denied them for so long.

We know that people were thinking about this on 26 July 1945 because that is what people were thinking about every single day; diaries and letters of the period are packed with longing references to food and the aching absence of it. People had endured rationing during the war, appreciating that the tractor factories were busy making Spitfires and food convoys were being attacked by German U-boats. But everyone had sort of presumed that when it was all over, they'd be able to sit down to a delicious traditional British meal of boiled fatty gammon with overcooked cabbage and cremated roast potatoes. No such luck. Rations were not suddenly lifted; to everyone's abject disappointment, they were increased. The bitter reality was that now Britain was occupying a large chunk of Germany, they had to help feed the people they had been trying to blow up only months earlier.

'Why have they suddenly introduced bread rationing now the war is over?'

'Well, it's so that we can feed the Germans.'

'Oh that's all right then, you should have said, we don't mind making a sacrifice, not if it's for such a worthy cause.'

The British public were urged to 'Eat Less Bread, Use Potatoes Instead'. A chip butty was just some chips in between two very big chips. 'Don't just think of potatoes as something you eat as a side vegetable,' said the government propaganda. Which translates as: 'You remember how those potatoes used to be served with a big piece of steak beside them? Well, now it's just the potatoes.' Even potatoes themselves became rationed in the years after the war, as bacon and other rations were also cut back, and such treats as powdered egg were denied to the British family as the financial crisis worsened.

For our bloated, paunchy twenty-first-century generation, constantly grazing on chocolate biscuits, kettle chips, mochaccinos and blueberry muffins, it is hard to imagine the prospect of going from empty larder to barren grocery store and discovering that there was literally nothing to eat. But for years after the war, just buying the basics could involve long queues and a fractious argument with the butcher or grocer about the measly weekly allocation being handed over the counter. That's why today's pensioners baulk at the wastefulness of throwing away a crust of bread with green mould all over it. 'You could scrape that mould off and make a nice green soup with it . . .'

The food that was available was generally of a pretty poor standard. Whale meat could be purchased in case you happened to have a couple of Eskimos coming round to dinner. One recipe recommended boiling the whale meat with an onion before throwing the onion away. 'As well?' quipped *Punch* magazine. Concerns about the shortage of protein prompted the government to import millions of tins of snoek – a little-known perch-like fish from South Africa (South Africa traded in sterling rather than expensive dollars). Snoek was launched with a host of exciting recipe ideas. 'Why have we never heard of this fish before?' wondered the ravenous British public as they eagerly raised the first forkful to their tastebuds. 'Ah – that's why.' Snoek ended up as pet food and even the cats were sniffy about it.

One rather cruel survey of this period asked people to describe their dream feast if there were no more restrictions and shortages. But this only served to remind them that it was impossible for the whole family to sit down to a hearty breakfast of bacon, sausages, tomato, mushrooms and toast garnished with a choice of scrambled, fried or poached eggs. And of course they were just plain and simple 'eggs' back then, not 'farm-fresh organic free-range Columbian blacktail eggs', because the post-war austerity also saw a severe shortage of superfluous adjectives. Today, we feast upon as many extra words as can possibly be fitted onto the packet and a 'cheese sandwich' is a 'pan-toasted Normandy Brie and cranberry triangle on wholewheat granary'. But back in the 1940s, adjectives for food were severely rationed and people had to save their coupons just to put one measly describing word in front of the root vegetable they were having for Sunday lunch.

Oh no – it's victory in Japan!

Although Japan was clearly losing the war in the summer of 1945, most people assumed that total victory would have to involve invading and occupying the Japanese mainland. This was a forbidding prospect. Japanese soldiers had not gained a reputation for saying, 'Oh shucks, look, this whole Pacific Empire thing was a terrible idea. Let's avoid further bloodshed – sod the Emperor, you win this time!' Some feared that the final and bloody end of the Second World War might not come until 1947 or 1948, such was the magnitude of the task. So it was something of a shock when the atomic bomb was dropped on Hiroshima on 6 August 1945. All at once people had to reconcile the feelings of excitement that the war might end so much sooner, pride that the Allies had such an impressive new weapon and fear that a terrifying destructive new power had come into the world.

The city of Hiroshima was described as a 'military centre', which is the usual description for any civilian location destroyed by bombing. A second bomb was dropped on Nagasaki a few days later, sending a clear message to Japan that more bombs would be dropped until Japan surrendered (even if America didn't actually have any more just yet). It is sometimes suggested that the United States dropped the atomic bombs as a show of force to the Russians, but the chronology of the Cold War does not support this particular conspiracy theory. The American government was not especially hostile to the Soviet government in August 1945; it might possibly be that Washington was motivated by the idea of sparing the lives of a million US servicemen.

However delighted people might have been when Japan surrendered, the sudden and unexpected end to the war in Asia was something of a calamity for Great Britain. Because the moment there was peace, President Truman ended the Lend-Lease Agreement negotiated by Churchill and Roosevelt that had kept Britain financially afloat for so long. If President Roosevelt, a great friend of Britain's, had not died in the last days of the war, it is possible the cash might not have been cut off quite so soon. But President Truman followed the letter of the law, and suddenly Britain was penniless.

Do you do 'cash back'?

After another national day of rejoicing to celebrate VJ Day, Britain counted up all the money it had left and worked out that there was just enough to send someone to Washington to beg for spare change. The brain-box economist John Maynard Keynes was quickly despatched in the hope of persuading the Americans to lend us a few billion, so that lots of left-wing election promises could be kept.

'So, Britisher, what d'ya need all this money for?'

'Well, the old place is looking a bit shabby, you know, so repainting our funny little pillar boxes, and er, washing the cricket whites, fuel to keep the beer warm, you know what we're like . . .'

'Don't forget our massive programme of socialist national-ization, sir,' chirped up his helpful assistant.

'Did that guy just say *socialist*?'

'No, no, no, not at all . . .'

'But, Mr Keynes, sir, on the way over you said our socialist government needed the loan to stop all the capitalist businessmen making huge profits at the expense of the workers—'

Britain's bargaining position was not a strong one, but Keynes argued long and hard. Britain may have become a debtor nation financially, but the country's refusal to make a deal with Hitler in 1940 made Britain a *moral* creditor. The terms were far from generous: the pound was devalued but British bankruptcy was avoided. It was hoped that once the economy was on its feet again it shouldn't take too long to pay the Americans back. The last instalment was finally paid in 2006. 'And thank heavens we won't be getting back into debt like that again for a very long time,' said the Chancellor.

Politician slammed for smart, clean appearance!

Shortages of food were the most obvious sign of the austerity, but pretty well everything was in short supply. Britain looked tatty, with peeling paint, leaky roofs, cracked windows and dirty buses and trains. Soap, for example, was hard to get hold of and so was not to be wasted on things like washing. Clothes were expected to be worn until they fell apart. It was unpatriotic not to make everything last. When Christian Dior's so-called New Look came in from Paris in 1947, Labour politicians criticized its indulgent, wasteful style that used up so much material in the name of vanity.

With all the rationing and counting points and clothes coupons that carried on after the war, you think just one person might have had the left-field idea that could have saved them all an awful lot of queuing and making do.

'I know this might sound like a crazy idea, but hear me out for a second . . . How about – *we just don't bother with all these hats?*'

'What?!'

'You know, all these trilbies and bowlers and cloth caps and ladies' bonnets and berets, why don't we all just decide that millions and millions of *hats* are a rather pointless drain on clothing material, coupons and factory space?'

'Don't be ridiculous – you can't just go outside without a hat. Everyone would be walking around in the open air with the tops of their heads visible!'

'You're right! Sorry, what was I thinking? The only time it is acceptable to be seen outdoors without a hat is when you are on a motorbike.'

'Exactly!'

Where accountants dare

The challenges the peacetime government set itself were in many ways just as monumental as the achievements of the previous six years, it's just that popular culture has always found the drama of war more exciting than the humdrum business of reform and reconstruction. Perhaps that's why there don't seem to be as many heroic films about the years after 1945; why there is no action adventure classic in which Alec Guinness and Donald Pleasance succeed against all the odds in organizing the welfare payments office in Newcastle.

'Right, men, here's the plan: we have to get in there fast, and process twenty-five million National Insurance contribution payments before the fourth of the month.'

'No, sah! It can't be done.'

'Pull yourself together, Johnson! Now I won't pretend some of you may not come out of there without repetitive strain injury, but those family allowances simply have to be issued!'

Much of Labour's ambitious domestic programme centred around 'the public ownership of the means of production, distribution and exchange', as it said in Clause IV of the party's constitution before Tony Blair changed it to: 'Everyone just try and be nice to each other.'

Labour's nationalization programme in 1945 wasn't just a matter of political dogma; many of these crucial industries had been badly run before the war, with underinvestment, poor planning and a demoralized workforce. The war had shown how crucial industries like coal and steel and transport were to the nation; their future could not be left to chance. That said, it was worth nationalizing everything just to annoy all those toffs who'd been making a fortune exploiting Labour voters all these years.

Taking the coal mines into public ownership was probably the least controversial of Labour's plans. The coal industry had been taken under state control during both world wars, and state ownership had long been demanded by the workforce. On 1 January 1947, signs were unveiled at pits across the country declaring: 'This colliery is now managed by the National Coal Board on behalf of the people.' It was a deeply symbolic day for Britain's 750,000 miners. They excitedly arrived at work to see who their new boss was. It was the same boss they had the week before with a different logo on his door. There were hopes that under national management and with strategic planning, coal production would now increase. The following month, it stopped altogether. In a frankly rather heavy-handed piece of imagery, the weather decided to empathize with Austerity Britain's frozen economic development and the country experienced the snowiest winter since Dickens's novels. Four million workers were made idle by power cuts, no coal could be dug, no stocks could be moved by train. Even the snowmen looked worried; at least they would have done if anyone could have spared any coal or carrots for their faces.

Power cuts and reduced gas pressure left people shivering in their homes and places of work, with little to look forward to but a nice big lunch of last night's leftover horse meat, in the hope that it might warm them up a bit. When the snow suddenly melted in March, thousands of people's homes were ruined by flooding. The Tories had warned them what life would be like under Labour.

The government got its own back on the water by nationalizing it. Roads, electricity and the railway companies were all taken into public ownership. Now that the trains were state controlled, everyone was confident that a sense of patriotic pride and public service would transform that surly man at the ticket kiosk. The Port of London Authority, the Post Office, civil aviation;* the impoverished government continued to pay out large amounts of compensation to the previous owners of nationalized industries while keeping their fingers crossed that the cheques wouldn't bounce. Herbert Morrison was Labour's nationalization expert from his experience in London government when transport had been brought under public control. The usual template was to set up a public corporation that would be responsible to the relevant minister. Obviously not everything that was nationalized had its own minister; they didn't have a Minister of Sewage, for example, even if it might have made cabinet reshuffles far more entertaining.

An Englishman's home is his prefab

In 1947 little plastic building bricks called Lego were launched in the United Kingdom. Architects saw their children cobbling together little square houses from whatever bricks they could find on the drawing-room floor and thought, 'Right, that's the design of all the new homes sorted!'

Housing was clearly an urgent priority and again the debate was about which sector could make the greatest provision. The Conservatives argued that private enterprise was best placed to rebuild the hundreds of thousands of homes destroyed by the Blitz. But Labour argued that the desperate shortage of materials

---

* On 1 January 1946, the first civilian flight took off from Heath Row. During the war a secret decision was taken by the Conservative minister Harold Balfour that this would be London's major civilian airport, despite its unsuitable position. Unlike nearly every other major city in the world, London has its major airport to the west. Planes have to fly into the prevailing westerly wind, in London's case directly over the most populated area of the country, thereby creating the maximum disturbance and risk to the population below. If you are woken up at half past five in the morning by aircraft noise, blame Harold Balfour for deceiving the government that his pet airport project was for military aircraft only.

would drive up prices and the free market would end up building homes only for the middle classes, as it had tended to between the wars. The thousands of homeless couldn't wait much longer; some of them were already squatting in empty office space, and those in the 160,000 temporary prefabricated cabins were starting to realize that this solution wasn't so short-term after all.*

Instead of taking it on directly, the government entrusted this massive task to the local authorities, who built whole new council estates, and then inspired generations of residents by naming the blocks after members of the Housing Committee. Whole new towns were planned such as Stevenage and Harlow. There were concerns that these places stuck out as a bit bleak and soulless, but this was eventually remedied by making every other town centre in Britain bleak and soulless as well.

Despite all the shortages and financial restraints, one and a half million new homes were built during this period, an incredible achievement considering the state the country was in. Admittedly the period may not be the zenith of British architecture and design, but almost a thousand new homes were completed every day and by the time of the 1951 census there were more occupied dwellings than had been counted in the last census twenty years earlier. If such a challenge were attempted today, the prefabs would arrive with various bits missing, the self-assembly instructions would be incomprehensible and the homeless would be left with various unconnected wooden sections and a bent Allen key.

'NHS online' postponed till invention of internet

But the greatest of all the domestic achievements of the post-war Labour government was surely the creation of the National Health

---

* Neil Kinnock was one of the post-war children to grow up in a prefab.

Service. The proposal was as radical as it was straightforward. Indeed, the very simplicity of the idea made it very hard for its opponents to pick away at the details: a universal health care system, free at the point of delivery, available to all, irrespective of income, status or nationality. The minister responsible for delivering this revolutionary idea was Aneurin Bevan,* perhaps the most iconic of Labour heroes, capturing both the passion and the ambiguities of the people's party. He was an ardent and persuasive campaigner in opposition, but a minister conflicted with the compromises of power once in office. One of ten children born to a Welsh mining family, Nye Bevan was secretary of his trade union branch by the time he was nineteen, but the colliery manager had him sacked as a troublemaker. The British Medical Association (BMA) would later wish they could do the same thing.

Nye Bevan's idealistic vision was that one day every town would have an Accident and Emergency department, where violent drunks could end up after closing time, knowing that they would get free medical treatment for injuries sustained in the fight they had just started. He dreamt that the war-weary British, fed up with queuing for bread and meat and petrol, could join a waiting list for heart-bypass operations as well. In fact, what was revealed by the first few months of the National Health Service was the extent to which vast numbers of ordinary people had endured painful and dangerous medical conditions because they could not afford to have them treated under the old systems. Until the creation of the NHS, millions of people died decades earlier than they would have done if they had had access to proper medical health care. And then they all lived to old age, and the planners went, 'But we never budgeted for them all staying alive like this.'

---

* With Nye Bevan responsible for housing as well as health, the joke was that the government 'only had half a Nye on housing'.

Back in 1945, the vast majority of doctors were vehemently opposed to the government's radical health plan, and didn't take too kindly to having this brusque Welsh oik telling them they had no choice. Bevan was called a 'medical führer' and accused of treating the doctors like 'West Indian slaves'; it looked as if the high ideas of a national health service might be laid low by the superbug of the doctors' intransigence. Had it occurred to the BMA to put a GP's receptionist in the way of the plans, they probably could have delayed things for another decade or so. But gradually Bevan wore them down. The doctors were reassured that they would be permitted to continue with their private practice and their handwriting could remain as illegible as always. The consultants' anger diminished when they were offered an extremely generous pay scale; 'I stuffed their mouths with gold,' said Bevan later.

It was very much Bevan's personal resolve and political will that forced through the NHS where others would have been defeated. The Conservatives had paid lip service to some sort of universal health care in their own manifesto, but no Tory minister could have pushed through such a radical plan in the teeth of the vehement opposition that came from the professional classes the Conservatives represented. The NHS came into existence on 5 July 1948, and would remain in place whoever was in power: criticized for the unwieldy nature of its bureaucracy and the problems of ever-growing costs, but still a miracle to those who remember the uncertainty and fear of illness before the war. It became the sacred cow of British politics; even if this particular sacred cow had caught some hospital superbug and was still waiting for a hip operation.

'From cradle to grave' (if you die before Thatcher gets in)

On the domestic front, the government achieved much else. Taking its cue from the Beveridge Report, Labour abolished the Poor Law and brought in a universal entitlement to pensions, family allowances (crucially made payable to the mother of the child), benefits for those suffering unemployment, maternity payments, funeral grants and a large one-off payment for one young unemployed London girl, who was marrying an immigrant she'd met on holiday.

By November 1947, Princess Elizabeth had saved up enough of her diamond coupons and pearl rations to finally get herself hitched and so the nation's gloom could be temporarily lifted by the advent of a royal wedding. Princess Elizabeth had chosen her true love from the wide choice of suitable man available; as befitted a future Queen of England, they had found her a nice local boy called Philippos Schleswig-Holstein-Sonderburg-Glücksburg (no, *really*). He was advised he might want to change that surname, oh, and maybe give up the Greek Orthodox religion thing as well. 'The Duke of Edinburgh', as he became on the day of the wedding, solemnly pledged to serve the British crown 'with a lifetime of embarrassing right-wing outbursts and vaguely racist gaffes'. Their first child, Charles, was born less than twelve months later (though thankfully more than nine). He was sent off to boarding school the following day.

Olympic Games: British athletes bring a note

Since they didn't have much else on, in 1948 the British also hosted the XIV Olympiad. London had originally been selected to host the 1944 Olympics, but the Health and Safety bureaucrats cancelled it due to some petty regulation about a world war or something, and London was awarded the following games without a vote. The proposed hosts of the cancelled 1940 games in Tokyo thought it best not to make a fuss. However, in post-war austerity Britain, the Olympics were not quite the glitzy national showcase we tend to expect these days. 'And now we go over to the Empire Stadium for the final heats of the clearing-up-the-rubble followed by the 10,000-metre bread queue.' It must have pained the government to watch all those gold medals going out of the country.

A huge sign above the stadium said: 'The important thing in the Olympic Games is not winning but taking part', and the hosts did indeed 'take part' in many events, winning only three golds in the 'mucking about in boats' category. A Great Britain football team won a quarter-final against France at Craven Cottage only to lose the semi-final to Yugoslavia.* Most Olympic competitors had to bring their own towels, and were ferried to events on London buses. When one event overran, the absence of floodlights was overcome by commandeering a number of motor cars to park in front of the track and turn on their headlights. The games were the first to be televised, and also saw the first ever political defection when one Czech gymnast refused to go home, protesting against her country's inclusion in the Soviet bloc. When it was all over, the Olympic committee agreed it had been a lovely way to spend a couple of weeks in post-war London and they very much looked forward to coming back again soon. Like in 2012.

* There had been three football World Cup competitions in the 1930s but the Home Nations had so far declined to enter a team. England finally made their World Cup debut in 1950, and were thought to have a good chance of winning it. Instead they were beaten 1–0 by the United States in a shocking national humiliation (before footballing humiliation ceased to be shocking).

Britain reduced to bronze medal for 'Most Important Country'

Britain's international status was now clearly below that of America and Russia, but with its surviving empire and dominions, its pivotal role in the Second World War and the aftermath, not to mention its exciting groundnut scheme in Tanganyika,* Britain was at least way ahead of the rest of the pack. And so when the French proposed a European Coal and Steel Community, which would provide a free trade area in these crucial commodities, the Labour government turned it down with barely a moment's thought. 'Yeah, you go off and form your little common market . . . Let's see what becomes of that!'† Attlee said of the six countries that were about to join together: 'Know them all well. Very recently this country spent a great deal of blood and treasure rescuing four of them from attacks by the other two.'

Despite their socialist politics, the idea of British Empire still counted for a great deal for the Labour ministers who had grown up in the jingoistic atmosphere of Victorian and Edwardian England. They looked to Britain's influence across the whole globe, rather than just Europe. When the voters of Britain elected a Labour government they were turning from the international agenda to focus on domestic issues. But Labour's ambitious plans at home were constantly hampered by the complexities of the global situation as the dust settled from the Second World War.

Britain was central to the establishment of the United Nations, which held its first meeting in London in January 1946. Although

* The plan to grow peanuts for cooking oil in Tanganyika (the larger part of modern-day Tanzania) was a much lampooned and ultimately disastrous government plan that cost nearly £50 million and was eventually abandoned. The phrase 'groundnut scheme' became a catch-all phrase for badly planned government projects.
† Ernest Bevin's reaction to the idea was: 'The Durham miners would never stand for it.'

the UN would initially work with five official languages, it was English that came to dominate. And it was agreed that the version of English used would be 'British English': using the spelling, grammar and vocabulary of the United Kingdom. Presumably they meant standard BBC-type English. It would be hard to imagine the Russian delegate denouncing Western Imperialism in the British English spoken in Newcastle: 'Whay-hey, man, yers no reet like, wi' ya Berlin Airlift, hoikin' all yers tabs and brun o'er wor toon.'

'Cold War' proves less dramatic sequel

In 1946 Winston Churchill had given a speech in Missouri, warning of an 'Iron Curtain' that was descending across Central Europe. Churchill wasn't pandering to American anti-communist prejudices with this speech; he was trying to alert them to something they did not want to see. For a brief moment after the war, the United States were the ones imagining they could still work with their former allies; it was the British who were under no illusions about Stalin. The British Foreign Secretary Ernest Bevin was particularly hostile to the communists, having had his fill of them when he was general secretary of the Transport and General Workers Union. 'Bloody commie entryists. You watch what they do in Czechoslovakia: it'll be just like when they tried to take over the Dudley branch of the TGWU.'

Soon the Americans were persuaded that Stalin hadn't liberated Eastern Europe from the Nazis in order to leave the locals free to buy jeans and listen to country music. Political cartoonists racked their brains for an image that might convey the relationship between Stalin and the new communist governments of Eastern Europe.

'So what you are saying, Mr Cartoonist, is that these leaders are like "puppet governments"?'

'Yes, that's why I've drawn them as puppets in a puppet show . . .'

'I see, I see, and Joseph Stalin here, you've got him controlling these puppets on the end of his hands . . .'

'Yes, in this satirical image that I have created, he is the *puppet master* of the *puppet governments*.'

'Right, well, thank you for explaining that, it's certainly much clearer now.'

To prevent any more poverty-stricken Europeans from succumbing to communism, a massive programme of assistance was agreed for Western Europe which became known as Marshall Aid. Refused by Stalin for the countries in the Russian sphere, it was this anti-communist insurance policy that funded much of Labour's socialist programme. So when you are boasting to an American about Britain's wonderfully inclusive health care system, it's probably best not to mention that they paid for it.

A principled stand was made over West Berlin, the Western-held sectors of the German capital that lay cut off deep inside the Soviet zone.* As relations between East and West deteriorated, Russia severed road and rail links to West Berlin in an attempt to force the Western Powers to surrender the city to them. With memories still fresh about the failure to stand up to Hitler, there were many (including Nye Bevan and Churchill) who believed that Stalin's bluff should be called while America had atomic weapons and the Russians didn't.

'We should send an armoured column escorting food supplies to West Berlin and dare them to fire upon it!'

'OK, who wants to drive the first truck?'

---

* As well as occupying a section of Germany after the war, each of the victorious Allies (and France) took responsibility for a section of the German capital. The Russian section became East Berlin, and the British, American and French sectors merged to become West Berlin, an island of capitalism in the middle of communist Eastern Europe.

Rather than provoke another war when they were still tidying up after the last one, Britain and America organized a massive airlift to feed the people of West Berlin. For nearly a whole year after June 1948, huge quantities of food and medicine were flown over Soviet-occupied Germany to the beleaguered Berliners: 'Oh, hang on – they've left a note saying they want organic semi-skimmed, we'll have to fly back to the depot.' Little packets of sweets were attached to tiny parachutes for the children of West Berlin; a PR stunt that must have gone down particularly well for all the British kids who would have their sweets rationed until 1953. After nearly a year the Russians lifted the blockade, thereby conceding that West Berlin would remain outside the communist zone. A line had been drawn in the sand. Henceforth any fighting in the Cold War would be far away from the frontline of Checkpoint Charlie, which instead would be used for frosty exchanges of captured spies in John Le Carré novels.

Despite its role in the establishment of the United Nations in 1945, there were many in Washington who would have liked America to extricate itself from Europe now that the Second World War was over. But Britain was eager to secure a formal military alliance while the Cold War was hot. A military agreement between Britain, France* and the low countries had been established in 1948 but one sensed that Moscow wasn't quivering with fear thinking, 'Oh no, now they've got Belgium *and* Luxembourg.' Bevin was desperate to get the Americans to join this alliance.

'But I thought you were England's Minister for Health?'

'No, that's Nye Bevan. I'm Ernest *Bevin*. I'm Britain's most influential Foreign Secretary of the twentieth century.'

'Oh sure, I remember. Nye Bevin, the Welsh one?'

Ernest Bevin used the crisis of the Berlin Airlift to push for the

---

* France ended up leaving NATO in the 1960s, having spent years annoying everyone else by calling it 'OTAN'. De Gaulle said he wanted all American troops to leave French soil, which prompted the response, 'Including all the dead ones?'

creation of what would become the North Atlantic Treaty Organization. This military power bloc was created in order that Western Europe could be rude to the Russians and then run and hide behind the legs of the American President. 'At last,' Britain thought, 'we can sleep easy.' Four months after NATO was formed, Russia tested its first atomic bomb.

Middle East solutions: answers on a postcard, please . . .

Rather inconveniently, the British discovered that Palestine had somehow ended up as part of the British Empire after the First World War. They had a look back through the old minutes to make sure no one had said anything stupid, and there was only the minor matter of the 'Balfour declaration' of 1917 vaguely promising a Jewish homeland in Palestine.

'Well, I'm sure no one remembers us saying that . . .' they whispered, looking around in the hope that they might have got away with it. But by now thousands of Jewish refugees were heading to the sacred homeland they had been promised by Jehovah (as well as the British Foreign Secretary Arthur Balfour, so that made it doubly legitimate). The holocaust had left an enormous well of sympathy for the Jews who had survived the Nazi reign of terror in Europe, but the Arabs who had lived in Palestine for millennia were understandably not that wild at finding themselves overwhelmed by a massive influx of Jews who claimed this land as their own.

The proposed Anglo-American solution was a partition of Palestine, but neither side could agree on the terms. Violence was increasing in the British mandate as the number of Jewish arrivals exceeded the quotas that had been established to mollify Arab opinion. With Nazi war criminals still being tried in Nuremberg,

Britain decided it might look good if the Jews arriving in Palestine were now imprisoned in internment camps, and thus it was that Britain found itself responsible for putting holocaust survivors behind barbed wire against all the advice of the PR guys.

British soldiers were being alternately stoned by Arabs and blown up by Zionist terrorists (some of whom would go on to be Israeli ministers) and with Egyptian and Syrian armies gathering on the borders, Britain washed its hands of Palestine in 1948, saying to the United Nations: 'Is it all right if we leave this one with you?'

The State of Israel was declared before the UN had finished colouring in the map of their messy-looking partition; an Arab-Israeli war broke out, the first of several such conflicts which have seen the Middle East earn its special status as 'most likely spark of World War Three'. Fortunately in 2009 a caller to a radio phone-in show was able to offer the solution to the seemingly intractable Arab-Israeli conflict. 'They should just sort it all out,' suggested the late-night contributor to Radio 5 Live. 'Somebody needs to get in there and bang some heads together.' Peace is expected to follow as soon as this formula is implemented.

The partition of India: Mountbatten draws map on poppadom then snaps it in three

In India the partition solution was at least accepted in principle, even if each side believed that its rival should only have that bit of land that's exposed when the tide is out. India had played a major part in the war, without ever being consulted whether it wanted to be involved or not. By the time Japan surrendered, the clamour for Indian independence was unstoppable, despite Conservative outrage at the Labour government apparently allowing the 'jewel in the crown' of the British Empire to be given away. Indeed if

Winston Churchill had won the 1945 election, one shudders to think of the bloodbath that would have followed had the clamour for Indian independence been refused.

Lord Louis Mountbatten was given the task of viceroy, and arrived in his new job with leisurely thoughts of maybe convening a high-level conference on the various options for self-government at some point in the next few years. Within a couple of hours at his desk he realized that Britain's best interest would be to get out of India as quickly as possible. Despite the peaceful campaign of Mahatma Gandhi that had seen him locked up during the war, violence was escalating, with regional and religious rivalries threatening civil war at the same time as a general war of independence. With Muslim and Hindu rivalry intensifying, Mountbatten proposed the partition of India. He dug out an old map of India, drew a big line across it with his marker pen and said, 'Right, this bit can be Muslim Pakistan. And this bit we'll just call "India". And then way over here, we'll give this big delta to Pakistan as well, and call that "East Bengal" or "East Pakistan" or something. Yes, that will work well. One Muslim country split into two parts, thousands of miles from each other, with their greatest rival slap in the middle. I definitely can't see that going wrong . . .'*

Independence Day was set for 15 August 1947, just two years after the departure of thousands of British troops who had been stationed there to stop Britain losing India during the war. There was hardly time to print a few 'The Mountbattens are moving' cards.

'But, Lord Mountbatten, the ruler of Muslim Kashmir is Hindu, he has opted for the wrong country.'

'Erm . . . well, we've sort of done the new maps now . . .'

'And Mr Viceroy-Sir, hundreds of thousands of refugees are

---

* In 1971, East Pakistan seceded from its larger partner and after a small war, which got a lot bigger once India joined in, became the independent state of Bangladesh.

fleeing their homes to be on the right side of the border when it comes into existence, and not all of them will make it.'

'Right, OK, I hear what you're saying, but we're going now, so can we just leave you to sort all that out? I've left a fiver for the gas and electric. The lady who cleans the Taj Mahal normally comes on Thursdays . . .'

Colonies reunited

In 1949 the prefix 'British' was dropped from what became known as the 'Commonwealth of Nations', in an attempt to pretend that it wasn't a self-help group for victims of imperial abuse. They continued to meet in echoey church halls where they'd sit around in circles saying, 'My name is Burma, and I am a survivor of colonial exploitation.' Then a gentle but encouraging smatter of applause at this new recruit's courage to confront his harrowing mistreatment at the hands of an invading foreign power, while the British delegate shifted self-consciously in his plastic chair.

In order to get their own back on the British, a large number of its newly independent colonies* kept the British monarch as their head of state, so that the King or Queen would have to try not to blush or giggle at displays of aboriginal war dances that involved a lot of naked bottoms or jiggling bare breasts. If the royal family still weren't embarrassed, then one of the Commonwealth leaders would occasionally turn into a mad dictator, massacring his own people and declaring himself the World Kung Fu Champion or something, to see at what point they might earn a mild

---

* All members of the Commonwealth of Nations were of course former British colonies, though for some reason the former Portuguese colony of Mozambique managed to sneak into the clubhouse in 1995, and though various guests at the banquet were whispering, 'What are they doing here?' nobody was quite brave enough to ask them to leave.

rebuke from the uncomfortable former colonial power.

Not all of Britain's former colonies opted to join the Commonwealth, however; those who are not members include Iraq, Kuwait, Jordan, Somalia, Sudan and Israel. When you look at the disaster areas on this list, you can't help thinking that somebody in London just pretended to lose their application forms.

On being reminded that it still had links with Britain, Southern Ireland withdrew from the Commonwealth in 1949, declaring itself a republic. Although many Irishmen had fought with the Allies during the war, Ireland had maintained a strict neutrality during what it had rather quaintly called 'the Emergency'. The Royal Navy would have gained great advantage from use of the Irish ports, and in June 1940 Churchill was so desperate for Eire to join Britain in the war that he offered to cede the six counties of Northern Ireland to the Irish Free State. De Valera turned him down flat. Immediately after the war, the two of them took turns to broadcast rude things about one another, a sort of diplomatic *Jerry Springer Show*: 'Coming up after the break – neighbours who hate each other more than the Nazis.' Had De Valera accepted Churchill's offer, the six counties under British rule would have been reunited with the rest of Ireland at a time of such dire national emergency that the Unionists could not have resisted, and the Irish problem might have been solved for ever. But De Valera had no reason to trust Churchill, nor the British, and in any case Irish public opinion would never have stood for it. 'Ah well, not to worry,' they would have snapped.

Welcome to Britain (please use tradesmen's entrance)

The Irish continued to emigrate to England in large numbers, looking for work as builders or twinkly-eyed television presenters. They still endured discrimination, but soon there would be new arrivals for the British to be prejudiced against. There was a stark contrast between the romantic notion of the British Empire being a global nation of equals under the King, and the reality of British attitudes to foreigners, particularly those with a different-coloured skin. Although black American GIs had found British attitudes to their race refreshingly polite, there was still an almost unquestioned assumption that the white man was superior to the black, and that it was perfectly acceptable for the Dam Busters to have a black Labrador called Nigger.

When the British government passed the British Nationality Act in 1948, affirming the right of Commonwealth subjects to British citizenship, they had in mind all those hearty Canadian lumberjacks and Australian sheep farmers and rich white South African diamond traders. It never occurred to them that ordinary Jamaicans or Indians or Pakistanis would have the initiative, or indeed the money, to up sticks and move to Leicester, or that companies like London Transport would turn to the Caribbean to solve local labour shortages. The transformation of Britain into a multiracial country did not happen because of any planned government policy; it happened when no one was looking. It is only retrospectively that they all pretend they were always in favour of it, so as not to appear racist.*

In 1948 the former troop carrier *Empire Windrush*† set sail from Jamaica, destined for Tilbury Docks and pride of place in Black History Month. When 492 West Indian immigrants disembarked on 22 June, there was widespread alarm at the prospect of what this might lead to. All the white liberals would have to pretend to

---

* At this point the destination of choice for most West Indian migrants was still the United States, but the door was slammed shut by their Immigration and Nationality Act of 1952. Not that the UK was second choice or anything.

† The *Windrush* was originally a German ship, but was seized towards the end of the war. The boat that came to symbolize the beginnings of Britain's multicultural society had previously been used for holidays for high-ranking Nazis.

enjoy the crush of the Notting Hill Carnival, for a three-second glance at a Jamaican lady in exotic costume. The TV news producers would have to find a white policeman who was prepared to fake laughter while dancing with a fat black grandmother. Mass immigration had always happened, of course, but now you'd be able to spot a foreigner before he opened his mouth. Nobody had thought any of it through, with the result that it was racists who would set the agenda with their own reactions to the changes that followed over the next couple of decades.

Many of the new arrivals were found temporary housing in the deep underground tunnels at Clapham North and in tents on Clapham Common. One hundred and fifty years earlier, the Clapham Sect had met in the houses around the common and began the campaign that would end the transportation of slaves from Africa to the Americas. Now fifteen decades later, the descendants of some of those slaves came back across the Atlantic, to the very place where the emancipation of their forefathers had begun. But you try explaining the wonderfully symmetrical history of Clapham to a cabbie at half past midnight, and he still won't take you south of the river.*

Shortages to be rationed

The mood in Britain remained stubbornly gloomy as the patient British public joined the back of the queue for the 1950s. Shortages of goods and raw materials didn't just limit what you could eat or wear, it was much harder to make improvements to your home, or to buy new furnishings or the occasional luxury or treat. You couldn't just go into Ann Summers and buy sex toys for

---

* The nearest Labour Exchange was in Brixton, and so a number of the West Indian immigrants ended up settling there.

your sister's hen night, you had to queue up behind all the other housewives in headscarves clutching their vibrator coupons and moaning about the rationing of chocolate willies. Foreign holidays were almost impossible while travellers were forbidden to take more than £30 out of the country, and a web of regulations and high taxation stifled those entrepreneurs who aspired to develop private businesses.

This was the price paid by the middle classes for the banishing of unemployment and poverty that had blighted millions of lives between the wars. Being told that a family in Jarrow have stopped worrying about hunger and rickets is all well and good, but it doesn't help solve the more pressing issue that petrol rationing is preventing you from speeding around the leafy lanes of Surrey in your new motor car.

In the run-up to the 1950 election, the government made an effort to abolish as many regulations and restrictions as was practically possible. The president of the Board of Trade was a precocious young minister called Harold Wilson, only thirty-one when he joined the cabinet, and he declared his ambition to create 'a bonfire of controls' and to see that coupons and regulations went up in smoke. The government succeeded in ending rationing in most foods and commodities; now there would just be runaway inflation so you couldn't afford the stuff anyway.

Election '50: 'We'll change things less than you would'

Having had such a radical manifesto back in 1945, Labour thought it would keep one step ahead of the electorate in 1950 by boring them into submission. Whereas previously the people's party had advocated state ownership of such giants as coal, steel, ship-building and health provision, now it attempted to stir the idealists' imagination with proposed nationalization of the meat wholesaling industry. And the visionaries weren't going to stop there – the 1950 manifesto also promised the people that they could become the proud owners of the cement industry and sugar-refining plants as well. To campaign against the latter, Tate & Lyle launched the 'Mr Cube' character, a determined-looking cartoon sugar cube armed with a sword, who presumably intended to stab anyone who attempted to carry out government policy.

But what is significant about the 1950 election isn't what Labour put in its manifesto, it was what the Conservatives left out of theirs. Despite having opposed every nationalization and reform of the Labour government, Churchill's opposition now accepted the welfare state as a fait accompli and offered no proposals to put the nation's health, coal or indeed sewage in private hands. Quite apart from the logistical problems this would involve, Labour's reforms were on the whole very popular, with the National Health Service judged to be a particular success even by most of the doctors who had so vigorously opposed it. It shouldn't be forgotten that Winston Churchill was a former Liberal, a key figure of the reforming government elected in 1906; the foundations of the welfare state had been laid by Lloyd George with Churchill at his side.

Labour won the 1950 election,* but with a greatly reduced majority. It was clear that a second election would have to follow soon, and despite Labour riding high in the opinion polls, the collapse of the Liberals with most of their votes going to the Tories would see Labour defeated and out of office for thirteen years.

---

* This was the first 'one person one vote' general election in British history. Prior to the abolition of the university seats in 1948, graduates had a second vote to elect Conservative Members of Parliament who couldn't find a seat anywhere else. Labour candidates were never elected to university seats – not even when H. G. Wells stood for London University.

A massive 30 per cent devaluation of the pound the previous year had been a further knock to British prestige, but it would actually be another war that would help the great war leader Winston Churchill return to office.

The Korean War: what is it good for? Answer: M*A*S*H* *

When North Korea attacked the South in 1950, Britain was starting to wish it hadn't been quite so hospitable to Karl Marx when he wrote down all his ideas about communism. Back in 1945 the Korean peninsula was divided into two occupation zones by the future US Secretary of State Dean Rusk. He did this in under half an hour using a National Geographic atlas. Japanese forces north of the 38th parallel would surrender to the Russians, those to the south would surrender to the Americans. This arbitrarily drawn line pretty well remains the border between the two countries today. But only after a three-year civil war that drew in around twenty other countries and left over a million dead.

Having watched China go communist, America did not feel particularly like standing back and allowing the Reds to take over a country it had effectively liberated five years earlier. They were determined to prevent South Korea and Japan from falling into the communist bloc, in order that they could develop free-market economies and then wipe out the American car industry a few decades later. President Truman made some alarming noises about using the atomic bomb and Clement Attlee flew over to Washington to try and talk him out of it. Thus it was that Britain found itself reluctantly dragged into a

* Set in Korea (although really a covert critique on the war in Vietnam), the American sit-com M*A*S*H* ended up lasting three times longer than the Korean War itself.

41

conventional war under the auspices of the United Nations.*

Britain sent sixty-three thousand troops out to the Far East. Luxembourg sent forty-four. North Korea was completely over-run, and then China intervened and South Korea was completely overrun, so they decided to go back to roughly where they had started and leave things as they'd been before it all kicked off. Since the ceasefire in 1953, there has been very little notice given to what became known as the 'forgotten war', although interest might be rekindled now that North Korea has got nuclear weapons and looks mad enough to use them: precipitating all-out atomic warfare and the end of life on Earth.

Although no regime change occurred in North or South Korea, thousands of miles away in London the financial burden of increased defence spending proved to be too much for the exhausted Labour government. The communists of North Korea finished off Britain's socialist government. Not that there was very much similarity between the British brand of socialism and the version developed in North Korea; Clement Attlee's birthday was not celebrated by a thousand schoolchildren performing a synchronized dance in the National Square of Salvation. 'Oh Clement Attlee, father of our nation, shining sun of a thousand suns, bringer of life to our farm animals and rice field irrigation system, let us sing the joy in our hearts at our glorious leader, Clement Attlee!' He would have puffed on his pipe and said, 'Well, let's not get too carried away, chaps!'

---

* Russia was boycotting the UN at the time, so just to annoy them, the others used the United Nations as the agency by which the North Korean aggression would be countered. And to really rub the communists' noses in it, China's seat on the UN was occupied by the exiled Chinese government now on the island of Taiwan.

The Festival of Britain (indoors if wet)

But with a mood of fatigue and drabness rather smothering smog-bound Britain, the idea of some sort of modest national party seemed like a good idea. Labour's deputy prime minister, Herbert Morrison, was determined to lift public spirits with his project of the Festival of Britain. It was described as 'a tonic for the nation' to be held on the centenary of the Great Exhibition of 1851, though many suggested the money would have been far better spent on housing. A large section of the south bank of the Thames was cleared of bomb-damaged slums and warehousing to create a riverside walkway beside what would become the Royal Festival Hall. 'Yes, and we can have a graffitied concrete undercroft full of teenagers skateboarding or drinking WKD . . .'

In terms of visitor numbers the festival was a great success, even if its legacy was rather diminished by the fact that most of the buildings, including the huge Dome of Discovery, were subsequently destroyed; judged 'too modernist' for the taste of the incoming Conservative government. No doubt in later years Herbert Morrison would have sat his grandson on his knee and told the young Peter Mandelson all about this whacky idea of building an expensive dome on the south bank of the Thames. 'Granddad is losing it,' he must have thought.

Cabinet split in two by NHS dentures

One of the icons of the festival was a large cigar-shaped sculpture called the Skylon that was suspended above the south bank. This futuristic symbol of modern Britain was proudly described as having 'no visible means of support'. 'Much like the British economy,' it was joked.

The dire economic situation and increased defence spending

meant the Exchequer was compelled to find a new source of revenue. It had become apparent that two areas of NHS spending were costing the government far more than anticipated. Rotten teeth and fading eyesight were revealed to have been two burdens people had suffered from in poverty for years (blindness from cataracts was suddenly reduced by a quarter), and that had now become a huge financial drain on the Treasury.

But when the cabinet finally agreed to the introduction of charges for spectacles and dental work, Nye Bevan resigned in protest. The father of the National Health Service argued (correctly as it turned out) that if Labour crossed the line of charging for medical attention, then the Tories would be able to go much further.

His resignation from the cabinet highlighted a bigger split: should there be more nationalization, or would that further alienate the Liberal voters who were switching to the Tories? The debate was becoming public and increasingly bitter, and when Labour lost the 1951 election, each side blamed the other for the defeat.

The policy of nationalization as pursued by Attlee's government has not had a good press in recent decades. Because of our memories of the doomed state-owned monoliths of the 1970s, we associate them with industrial unrest and appalling haircuts. But what we've forgotten is how badly these industries were run in the century before they were under public control. People didn't moan about overzealous Health and Safety officers back then. They just dug coal for a pittance until they were crushed at the pit head or died of pneumoconiosis. Unplanned railway development led to a chaotic system of competing lines and companies often serving the same area; London is still littered with overground railway stations that don't link up with one another or provide an integrated service. And the brutal and exploitative nature of unfettered private enterprise actually made capitalism less efficient. In the five years after the First World War, 178 million working days were lost to strikes. In the equivalent period after 1945, only 9 million days were lost.

At the end of the 1940s, there were many who thought the problem with Attlee's government was that they hadn't nationalized enough.

'Do you think any Labour government will ever be left-wing enough to nationalize the banks?'

'Well, maybe in the far-off future, like, say, in 2009 or something, there might be a Labour government so socialist that they take a majority share in all the investment banks and building societies. But I doubt it . . .'

Election '51: Labour lose power after getting most votes

But the British people didn't reject the Attlee government in 1951 for being too left-wing or indeed for failing to go further. In fact, the government remained incredibly popular, gaining over a million votes more than the Conservatives. But with the Liberals all but withdrawing from the contest, the Conservatives made twenty-five gains in key seats to see Winston Churchill return to power. Popularly believed to be Britain's greatest ever Prime Minister, Winston Churchill served two periods of office at 10 Downing Street without ever winning a mandate from the British electorate.

And so one of the most remarkable British governments in history came to an exhausted end. In six hectic years they had transformed the relationship between the individual and the state, taken the key industries into public control, created the NHS, managed the aftermath of war with Germany while trying to avoid a new one with Russia, withdrawn from India and Palestine, and taken a lead role in the establishment of the United Nations and NATO. And yet it seems all anyone could think about was the distinct lack of chocolate biscuits.

The late 1940s and early 1950s have become synonymous with austerity; shortages, rationing and people in unconvincing cockney accents telling the butcher, 'Lawks a lordy, how am oi gonna feed the whole family on that tiny bit o' bloomin' gristle?' But despite the allegations from some quarters of malnutrition, people were in fact healthier than they had ever been and certainly had a better diet than they do today. We have to remember that the history of those years was written by the middle classes; that the opinion-formers, such as journalists and novelists and diary-keepers and letter-writers, were predominantly the people who had never experienced the dire poverty of the 1930s and were now enduring *comparatively* mild peacetime shortages for the first time.

For the great mass of the British people, the daily calorie intake was higher than ever before; the centuries of genuine hunger were over. Children were growing taller; free school milk and cod-liver oil were helping to banish the preventable, poverty-related diseases of the Great Depression. Nobody was starving, even if the prospect of *snoek piquante* might not have been particularly appetizing.

Increased government expenditure meant higher taxes for those who could afford it and there is no denying that for the better-off, life was not as comfortable as it had been in the 1930s. The middle classes were still looking at the enormous pile of washing up that had been growing since 1939 and wondering who was going to do it now they no longer had domestic servants. The incomes of manual workers were reckoned to have increased by about 10 per cent since 1938, while the middle classes dipped by about 20 per cent, even if they still earned twice as much. So it was the professional salary-earners who felt the pinch, and that is why the era has become synonymous with austerity and petty officialdom. If the three-quarters of the population who made up the working classes had written the history books, the war and its aftermath would be remembered as a golden age of plenty. And then their 'superiors' would have tutted at their use of regional idioms and appalling grammar. The post-war period was that narrow window in British history when the British people were finally healthy: no longer visibly undernourished and suffering the diseases of poverty, but before they all stuffed themselves with burgers, fries and Dunkin' Donuts and developed obesity, heart problems and type-2 diabetes.

And so with a new government, and shortly a new monarch, the British hovered at the threshold of the 1950s, saying, 'After you.' 'No, really, you first.' Despite six years of socialist government, Britain was still a very class-bound country; reverence and respect for the middle and upper classes was the norm.

But Labour needn't have worried that it hadn't done much to change the culture of unquestioning deference towards the rich and well educated. Now the socialists just had to let the upper classes have another turn in government, and the aristocracy would do the job for them . . .

2

1951–1963

*How the ruling class lost the British people's unquestioning respect
just because they were exposed as a bunch of self-serving,
philandering liars*

In 1955 a mad scientist working alone in a laboratory in California
mixed together the compounds of bubblegum, vinyl and over-
active hormones and created a monster that was before long
rampaging out of control. *The Attack of the Scowling Teenagers*
brought terror to normally quiet and respectable communities;
crowds turned and fled in panic as hordes of these hideous, acne-
covered humanoids closed in on suburbia, chewing and sneering
and failing to maintain adequate standards of personal hygiene.
Dawn raids on suspected adolescents were useless as nobody
could wake them up. An attempt to arrange high-level peace talks
failed when no one could understand their mumbling.

Before the 1950s, young adults generally went straight into
work or were stuck in a uniform and packed off to catch venereal
disease in some far-flung colony. But this was the decade when
teenagers would no longer aspire to ape their mothers and fathers.
They would develop an entirely separate youth culture all their
own, one that revolved around music, clothes and spending their

parents' money. The energy and attitude of American rock 'n' roll was adopted wholesale by Britain's working-class youth (middle-class students continued to prefer jazz for a few years until eventually they realized it wasn't as good). This was the decade when the Americans gave us Elvis Presley, Buddy Holly and James Dean. And Britain hit back with Cliff Richard. As if the Suez Crisis wasn't humiliating enough.

But the 1950s was also the period when the great British public reached a sort of shared national adolescence. The teenagers thought they had found something new in this shocking idea of sneering at the establishment, only to find their parents doing it as well. A series of scandals and political disasters left large sections of the British public wondering if their elders and betters (and their rulers generally were the former) deserved their un-questioned deference after all. And so they matured from their child-like state of naive trust and unwavering respect for their 'superiors' into a sort of grumpy political puberty: '*OMG, my Prime Minister is like, so embarrassing!*' and '*Chancellor: UR ruin-ing my life!*' and '*I'm like, totally old enough to read* Lady Chatterley's Lover *and there's nothing you can do to stop me!*'

Churchill the sequel: 'This time he's old'

Winston Churchill was seventy-seven when he returned to 10 Downing Street. He suffered a couple of strokes while in office, but his doctor decided he ought to remain in public life in case retirement demoralized him and led to further deterioration in his health. Fortunately for the British people, this reasoning was not made public at the time: 'He's not really up to it, but I thought he ought to be Prime Minister just so he's got something to do ...'

Churchill surrounded himself with a number of wartime colleagues, many of whom sat in the House of Lords, but a couple of future stars began to make names for themselves in the cabinet. Both Harold Macmillan and Rab Butler had ambitions to become Prime Minister, though only one possessed the killer instinct to finally make it. But the immediate heir apparent was Anthony Eden. Eden had been Foreign Secretary before the war, resigning in protest at Neville Chamberlain's policy of appeasing Adolf Hitler. This gave Eden a certain number of brownie points later on when it turned out that the anti-Semitic fascist dictator was actually one of the bad guys, and so he emerged as the man who would eventually succeed Churchill. But like Gordon Brown waiting for ever for Tony Blair to retire, Eden became deeply frustrated that the top job seemed like it would never be his. Eden actually married his boss's niece, but rather disappointingly Uncle Winston didn't give the happy couple the keys to Number 10 as a wedding present.

With the cabinet full of crusty old ministers covered in cobwebs, the new government did not bring a particularly fresh feel to the new decade. The ageing nature of the government was further highlighted by the accession of a 25-year-old Queen Elizabeth. The young Princess, who, when she was a child, had not been expected to become a monarch inherited the throne in February 1952 after the premature death of her sickly, chain-smoking father. She had actually been on holiday in Kenya when news came that her father had died; now she was to fly home as Queen. Whether she managed to persuade the airline to give her an upgrade is not recorded.

Queen Elizabeth II's* coronation the following year was the event that popularized television. For the first time, this ancient ceremony was watched by millions of people around the globe. In Britain sales of TV sets rocketed, and those who couldn't afford the latest electrical gadget all crammed into their neighbours' front

---

* In Scotland she became Queen Elizabeth I, as the Scots had not been ruled by Elizabeth Tudor. Prince Charles will be Charles III north and south of the border, even though this was the title Bonnie Prince Charlie gave himself.

rooms to witness the crowning of their monarch and then to watch the action replay while the pundits back in the studio analysed the action: 'Look at the Archbishop of Canterbury – he picks up the crown there, he knows what he wants to do with it, and bam! Straight onto the Queen's head, inch perfect!'

The papers boldly talked of the 'New Elizabethans', and her subjects obliged by a string of notable achievements. The New Zealander Edmund Hillary and Tenzing Norgay climbed the highest mountain in the world; Roger Bannister ran a mile in under four minutes, and most important of all, Watson and Crick discovered the structure of the DNA molecule, which everyone agreed was a splendid achievement, though not quite as easy to understand as running fast or climbing mountains. Ian Fleming published his first James Bond novel, and in the West End a new Agatha Christie murder mystery play opened called *The Mousetrap*, which is still running today, in case you wanted to drive past all the tourists queuing up outside St Martin's Theatre and shout out who did it.

Britain gets atom bomb to keep up with the Joneses

To add to Britain's list of 'achievements', Churchill announced that Britain now had its own atomic bomb. It was very big and powerful and its arrival must have been a huge consolation to all those people still queuing up for their meat ration. British scientists had of course played a major role in the development of the bomb during the war, and Churchill now revealed that Roosevelt had assured him that he would never use this terrifying new weapon without the British Prime Minister's agreement.* But after the war, America had ended its atomic cooperation with

* By the time of Hiroshima, however, Roosevelt had of course died, and Churchill was out of power. Attlee contacted Washington to give his approval in any case, as if anyone cared.

Britain, and so the Attlee government had resolved to go ahead with a programme of its own. The story goes that in 1946, a cabinet sub-committee chaired by Attlee was close to deciding against building a uranium-enriching plant on the basis of cost, when Ernest Bevin arrived late and said, 'We've got to have this thing . . . I don't want any other Foreign Secretary of this country to be talked at or to by the Secretary of State of the US as I have just been.' So it is quite possible that if James F. Byrnes had been a little more polite and tactful to Ernest Bevin, Britain would never have embarked on an atomic weapons programme.

The project was kept secret from the cabinet and of course from the leader of the opposition (much to Churchill's irritation), but it was not until he returned to power that Britain was ready to test its first weapon. And so in October 1952, Operation Hurricane saw Britain's first atomic bomb tested off the coast of Western Australia. The bomb was taken to this location aboard HMS *Plym* and detonated inside the hull of the ship. The ship was not really worth repairing after that.* It was a moment of some pride for Britain, and the news reels cheerfully reported the fun of it all: *Yes, being in the British army can sometimes be pretty hot work, especially for these lucky young soldiers who were allowed to top up their suntans by watching the testing of Britain's first atomic bomb! Some of the soldiers reported feeling a little queasy afterwards, but it was probably just the excitement of it all!*

Britain became the world's third atomic power; the Russians had tested their first bomb three years earlier, thanks to the generous assistance of half the staff of MI5 whose communist sympathies could not have been more obvious if they had worn little furry hats and sold the *Morning Star* outside Woolworths. The shock defection of Guy Burgess and Donald Maclean to the

---

* The Royal Navy had more ships than it knew what to do with after the war. Many were towed out to sea and simply used for target practice.

Soviet Union in 1951 had confirmed American suspicions that the British security services were riddled with spies, and rather justified their decision not to share nuclear secrets with their former ally. Much was made of the homosexuality of these spies. Being 'queer' and being a traitor became rather mixed up in the minds of the British press, who somehow imagined that the Cambridge spy ring were not only leaking nuclear secrets, but also the latest British developments in window dressing and musical theatre.

Let them eat toffee apples!

There was some hope that the Cold War might warm up a bit with the death of Stalin in 1953, but this proved short-lived. Before long the government would be issuing the first nuclear civil-defence manuals, which recommended wearing a hat and gloves and using lots of soap and water. But the end of the Korean War did help improve the government's finances, while standards of living began to improve noticeably. The number of cars on the roads rose from 2.5 to 6 million between 1951 and 1963, and with no parking restrictions, even in central London, it was possible to drive to work and leave your car outside the office all day. The number of households with fridges rose from 5 per cent to 37 per cent and millions of hours were lost as people tried to see if the light went out when you shut the door. Thousands of British people were now buying television sets so they could be patronized by tiny blurred upper-class presenters lecturing them on high culture from the corner of their living rooms. The launch of commercial television in 1954 brought its own cultural shift; being presented with a choice between the BBC's Reithian mission to educate and inform, or independent television's more populist American-style game shows and light entertainment, millions of Britons opted for the latter. It was still considered a little 'common' to watch ITV for decades afterwards, until the Sky Monster Trucks and Lager Channel finally came along and made ITV look positively highbrow.

The feel-good factor was augmented when sweets and sugar came off ration in February 1953. One firm in Clapham gave away free lollipops to 800 schoolchildren, throwing them off the back of a lorry into a crowd of joyful kids. The following year saw rationing end for butter, cheese, margarine, cooking fat and finally, in July, meat. The end of rationing was a huge psychological step forward for the British consumer, and with the abolition of identity cards around the same time, drew a line under the extended hangover from the Second World War.

One meat that had been a popular alternative in the countryside during the years of shortages suddenly disappeared. In 1953, Britain's rabbit population became infected with the myxomatosis virus that had devastated the French rabbit population and was deliberately introduced by a handful of British farmers and landowners. Children accompanying their parents on country walks would suddenly stumble upon a diseased flea-ridden rabbit that was too sick and disoriented to run away. 'Mummy, Mummy, I've found a rabbit! Can we take it home for a pet? I'm going to call him Thumper!'

'Er, no, dear, put Thumper down, I think he's a bit poorly and needs to go home for a very long sleep. Why don't we get you something more hygienic? Like a rat with Weil's disease?' Britain's rabbit population was reduced by about 95 per cent and it took another couple of decades for the rabbit population to recover, by which time everyone had cars and they all got run over instead.

Government and opposition agree to agree

The economy was finally recovering from the post-war depression, though it was the Conservatives who could now take credit for the mini-boom that eventually followed Labour's unpopular devaluation of the pound. But in both foreign and domestic affairs there was little to choose between the two parties. When he returned to power Churchill could hardly reverse everything achieved by the previous 'socialist government'. 'Excuse me, India, I know we made you independent, but would you mind coming back in the Empire now?' Churchill lived with Labour's welfare state, introducing prescription charges, but not daring to dismantle the popular provisions for young and old. The main political parties were so close that they had to find something else to argue about at Prime Minister's Question Time. 'I cannot accept the leader of the opposition's assertion that cats are cleverer than dogs. When did you ever see a cat fetch a stick?'

'Because cats don't want to. They're too clever.' Further heated debates ensued on whether milk should be added to tea before or after and on the correct length for a piece of string.

Such was the similarity between the parties that the political philosophy of the day was dubbed 'Butskellism', an amalgam of the Tory Chancellor Rab Butler and his opposite number Hugh Gaitskell. And yet there was a moment when the entire post-war consensus was nearly blown apart, when the government was days away from adopting a radical economic policy that would have seen unemployment rocketing towards a million. Nicknamed ROBOT after the initials of the three civil servants who championed the proposal (one of them was the father of Charles Clarke, the future Labour minister), the secret plan was to let the pound find its own value on the world markets, regardless of what it did to jobs or the government's ability to fund the welfare state, its house-building programme or extensive overseas commitments. If the monetarist ROBOT scheme had not been abandoned at the last minute due to the fierce opposition of Harold Macmillan and Anthony Eden (who threatened to resign), then the entire history of post-war Britain would have been very different. British manufacturing industry would have had a huge boost from cheaper exports, but it is impossible to guess whether the welfare state could have survived. Churchill was not prepared to go through with such a high-risk and socially divisive policy. Although she always enjoyed the comparison, Churchill, it transpired, was no Margaret Thatcher.

The cabinet was furious about the way this radical proposal had been put to them so soon before the budget, and individual ministers were regularly outraged by the careless, high-handed way Churchill would announce summits or new initiatives without informing them first. He was far more considerate to those outside the Conservative Party; he invited the leader of the Liberal Party to join his cabinet (who declined) and talked of coalition if the economic situation deteriorated. Without telling his Chancellor, he gave in to all the demands of the railway unions, so that people travelling home for Christmas would not be disturbed by a railway strike. The growth of union power in Britain is generally associated with the Labour Party but it was during the Conservative 1950s that the trades unions became seemingly unassailable. Ironically for a man who had lived his entire life as an indomitable fighter, Churchill's peacetime premiership was spent avoiding conflict and thus storing up problems for later.

It's the ~~economy~~ Empire, stupid!

Britain's improving situation could not hide the fact that her economic growth was still lagging behind that of her competitors.

The European Coal and Steel Community* was proving to be something of a trading bonus for its founding members, while bizarrely Britain still looked to the distant Dominions as its natural trading partners. The legacy of Empire wasn't just a financial burden in terms of Britain's military commitments around the globe, it also affected the country's outlook: the former imperial power failed to recognize where its future lay. All the harsh economic indicators suggested that Britain should focus on trading with Europe; all the sentimental arguments pointed to concentrating on New Zealand. It took them a decade and a half to work out that France was much, much nearer.

With better leadership, Britain could have been *the* dominant European economy after the war. British industry had a huge headstart on Germany in 1945. So how did it come to the point twenty-five years later when *the* second car to buy for the wife and kids in the United States was the Volkswagen Beetle, and not the Morris Minor? It can't all be put down to the persuasive power of *Herbie Goes Bananas*. Some blame an economic system that kept the pound artificially high, others the power of the British unions or a lack of entrepreneurship.

The nation's progress was also stymied by that peculiarly British problem of class. In the UK, the heads of industry were not trained as engineers or technicians; that would have involved getting oil on your hands and talking to people who took sugar in their tea. No, what better preparation for running a sector of Britain's manufacturing industry than studying Classics at Oxford or Cambridge? To say that one was an 'engineer' would have cost you your invitation to join the golf club to tut at that oik

---

* The 'Common Market' was an evolving alliance, but most date the creation of the European Economic Community from the signing of the Treaty of Rome in March 1957. This came about after various French overtures about closer cooperation had been rejected by the British government, including even one suggestion from the French Prime Minister that France join the British Commonwealth.

attempting to enter the clubroom without a tie. The more common members of Churchill's cabinet like Rab Butler had gone to public schools such as Marlborough College, rather than Eton or Harrow like the PM and his deputy. Other names around Churchill's cabinet table were Lord Woolton, Lord Simonds, Lord Ismay, Lord Leathers, Lord Cherwell and the Marquess of Salisbury; Marquesses as well as Lords, so there was some social variation.

In a rare concession to the changing times, the Queen eventually decided to end the tradition of having the debutantes presented at court. Until the 1950s, the daughters of aristocrats 'came out' (no, not like that) by being presented to the reigning monarch, after which they would attend the social events of the season such as Ascot, Henley Regatta and Monsters of Rock at Castle Donington. Then they would get married, produce an heir, find their husband was cheating on them, start drinking heavily while remaining stoic and loyal, before finally having a nervous breakdown on being informed that their only child was now seven years old and was being sent off to boarding school.

The happiest days of your life (Christian Brothers pupils excluded)

One of the latter-day criticisms of the Attlee government was that it missed the opportunity to abolish public schools at the one point in British history when this might have been politically possible. This is perhaps a little unfair, considering what else the Labour government achieved in just six years, but also presumes that Attlee would have wanted to do such a thing. The Haileybury old boy had fond memories of his own public school, but more importantly, a major education reform had been enacted by the coalition government the year before Labour came to power. The man who was now Chancellor of the Exchequer, Richard Austen Butler, commonly known as 'Rab', had piloted the 1944 Education Act which had created the so-called tripartite system of education, creating grammar schools, secondary moderns and technical schools (although in practice the latter were very few in number).*

Now every 11-year-old in the state system took an examination to sort out the minority that would go on to get qualifications and possibly proceed to university. 'Right, children, this little examination is nothing to worry about, it's simply to determine whether you spend your adult life in a nice warm office earning a comfortable salary, or whether you will be out in the rain from the ages of sixteen to sixty-five, digging the road for a pittance. Barry, why are you crying?'

It was a bit like the sorting hat in Harry Potter: if you looked better in a cloth cap, you were designated working class and sent off to learn about metalwork and burglary. And if the bowler hat was a better fit, then you were clearly middle class and were destined to study English, Maths and fiddling your tax expenses. Under the grammar-school system, the life chances of most children were effectively written off before they were twelve, since only between 15 and 25 per cent of children would get a place at a grammar school (depending on where you lived). The uniform of one school signified success, the other signified failure; a division that often cut across the same family. Bobby Charlton, for example, passed his eleven-plus and ended up playing as an attacking midfielder for England's World Cup-winning team. But Jackie Charlton failed his eleven-plus, so he had to go in defence.

---

* Rab Butler's Education Act had also allowed for the creation of what was called a 'comprehensive school', which would educate all the children together, and the first one opened in Anglesey in 1949.

Churchill retires exhausted after four years doing nothing

Churchill now spent a good deal of time at Chequers gardening and painting. 'Sir Winston', as he now was, had always been irritated by one of the priceless works of art at the Prime Minister's country retreat. A large original painting by Snyders, it featured a mighty lion trapped in a net, being released by a little mouse gnawing at the rope. Churchill decided that Snyders had failed to make the mouse big enough, and so he painted a great big rat over it. It takes a certain sort of self-confidence to correct the priceless painting of a seventeenth-century Flemish master. Another painting was 'improved' in a more direct way. When his fellow MPs gave him an eightieth birthday present in the form of a portrait by the great British artist Graham Sutherland, Churchill damned the work by praising it as 'a remarkable example of modern art'. He actually detested the painting and later had it thrown on the fire.

The eccentric old man's health was deteriorating and he was visibly tired. His depressions (what he called his 'black dog') were more frequent and had he not been the clear favourite to win the BBC's Great Britons poll coming up in 2002, he would have been told to step aside for a younger man. He was not even well enough to collect his Nobel Prize for Literature, an award that makes him unique among Conservative Party authors until writing's greatest prize is won by Jeffrey Archer, Ann Widdecombe or Edwina Currie.

As the government entered 1955, with an election looming it was clearly time for Churchill to make way for another man. 'Who should it be?' he would wonder out loud in front of his Foreign Secretary, as Eden tried not to explode with frustration. Churchill had first identified Anthony Eden as his successor back in 1942. Thirteen years later the impatient deputy finally got the top job he had coveted for so long. He lasted just eighteen months.

Eden wins election, loses British World Power status

Anthony Eden's arrival at 10 Downing Street was greeted with a warm glow of self-congratulation by the Conservative establishment. The debonair old Etonian had a long and distinguished record of serving his country, dating right back to the First World War when he and Hitler quite possibly faced one another in opposite trenches at Ypres. In 1955 the new Prime Minister quickly called a general election to secure a personal mandate, and with rationing now ended, standards of living improving and an experienced statesman at the helm, British voters saw no reason to change governments. The defeated Labour legend Clement Attlee retired with a hereditary peerage, so that eventually his grandson could become a Conservative member of the House of Lords.

But very soon a few people began to have their doubts about Anthony Eden, worrying that this lifelong understudy was not up to playing the starring role. Poor management of the cabinet and the economy meant that his stock was already falling by the time of the crisis that would forever overshadow all his previous achievements.

To understand the Suez Crisis of 1956 it is necessary to give a little background on Egypt. Around 2500 BC, during the Third Dynasty, Cheops began work on the Great Pyramid at Giza . . . Hang on, skip a bit . . . In 1954, Gamal Abdel Nasser came to power in Egypt, following a revolution he had helped initiate a couple of years earlier. He was keen to press ahead with ambitious plans for a dam across the Nile, but Britain and America changed their mind about lending Egypt the cash. So in 1956, having cut Egypt's remaining ties with Britain, Nasser nationalized the Suez Canal.

The reaction in London was little short of hysterical. Britain's press and politicians came up with all sorts of carefully thought through historical analogies: 'He's like Hitler' or 'It's Adolf Nasser' or 'Taking control of a waterway that runs through his own country is exactly the same as starting the Second World War and killing millions of innocent people'. The previous decade the British government had nationalized the railways. If an Egyptian company had had 44 per cent of the shares in Great Western Railway, it's hard to imagine the Cairo government launching an invasion of Swindon to take them back.

The canal was certainly important to British trade; two-thirds of Europe's oil passed through the canal. But Nasser had no intention of halting this traffic. It was exactly because he needed those tolls that he nationalized Egypt's greatest asset. Although Nasser had not acted illegally, Eden was obsessed with the Hitler analogy and determined not to allow this Arabic revolutionary to 'have his thumb on our windpipe'. The French, who had originally built the canal (before Disraeli bought it on eBay), were equally outraged and a secret deal was done at Chequers between Britain, France and Israel. The clumsy plot was that Israel would invade Egypt, and then France and Britain would feign shock at this development, and be forced to intervene to make the canal safe for the world.

Nobody was fooled for a minute. A build-up of British troops at Cyprus prior to the Israeli invasion made it clear that military action was coming. More significantly, the American President was up for re-election the following month, so what better time to publicly humiliate him by not letting him in on the secret plans? Eden deceived the House of Commons and the British people, but worse still, Arab and Israeli soldiers lost their lives during the obliging Israeli invasion that was only mounted to allow Eden and the French government to save face. Britain and France duly issued their stern 'ultimatum' to Egypt and Israel.

'Oh, I recognize this . . .' said Israel. 'We helped you write it.'
'Shhhh!'

Showing even less political nous than they had demonstrated in
the lead-up to the crisis, the former imperial powers began their
invasion of Egypt in the week of the US presidential elections.
The Europeans had no moral case for the seizure of the canal, and
an angry President Eisenhower, feeling betrayed and deceived by
his allies, had their actions condemned at the United Nations.
The UN General Assembly voted for a ceasefire and for a UN
force to occupy the canal zone. The American government
threatened to sell US reserves of sterling, leading to a collapse in
the value of the pound.

Facing economic sanctions from the United States, Eden
ordered British forces to halt just as they had nearly achieved all
their military aims. It turned out that the 'thumb on our windpipe' wasn't Nasser's after all, but the American President's. 'I am
not sure I should have dared to start, but I am sure I should not
have dared to stop,' said Churchill. 'Why on earth didn't you go
through with it?' asked the American Secretary of State. Eden was
wrong to invade, but having invaded he was stupid to stop so short
of having achieved his goal. British prestige was shattered on two
fronts, morally and militarily. Eden had deceived his American
ally, and, to cap it all, failed to consult properly with the French
about pulling out.

With Western imperialists flexing their muscles, Russia sent
tanks into Hungary to suppress an anti-communist uprising and
NATO could hardly make a principled objection about the use of
force. All the moral authority that Britain had possessed since its
lone stand against the Nazis in 1940 had evaporated in an instant.
Anglo-American relations were severely damaged and perfidious
Albion had been humiliated on the national stage, losing its status
as a world power overnight. *At the time I remember feeling very
strongly*, wrote Britain's representative at the UN in his diary, *that*

we had by our action reduced ourselves from a first-class to a third-class power. The only positive that can be drawn from the Suez debacle was that at least they invaded the right canal. Given the incompetence and poor judgement that characterized the entire episode, we should just be grateful that British troops did not storm the Storybook Land Canal at Disneyworld.*

Tommy Steele was number one with 'Singing the Blues'. Maybe they should have bought Anthony Eden a copy for his surprise retirement party.

'I didn't know I was retiring.'

'That's the surprise!'

The Prime Minister's health had deteriorated under the strain, and he stepped down in January 1957. A recent biography has claimed that President Eisenhower insisted he be replaced. Harold Macmillan, the man who had egged him on throughout the crisis and assured him that the American President would 'lie doggo', now stepped nimbly into his place.

'Are there no good worthy causes left?'

The national humiliation of the Suez Crisis crystallized the vague feeling that Britain was being badly led by a smug and stuffy clique of Edwardian toffs, a feeling that had been nagging away at people for . . . well, the previous two thousand years.

A whole new breed of writers was soon spitting bile at the complacency of the older generation; chief among them was John Osborne, whose drama *Look Back in Anger* marked him out as the most infamous young man. In reality this phrase was just convenient journalistic shorthand for any slightly grumpy writer who

---

* In fact, the famous theme park did play a small part in the Cold War. When Nikita Khrushchev visited the United States in September 1959, his mood turned angry when he was denied a trip to Disneyland.

was under sixty and had anything at all to say. But the genteel plays of Terence Rattigan and Noel Coward were beginning to look very dated, as dignified Ealing comedies began to give way to films about the gritty lives of the working classes, full of brooding handsome northerners saying, 'There must be more to life than this, pet,' and then he drinks too much ale and gets her pregnant and they have to get married and all his dreams are over, the end.

Osborne was asked by Laurence Olivier to write something for him, and the result was *The Entertainer*, the story of a rather pathetic music hall star whose decline was an allegory for the fading glory of imperial Britain (according to Brodie's Notes anyway). There was a rash of navel-gazing books about Britain's intractable problems with titles like: *Why is Britain like, so completely rubbish and like, no good at anything?* Or: *Is Britain doomed to decline – especially when it is led by a bunch of public school homos like this lot?* Basically you didn't have to read the book, you got the idea from the title.

The old order was directly challenged by Penguin Books in 1959 when they published *Lady Chatterley's Lover* by D. H. Lawrence. Written in 1928, it had been banned for its overt sexuality and foul language (on page 134; it falls open naturally at that bit). In the United States, one 1930s senator said the book was 'written by a man with a diseased mind and a soul so black he would obscure even the darkness of hell'. (Only three out of ten people found his Amazon review helpful.) But in 1959 Britain's new obscenity law allowed for such material if it could be proved that the work was of literary merit. Penguin decided to test the act with the unpublished classic and were duly taken to court. The trial became a national sensation and the prosecution counsel became a laughing stock for asking the jury, 'Is this the sort of book you would wish your wife or your servants to read?' The jury obviously thought it was, and found Penguin not guilty in what became a landmark case for censorship in the United Kingdom.

But did it either a) *Result in a huge surge of interest in the novels of D. H. Lawrence and his poetic studies of the dehumanizing effects of industrialization?* Or b) *Result in the publication of lots of smutty soft-porn novels?*

Is it a bird? Is it a plane? No, it's Supermac!

Harold Macmillan was indeed yet another grey-haired old Etonian with a moustache, but he was clearly a deft political operator to have secured himself the top job when he shared so much responsibility for the disaster that had seen off his predecessor. Outsiders thought Rab Butler the most likely successor, but apparently he had not managed to ingratiate himself into the so-called magic circle, so that just left Harold, Derren Brown or Paul Daniels.

As Chancellor he had introduced Premium Bonds, a controversial idea at the time given the element of gambling involved. Investors could buy Premium Bonds at £1 each; the difference between them and the National Lottery that came four decades later is that you still kept your pound. But it wasn't quite as exciting because players would only fail to win a top prize of a thousand pounds instead of failing to win five million.

Macmillan was a one-nation Tory, perhaps more of an old-fashioned Whig than a Conservative, who as MP for Stockton-on-Tees had been shocked by the suffering and poverty he had seen in the 1930s. Tony Blair's search for a 'Third Way' had echoes of Macmillan's political manifesto *The Middle Way*, written just before the war. In his first year as Prime Minister he sent a note to the Director of Conservative Central Office, asking: *I am always hearing about the middle classes. What is it they really want? Will you put it down on a sheet of paper and I will see if I can give it to them.*

The *Evening Standard* cartoonist 'Vicky' was tolerated for his left-wing politics because his drawings were so good he didn't have to put labels on everyone saying who they were. He sarcastically portrayed the old duffer at 10 Downing Street as 'Supermac', for nothing could be further from an all-action superhero than the pompous old gent who talked slowly and generally acted with such compromise and caution. But as happens so often, the satire backfired, and the nickname became a badge of honour for the feted Prime Minister.

'The special relationship': trial separation ends

Like Churchill, Macmillan had had an American mother, and now worked hard to patch up Anglo-American relations. He met up with Eisenhower in Bermuda and thought it best not to remind the President that he would need his passport to visit the British dependency. He later explained that Britain's role in the modern world was to be as the Greeks had been to the Romans. It was the might of Rome that had disseminated the values and culture that originated with the Ancient Greeks, who latterly had to content themselves with being a civilizing force on the world's first superpower.

Britain's own imperial past was slipping away fast. Ghana became the first black African nation to gain independence in 1957; formerly the Gold Coast, by the time the imperial power had finished with it, it was just 'Coast'. Independence for countries such as Nigeria, Sierra Leone and Tanganyika soon followed. Territories with large resident white populations, like Rhodesia and Kenya, were more complicated since the ex-pats refused to consider majority rule. In Kenya, the so-called Mau Mau rebellion was brutally put down with murder and torture, much of which has only recently received the historical attention it deserves. Thirteen thousand Africans were killed during the hostilities, compared to ninety-five Europeans. 'A wind of change is blowing across this continent, whether we like it or not,' Macmillan told an audience of white South Africans in 1960. They greeted this acknowledgement of black nationalism with stony silence, and a year later they would be thrown out of the Commonwealth. 'No team in the Commonwealth Games for you!' Some worried the trauma might be too much.

Britain's granting of independence to its various colonies was messy, occasionally violent and very expensive. The best that can be said for Britain's retreat from Empire was that everyone else did it much worse. The Belgians saw the most acrimonious split in the colonial divorce courts: their chaotic withdrawal from the Congo was a model of incompetence and national humiliation, while the French experience in Algeria left the mother country utterly traumatized.

Macmillan had actually ordered an imperial balance sheet to be drawn up to work out the financial benefits to Britain from owning all these overseas territories, compared to the cost in terms of governing, occupying and defending them. You can't help feeling that as far as the British Empire is concerned, leaving this till the end of the 1950s was a bit late in the day.

Cuts were now made in Britain's crippling defence budget, and National Service was abolished, reducing the numbers in the armed forces from 690,000 to 375,000.* Other huge cuts were made to the navy and air force. The size of the garrison on the Rhine was reduced, as Britain abdicated some of its responsibility

---

* National Service was the 1950s equivalent of the gap year. Young men didn't go to Peru in search of self-knowledge and a certain spirituality; instead they were stuck in an ill-fitting army uniform and sent off to Cyprus or Kenya to be shot at by the natives. It was basically a continuation of the conscription introduced in 1939, with the difference that, unlike the Second World War, at least you knew when it would all be over.

for getting West German girls pregnant. Gradually Britain would become a less military society, young men in uniform would no longer be seen at every railway station and port, and adults entering the job market would not have had a year being bored in the services to prepare them for a lifetime being bored at work.

Little local difficulties (as well as the usual global ones)

Defence cuts were not enough to balance the books at 11 Downing Street, but despite pressure from more right-wing Treasury ministers, the new Prime Minister refused to cut public spending and allow unemployment to rise, causing his chancellor Peter Thorneycroft and two Treasury ministers, Enoch Powell* and Nigel Birch, to resign in protest. The old gent dismissed what should have been a major political embarrassment as 'a little local difficulty' and his image of the unflappable commander-in-chief was further reinforced. He actually spent a good deal of time rehearsing this apparent ad-lib, but the most successful politicians always work hard on making it seem effortless.

However, his government showed rather less concern for the underdog when it came to housing. Harold Macmillan had risen to national prominence in 1953, fulfilling the Conservatives' key election promises to build 300,000 homes a year (even if four-fifths of them were actually built by urban local authorities, most of which were Labour). The future Prime Minister had got himself photographed in a typical council house and managed to avoid asking where the ballroom was. Now his government set out

---

* Macmillan considered Powell to be something of a fanatic, and later asked that he be moved along from his seat in cabinet directly opposite the Prime Minister because he couldn't stand the 'steely and accusing eye' looking at him across the table any more.

to liberalize the private rental market with the controversial Rent Act of 1957. This bill, which allowed greater freedom to landlords to evict tenants and raise rents, was the most bitterly opposed of his first term.

Private renters were now subjected to swirly patterned carpets and erratic water heaters over the sink. It was compulsory for the creepy person in the room next to yours to make a strange groaning noise at odd times of the day. Landlords were allowed to keep their bicycle in the hall, so that you gashed your shin every time you went to get the morning post; electricity slot meters were designed to run out just as you sat down to watch the telly, and it was only permitted to take a bath every Sunday (that fell on 29 February). The most notorious of the exploitative landlords was Peter Rachman, whose high rents and corrupt practices, including the use of intimidation and violence to drive out tenants, frankly amounted to Rachmanism – it's the only word for it. Flats were divided and subdivided to squeeze in as many immigrants as possible, with flimsy partitions dividing the statutory window. More congenial properties were kept for his beautiful young mistresses such as Mandy Rice-Davies and Christine Keeler, whom the millionaire visited in a chauffeur-driven Rolls Royce from his large house in Hampstead. Yeah, but was he happy?

'Never had it so good'

But for most people, life seemed to be getting better. In the run-up to the 1959 election, Macmillan appealed directly to the naked materialism of a Britain that was enjoying the benefits of modern conveniences and increased prosperity. 'Let us be frank about it, most of our people have never had it so good!' The Conservative slogan was: *Life's Good With The Conservatives,*

Don't Let Labour Ruin It!, which was eventually chosen over: *Vote Tory, and we'll give you a big tax cut, a new washing machine, an Austin Seven and a choice of a Garrard record player or Goblin Teasmade.*

Macmillan now had a convincing mandate of his own and the Prime Minister who had initially suggested to the Queen that he might only last six weeks was returned with a majority of over a hundred. The Suez Crisis had not damaged the Conservatives now they'd changed the leader responsible. Indeed, working–class opinion had generally been in favour of military action, and Labour's criticism of its execution could then be portrayed as unpatriotic.

Hugh Gaitskell had not looked particularly appealing as a potential Prime Minister, and he made some rash uncosted promises in the lead–up to the election that severely damaged his credibility. Despite this, Labour had been confident it would do well and its defeat sent the party into a mood of depressed intro-spection. Labour's support had now dropped for four elections in a row, and the party began to worry that now that they had done so much to raise people out of poverty, the electorate no longer felt the need to vote for them.

Hugh Gaitskell responded by proposing to abolish the party's commitment to uncompromising public ownership, but the totemic Clause IV that Tony Blair would successfully do away with a generation or two later was stoutly defended, and the battle just made the party look unnecessarily divided. Splits over unilateral disarmament would also take their toll, and as the 1960s dawned the Left began to wonder whether the Conservatives were now the permanent party of government. Macmillan certainly looked safe for another full term. 'That was a good line, wasn't it? I say, Mr Profumo, you've never *had it* so good, eh? Why's he gone all red?'

But this would be the high point of Conservative fortunes.

When they got the bill for the pre-election spending spree, the Chancellor came over all faint and had to sit down. Indeed, the 1959 budget was later criticized by Margaret Thatcher as overgenerous, setting a pattern for overspending that continued for another couple of decades. Britain's annual rate of growth of 2.6 per cent was below any developed country in the Western world except Ireland, which didn't count because all its workers had left for Kilburn. Britain's share of world exports fell from 26.2 per cent in 1953 to 20.6 in 1961. The boom that had been engineered before the election quickly turned to bust, and within a few years all of Macmillan's grand schemes were to end in abject failure. It was hard enough for the British to have been humiliated by the Americans, but being humiliated by the French – that was going too far.

Non!

The Treaty of Rome which effectively created the Common Market came right after the Suez Crisis when Britain's 'special relationship' with the United States looked effectively over. Suddenly Britain felt isolated on both fronts, convinced that both gangs were standing on opposite sides of the playground pointing and laughing at their bizarre constitution and appalling cooking. Macmillan was the first British Prime Minister to judge that Britain's future lay within the Common Market and hoped that Britain's admittance would be a formality. So for a man who could walk into any club in Pall Mall, it must have been a shock to find himself hovering outside the European Club, trying to negotiate with a very tall and rather obstructive French bouncer.

Charles de Gaulle had got to know Macmillan well during the war. Indeed, it could be argued that without Macmillan, the British and Americans would never have recognized de Gaulle as leader of the Free French and he would never have gone on to become President. However, de Gaulle felt resentful towards the Anglo–American alliance and the annoying little ways in which it patronized France, like, er, liberating it from Nazi occupation. With West Germany still in the process of recovery, France was the dominant power in the Common Market and there was 'only room for one cock on the dung-heap', as was commented at the time.

De Gaulle strung Macmillan along during protracted summits and conferences, while Britain's chief negotiator Ted Heath clocked up thousands of air miles going back and forth between London and the continent. De Gaulle came to Macmillan's private home, where the cook refused to have the French President's emergency blood supply in her fridge. De Gaulle went shooting with Macmillan, standing and watching as the British Prime Minister bagged over six dozen birds while the Frenchman chose not to pick up a gun himself (having surrendered to the pheasants first thing in the morning). The national humiliation of France's defeat in the Second World War was still very raw and demonstrating the power to reject Britain was another step on the road to France recovering her self-esteem. And yet Macmillan seemed not to have seen it coming. And so in January 1963 when de Gaulle finally declared a very public '*Non!*', the British government was left looking foolish and humiliated. The English papers were obviously magnanimous about this rejection, and no bitter references were made to any military assistance that Britain might have given their French cousins in recent decades. The best response England could muster was for Princess Margaret to cancel a trip to Paris. Well, that certainly taught them.

Blue Streak and other useless fireworks

De Gaulle's reasoning had been that Britain was still too close to the United States; the evidence being an arms deal struck between Macmillan and the contrastingly youthful John F. Kennedy at Nassau. Although it was losing its empire, Britain had hoped that it might cling to a small degree of superpower status with the development of an updated independent nuclear deterrent. Britain had started out developing its own missile, but despite the exciting aftershave-type name, Blue Streak proved to be more of a white elephant. In fact, dropping an actual white elephant on Moscow would have been cheaper and more effective.

The missiles could not be kept in a constant state of readiness since they needed special liquid propellant that had to be carefully loaded prior to use (so long as the local garage was open at the time). The design was based on the presumption that in the event of atomic warfare, the Russians would do the decent thing and ring up to give Britain plenty of notice. Other British rocket designs were tried and rejected because the little blue touchpaper always went out or the milk bottle kept toppling over. Macmillan then invested everything in the purchase of Skybolt missiles from the Americans, which would have British warheads fitted to them by whichever engineer in the West Midlands had the right Allen key. But then without a thought to the consequences for their British allies, the Americans cancelled the Skybolt programme. The British Prime Minister had put all his atomic bombs in one basket and another of his grand diplomatic schemes ended in abject failure. Ultimately a humiliated Macmillan was forced to rely on American Polaris missiles, leading Harold Wilson to quip that the independent British deterrent was 'neither British, independent nor a deterrent'.

Ban the Bomb (but not the duffle coat)

The proliferation of atomic weapons gave rise to the Campaign for Nuclear Disarmament (CND), which had been founded at Westminster Central Hall in February 1958 by such luminaries as J. B. Priestley and Bertrand Russell. They organized marches from London to Aldermaston in Berkshire, the location of the Atomic Weapons Research Establishment, specially kitted out in duffle coats, college scarves and thick-rimmed glasses. The real scandal was that Macmillan had leased Holy Loch near densely populated Glasgow as a base for American Nuclear Submarines, but CND were buggered if they were marching all the way up there.

The campaign had prompted yet more divisive debate within the Labour Party, but its leader Hugh Gaitskell fought hard to stop the party permanently adopting a policy of unilateral nuclear disarmament. 'I will fight, fight and fight again to save the party I love,' he vowed. Nye Bevan split the left with his famous assertion that unilateral nuclear disarmament 'would send a British Foreign Secretary naked into the conference chamber', and when one thought of the ageing Macmillan or Earl Home, this was not an image to dwell upon.

With Labour divided and Macmillan looking increasingly accident-prone, the Liberals looked like they might make a comeback under their charismatic leader Jo Grimond. They won a stunning by-election victory at Orpington in Kent in 1962, and didn't go on and on about this at all. Macmillan was becoming paranoid about plots against him, and in July he sacked seven members of his cabinet as well as nine junior ministers in what became known as the 'Night of the Long Knives'. Amid the carnage, one insignificant Minister of War survived. Pretty soon, Macmillan would be wishing he had added the name of John Profumo to the hit list.

'We would like to apologize for the delayed arrival of the 1960s'

1963 began with the coldest winter of the century. Thousands were trapped in their homes without power. They couldn't even turn on the television to see endless news reports about how bad the weather was.

The political scene seemed frozen too. Macmillan was entering his seventh year as Prime Minister, Hugh Gaitskell had been leader of the opposition for even longer and there was no reason to suppose much was going to change. 'Yup, I think we're in for a pretty uneventful year,' said President Kennedy, looking through his diary for a good time to visit Dallas.

Then in January, aged only fifty-six, Hugh Gaitskell fell ill and died from a rare autoimmune disease. The shocking and unexpected nature of his death later led some to claim that the Labour leader had been murdered by the Soviet security services in order to allow supposed secret KGB agent Harold Wilson to become British Prime Minister.*

Wilson was in America when news of Gaitskell's death came through. An American friend immediately offered him $10,000 towards his campaign fund. Wilson declined it, explaining that that wasn't how it worked in England. He eventually sent his friend his accounts to show that his campaign for the leadership had cost fourpence – the cost of two phone calls.†

Labour deputy George Brown had at first seemed the favourite to inherit the leadership, but those who knew him better were

---

* This nutty conspiracy theory was even repeated in the 1987 book *Spycatcher*, by Peter Wright, which the government attempted to ban because it breached the Official Secrets Act and sadly not because it was so dreary and badly written.

† This story comes from Wilson's own memoir and thus is about as reliable as the Wikipedia entry for your local school that says, 'Form 8S are all gay.'

nervous about one or two of his minor policy issues. For example, his policy on the European Economic Community was to stagger out of the pub and then fight anyone who disagreed with him. On the complex matter of maintaining Britain's colonial territories east of Suez, his analysis was: 'Yersh all bashtards, I'll take on every shingle one of yer . . .' Later in the year, on the shocking day that President Kennedy was assassinated, George Brown appeared live on television slurring his words and becoming very aggressive to a fellow panellist who asked him how well he had actually known Kennedy. Off air, Brown physically attacked this other guest, and the memorable excuse made for the Labour deputy was that he had been 'tired and emotional'. Thanks mainly to the persistence of *Private Eye*, this label stuck with Brown ever after, eventually passing into the English language as a general euphemism for being drunk.*

Despite Brown's brilliance as a speaker and party organizer, Labour could not risk having such an unreliable and erratic character as their prospective Prime Minister, and Wilson saw his chance.

James Harold Wilson was a grammar-school boy from Huddersfield, who had been a brilliant scholar at Oxford and gone on to work in the civil service during the war. He had been taken to London at the age of eight, and a famous photograph shows the little boy standing on the steps of Number 10 Downing Street. 'Is that when you decided that you were determined to become Prime Minister?' asked the journalists. 'Er, no, actually,' confessed Mr Wilson, rather disappointingly. *It was at this moment that young Harold resolved that he was going to become Prime Minister one day*, they all wrote anyway.

---

* Brown's decline from influence was peppered with embarrassing displays of public drunkenness. When he finally quit the Labour Party in 1976, the impact was rather undermined by a photo of him lying in the gutter later in the evening. He eventually joined the SDP but they did their best to keep quiet about it.

At the age of thirty-one, he had become the youngest cabinet minister of the century when he was appointed President of the Board of Trade in Attlee's government, but then surprised everyone when he followed Nye Bevan and resigned over the introduction of National Health Service charges for dentistry and spectacles. He said he was resigning on principle, which is always the claim of people utterly without principles. The move marked him out as a leading figure on the left of his party, and would stand him in good stead later on as various rivals fell down dead or just plain drunk.

Married man has affair: Britain utterly traumatized

Historians have to make a value judgement as to how much scrutiny and analysis a particular episode deserves in any given period. Some events may seem more interesting and appealing to write or read about, but the overriding factor must always be: 'How much did any of this ultimately matter – what was its long-term effect on other events and the course of history?'

Superficially the Profumo scandal may seem important because so many others have raked over the details. But the real scandal of the early 1960s was the enormous budget deficit being built up by Chancellor Reginald Maudling. Yes, there may have been a titillating scandal involving members of the establishment, but this was nothing compared to the building financial crisis facing the country, and it is this economic conundrum that really merits several pages of detailed examination.

So anyway Christine Keeler was frolicking naked around the swimming pool of this gorgeous stately home, and before long she was having sex with a government minister and a shady Russian attaché as rumours spread of sado–masochistic sex games, upper-class orgies and black magic rituals . . .*

The potent combination of illicit sex, Cold War espionage, West Indian drug dealers, upper-class hypocrisy and a minister lying to the House of Commons created a perfect storm of righteous indignation that masked the real reason for all the scandal: that the British public are endlessly fascinated by the sex lives of the rich and famous.

John Profumo was a minor member of the British government, not even inside the cabinet. At the beginning of 1963, the only reason the British public might have been vaguely aware of him was that he was the husband of one of the greatest show-business names of the day. Valerie Hobson was the star of countless wholesome and jolly films and most recently leading lady in *The King and I*. 'Getting to know you, getting to know all about you . . .' she sang. Well, nearly all about you, anyway. The other detail that is often forgotten about the scandal is that the key events had all taken place two years earlier, but didn't emerge until 1963 when patience with the twelve-year-old Conservative government was wearing dangerously thin.

In July 1961, John Profumo had been a guest of Lord Astor at the magnificent country house of Cliveden, near Maidenhead. The guests took a stroll through the grounds and stumbled upon a number of young women swimming naked in the pool. They chuckled at their good fortune and continued on their way. But one of them in particular, Christine Keeler, had made something of an impression on the Minister for War. Maybe it was her views

---

* In the 1989 film *Scandal*, there is a corgi scampering about in the middle of one of these sex parties, but anyone who imagines that hints that a member of the royal family was present at these high-class orgies is reading much too much into the symbolism. The Duke of Edinburgh was nowhere near the place; Windsor Castle is a good five miles from Cliveden. The more persistent rumour was that the man in the mask was a senior cabinet minister, while nine high court judges were also supposed to have been present. Why don't the rest of us ever get invited to parties like that?

on defence procurement? Soon afterwards Profumo began an affair with Christine Keeler. She may have been too young to vote, but soon she would help bring down a government.

Keeler had been staying at the Cliveden cottage loaned to Dr Stephen Ward, a 'society osteopath' who had done wonders for his lordship's back by persuading another showgirl, Mandy Rice-Davies, to lie on hers. The security services were watching all of them because Keeler was also thought to be sleeping with a 'Russian naval attaché' (Cold War speak for 'spy'). Profumo was advised by the cabinet secretary to end the relationship, which he promptly did after only four weeks. 'Hmmm,' thought the minister, 'what's the best way to end this illicit and potentially explosive affair? I know, I'll give her a handwritten note. That definitely won't resurface later to incriminate me.'

For a year or so, Profumo might be forgiven for thinking he had got away with his little indiscretion. But as bad luck would have it, Keeler was called as a witness in an unrelated trial, and details of Stephen Ward's social circle began to circulate in the press. When rumour began to spread that the Minister for War had been sharing a girlfriend with a Russian spy, Profumo came under increasing pressure to make some sort of denial. And so in March 1963, he made his misjudged statement to the House of Commons, in which he stated categorically that there was no impropriety whatsoever in his acquaintanceship with Miss Keeler. Today that would be taken to mean, 'Oh, so he was obviously sleeping with her then.' But because of the sacrosanct convention for total honesty in the Mother of Parliaments, his statement was taken at face value. It was this lie to the House of Commons that was to be the undoing of the minister and nearly the entire government.

Fearing that he was being made a scapegoat for the dalliances of his young female friends, the increasingly unstable Dr Stephen Ward wrote shocking letters to the Prime Minister, the leader of the opposition and anyone else he could think of. 'Dear Milkman, two pints of gold top today, please. PS: I'm bloody telling you, Keeler was asking Profumo for details of nuclear movements in West Germany to pass on to the Russians!'

The *Daily Mirror* was in possession of the incriminating letter to Keeler and by now just about everyone between Fleet Street and Westminster knew that Profumo had slept with Keeler and then lied about it in Parliament. The Minister took his wife away for a few days in Venice. It was there he told her the truth, which rather took the edge off that ride in the gondola. On 5 June, he resigned as a minister and as a Member of Parliament, and Macmillan's government was plunged into its deepest crisis.

The new leader of the opposition asserted that he had no interest in the private life of a cabinet minister, it was simply the matter of national security that worried him. 'We are not concerned with who was watching this naked nubile nudie frolicking around the swimming pool, her pert breasts jiggling in the moonlight, as the glistening drops of water ran down onto her firm but tender buttocks . . . These matters are of no interest to us whatsoever . . .' The hypocrisy of the newspapers also reached new heights as they chastised the politicians for being distracted by 'harlots' and 'women of easy virtue', while poring over every sordid detail and simply inventing many more of their own.* The *Times* almost imploded with moral outrage; rereading the editorials and letters page today makes you wonder if they imagined no politician had ever been unfaithful to his wife before. The rest of the world looked on in utter disbelief at this hurricane in a bone-china teacup. The French shrugged their shoulders and wondered

---

* For example, young Christine Keeler was unfairly labelled a 'prostitute', and accused of sleeping with just about everyone who had a walk-on part in the affair. In fact, she had probably never even slept with the so-called Russian spy, Ivanov, but no one was ever going to believe that since the entire salacious episode depended on this so-called security scandal to give it any political significance.

why Macmillan hadn't taken the chance to sleep with her too. Only the Americans shared a little of the puritan moral outrage. Their President was due to visit Britain later in the month, but the *Washington Post* wondered whether he should stay well away. They wouldn't want a man of President Kennedy's impeccable fidelity corrupted by the lax sexual morals of the British Conservatives.

The Conservatives fell even further behind in the polls as the whole episode crystallized a feeling that Macmillan was out of touch and the Tory Party and British establishment were out of control. Even some on his own side were calling for Macmillan's resignation. In the debate on the crisis in the House of Commons, one former Tory minister turned to the Prime Minister and quoted Robert Browning's poem 'The Lost Leader': 'Never glad confident morning again.' And members gasped or laughed, in order to cover up the fact that they did not get the literary reference.

Although there had always been plenty of cynics who thought the worst of their elected representatives, the Profumo scandal was the moment when the British public's trust in politicians evaporated. Before Profumo it would have been considered slander to suggest that a member of the government might deliberately lie. Ever since, it has been the general presumption that that is what happens when a politician opens his or her mouth. When it was put to Mandy Rice-Davies in a court of law that Lord Astor denied having an affair with her, she famously replied, 'Well, he would, wouldn't he?'

Stephen Ward was convicted (probably unfairly) of living off immoral earnings, was abandoned by all his high-class friends and committed suicide before sentence could be passed. Six hundred white roses with the message 'In memory of a victim of British hypocrisy' were sent anonymously to his funeral. Profumo disappeared from public view and devoted the rest of his life to charitable works, for which he was later awarded a CBE. Sadly, he never talked publicly about the affair before his death in 2006.

Which is a shame, because after he had ruined his political career, publicly cheated on his celebrity wife and brought down the Tory government, it would have been interesting to know if the sex had actually been worth it. 'But was it a good shag, John? That's what we want to know. I mean, despite everything, do you still lie back in the bath sometimes and think about it . . .'

The satire boom: government brought down by Footlights Revue

With the government so visibly out of touch and disaster-prone, it was no wonder that people couldn't help but laugh at them. And so as the curtain rose at the Oxford Playhouse, an audience of dinner-jacketed and heavily bejewelled theatregoers waited to see what this satire business was all about. A hush fell across the auditorium as a couple of young chaps in polonecks shuffled out onto the stage and launched into a blistering attack on all that was wrong with stifling, hypocritical, class-ridden, backward-looking Britain:

```
'I put it to you, sir . . . that Her Majesty's
Government is . . . not very good!'
(Gasps from audience at very idea of audacious
young public schoolboys showing mild disrespect
to Church of England, the Empire and Laws of
Cricket.)
'And furthermore . . . I suggest that the Prime
Minister, the Right Honourable Mr Harold
Macmillan, MP, is rather old!'
(Increased shocked laughter from some; older
members of audience storm out of theatre
denouncing the outrageous decline in public
```

morals and need to bring back flogging,
National Service and Gold Standard.)
Musicians sporting goatee beards and thick-
rimmed spectacles then strike up trad. jazz
number as cast change into duffle coats for
damning pastiche of Mr Rab Butler's economic
policies.

The satire of the early 1960s might seem pretty tame to us now, but it has to be remembered that nothing like it had been seen for as long as anyone could remember. Deference, at least in public, was not just the norm, it was basic good manners. The pillars of the British establishment, such as the royal family, the Church, the army, the government, all of these were off-limits as far as public mickey-taking was concerned. But it became harder to give unquestioning respect to the great and good as it became clear that they were neither. From the Suez debacle onwards, there was a nagging sense that Britain's place in the world was falling fast and that the country was badly led by liars and hypocrites. A mild satirical rebuke seemed like a more civilized response than an armed insurrection.

But like any revolution, the satire boom was led by internal dissenters. Those who railed against the establishment were pre-dominantly public schoolboys themselves, graduates of Oxford or Cambridge whose fathers had served King and Empire. The editors of the new satirical magazine *Private Eye* had cut their teeth at Shrewsbury, while its new owner Peter Cook had been destined for a career in the Foreign Office.

The great Peter Cook was the godfather of the 1960s satire boom. He was only twenty-three years old when the acclaimed satirical revue show *Beyond the Fringe* hit the West End. His impersonation of the Prime Minister was a shocking demonstration of young people's lack of respect, but that didn't stop the Queen attending the show, or indeed Macmillan himself, who was spotted by Cook who then started to ad-lib insults directed at the Prime Minister. During an incredibly energetic few years, Cook also set up the Establishment, a comedy club in the heart of Soho.* The BBC commissioned a pilot TV show based on sketches performed at the club, but when a series was not immediately commissioned Cook answered the call of Broadway, where the *Beyond the Fringe* team were again successful. On his return he was disgusted to see David Frost fronting a reworked version of the programme, now dubbed *That Was The Week That Was*.

TW3, as it became known, was the most visible evidence of the boom in satire, and although today it looks rather weak and a little bit smug, its cultural impact at the time was immense. For ever after, TV executives would say to comedy writers, 'We're putting together a hard-hitting but really funny new satire show; it's going to be the new *That Was The Week That Was*.' And the world-weary writers would nod and contemplate suicide.

Macmillan refuses to go: prostate resigns in protest

In September 1963 Lord Denning published his inquiry into the Profumo scandal and it became a huge bestseller, disappointing thousands who thumbed through it hoping for detailed and intimate descriptions of the infamous sex parties. Plans for a pop-up edition were cancelled. Although the Denning Report concluded that there had been little real threat to security, it was nevertheless critical of Macmillan, just when he thought he had ridden out the worst of the crisis. He had refused calls to go at the time of the scandal, but now he fell ill and had the opportunity to exit the stage for his

* One of the bouncers was the huge bearded figure of Roger Law, who two decades later would continue the satirical tradition with *Spitting Image*.

85

own reasons and with a modicum of dignity. He was diagnosed (incorrectly) with inoperable prostate cancer, and on the eve of the Conservative Party conference he announced his resignation as Prime Minister, throwing the Tory Party into disarray.

The 1963 Conservative Party conference was suddenly turned into an early edition of *The X Factor*, with each of the likely candidates performing their platform speeches as an audition piece for a chance to fulfil their dream of becoming Prime Minister. 'It means the world to me. I'm doing this for my mum. And for a chance to abolish the Retail Price Maintenance.' But one after another the hopefuls taking the stage in Blackpool were falling flat. Rab Butler had already alienated many by taking the Prime Minister's vacant suite at the conference hotel, and insisting on taking Macmillan's slot in the conference agenda. When it came to his make-or-break speech, Butler was suffering from a heavy cold and failed to impress. Reginald Maudling was even more boring, while Lord Hailsham committed the greater sin of visibly wanting it too much, allowing his supporters to wear badges with his initials. But these elderly wannabes were not canvassing for the votes of members or MPs. The Conservative Party still had no established mechanism for appointing the new Prime Minister; previous party leaders had mysteriously 'emerged' after a brief chat between influential gentlemen. 'Lord Snooty? Tip-top chap but has that Brazilian mistress with the Adam's apple.' 'Could be embarrassing. What about Fforbes-Harris?' 'Hmmm, good man with figures, excellent war record, but was a day boy at Eton, not a boarder.' 'Dash it, can't have him then. Looks like it'll have to be Lord Winchelsea. I'll tell the Palace to send a car for him.'

Having followed events from his hospital bed, Macmillan consulted with the so-called 'magic circle' of Conservative grandees and decided that Earl Home was the chap best placed to stop that dreadful man Rab Butler, whom Macmillan himself had kept out in 1957. The young Queen was advised to send for Home, and that was that. This was how democracy operated in the Jet Age.

The fourteenth Earl Home

Home, pronounced 'Hume' (really posh people always have names that the rest of us pronounce incorrectly), was born in Mayfair to a ludicrously aristocratic family and was such a goody-goody at Eton that he married the headmaster's daughter.* He is the only British Prime Minister to have played first-class cricket, a talent that stood him in good stead at one election rally when a protestor threw an egg at him and he managed to catch it without it breaking. He had been Parliamentary Private Secretary to Neville Chamberlain, accompanying him to Munich in 1938 for the fateful meeting which surrendered Czechoslovakia to Adolf Hitler. With foreign policy triumphs like this on his CV, it is no wonder that Macmillan made him Foreign Secretary despite the fact that he sat in the House of Lords.

Had it not been for a young Tony Benn (or Anthony Wedgwood Benn as he was known back then), Home would never have been able to get into the House of Commons to become Prime Minister. Lord Stansgate, as Wedgie Benn had become on the death of his father,† fought a determined campaign to renounce his own peerage, even being re-elected to Parliament in a by-election when the voters of Bristol South-East knew that their choice would be legally disqualified. Eventually the government accepted that the

---

* Elizabeth had previously been engaged to the future cricket commentator Brian Johnston.
† Tony Benn's father, a former Liberal and then Labour MP, had been made a hereditary peer by Winston Churchill in 1942, and when Benn's older brother was killed in the war, Anthony Wedgwood Benn became the next in line.

situation was untenable, and the Peerage Act of 1963 allowed Benn to throw off his ermine robes. But it also opened the door for Lord Home (and Douglas Hogg) to do likewise to challenge for the Tory Party leadership, and so on 24 October Wedgie Benn finally returned to the Commons expecting a hero's welcome, only to be upstaged by the arrival of the new Prime Minister. The bitter irony was that Benn's victory on behalf of the Commons over the Lords had resulted in an elderly lord stepping in and becoming the head of the government. Maybe the whole thing was an elaborate plot just to annoy him.

Alec Douglas-Home would be the last of the upper-class patricians who had dominated British politics throughout the 1950s (and most of the previous centuries).* The following decade would see the arrival of a new breed of politician: grammar-school boys like Harold Wilson and Ted Heath, men who could claim to have risen on merit from the slightly wider gene pool of the middle classes.

Trusting the ruling class to know best had been tried and patently failed. The Suez Crisis and the Profumo scandal were the twin peaks of British disillusionment in this long decade. The former was an unmitigated catastrophe, the importance of which has grown down the years as more has been revealed about the incompetence and duplicity of those involved. The latter was actually trivial in terms of any threat to national security and the political status of those involved, but it acquired huge significance because it seemed to represent everything that people already felt was wrong with the privileged clique who presumed to rule over

---

* Home was an old Etonian, like his two predecessors. Before that the leaders of the Conservative Party were from Harrow (Churchill and Baldwin), Rugby School (Chamberlain) and Eton again (Balfour). But after Alec Douglas-Home, no Conservative leaders were from a major public school until the election of the old Etonian David Cameron. There would not be a privately educated Prime Minister after Alec Douglas-Home until Tony Blair.

them. Politics would never be the same again. The Conservatives would be thrown out and then the British people would find completely different things to be disillusioned about.

Young vandal ticked off without fear of stabbing or calls to ChildLine

But as far as these things can be measured by data, twentieth-century Britain seems to have been at its most content in the 1950s. Indeed, the Isle of Wight liked the 1950s so much they decided to stay there for ever. With the nation now at peace, a generation that had known real deprivation didn't need to be told how lucky they were to have a home, a full larder and children who were going to live to adulthood. Though their grandparents told them anyway.

And so the 1950s are gazed upon nostalgically as the golden age of a unified society, a time when we all looked out for each other and everyone did their bit. 'Ah yes, the kids could play out in the street, dodging the speeding cars and motorbikes before deciding it was safer to go to the park to fall in the dog mess that had been left in the sandpit.' People didn't just hog lung cancer all to themselves, they shared it out equally by puffing away on their pipes and Capstan Full Strength in every cinema, pub and tram. Millions of homes did their bit to pump out sulphurous coal smoke, creating a smog so severe that 12,000 Londoners died in the winter of 1952. If a man beat his wife that was a private matter; you didn't get busybodies from the authorities poking their nose in. Child abuse obviously didn't happen because it wasn't in the papers. Maybe there were one or two tragic chaps who suffered from the disease of homosexuality, and the best cure for them was to lock them up with lots of other men. If you were an Irish or West Indian immigrant, you knew exactly where you stood, with the sign in the boarding-house window that said, 'No blacks, Irish or dogs.' Ah yes, they were happy, innocent times.

The social conservatives who look back to the 1950s so fondly must imagine that all those nasty sordid things that blight modern Britain didn't exist until Roy Jenkins and the Rolling Stones came along in the 1960s and invented permissiveness. But 1950s Britain was a deeply hypocritical society, in which anyone who was different or socially unacceptable was forced to live a lie or feel ashamed and excluded. The century before the Second World War had seen the struggle for major political freedoms: the right to vote, to join a trade union, to be safe from unjust dismissal or random eviction. Now the campaign for *social* freedom was really beginning. 'I have a dream,' as Martin Luther King might have said, 'that one day a divorced woman in Cheltenham might actually get invited to that Rotarians' cheese and wine buffet.'

By the end of the next decade such exclusion would be a thing of the past. Everyone would be dancing at free rock festivals and having instant, uncomplicated sex with beautiful people they had just met on an acid trip. Well, that's what it said in the papers anyway. And then everybody in the whole country felt excluded, presuming they must be the only person who was missing out on it all.

3

1963–1970

How Harold Wilson and The Beatles won the World Cup for England (but weren't allowed to melt it down to save the economy)

It was a sombre milestone in the story of Britain's seemingly inexorable decline when in 1967 Harold Wilson appeared on national television to address the British people with the grim news that many had been dreading since the decade began. The United Kingdom would finally be going over to flared trousers. 'This won't mean that your own trousers, or the trousers worn by your family, will suddenly be flared,' claimed the Prime Minister, but there was no hiding the national humiliation. Viewers could only see his dark jacket and narrow tie, but below the desk he was already wearing an outrageous pair of psychedelic loons, with paisley triangles sewn into the bottom to make them so ludicrously wide that they overhung the toes of his purple platform shoes.

The clichéd adjective for the 1960s is 'swinging'. By this is meant that it was perceived as a time of exciting change and youthful dynamism, of great pop music, vibrant fashion and social liberation; it is not called 'swinging' in the sense that Harold Wilson was swapping wives with President de Gaulle and Prince

Philip at sex parties in the suburbs. The cultural and social history of the decade is so appealing to anyone looking back that the true story has tended to be obscured: that it was a time of almost unremitting economic crisis, of desperate short-term financial fixes and cobbled-together Treasury cutbacks. Today any attempt by history lecturers to explain the 1960s in terms of the balance-of-payments deficit and the devaluation of sterling rapidly finds the students playing Dogz 3D on their mobile phones; a situation which can only be remedied by showing another clip of The Beatles on *The Ed Sullivan Show* or the mounted policeman beating up hippies outside the American Embassy.

And so we keep coming back to the music and the fashions and the protests. 'Young people marched and demanded a different future' – a future in which they would produce endless Radio 4 documentaries and *Guardian* features on all their student protests back in the 1960s. They used to say that if you can remember the 1960s you weren't there. Now, if you can't remember the 1960s it's because you aren't old. I cried the day that JFK was shot. My rusk fell out of the cot.

For all the frankly rather tiresome talk of how incredible the 1960s were, it has to be remembered that, for most people, they weren't. Most of the younger generation were not experimenting with pot in a groovy flat in the Kings Road. Most students were not dropping out of the London School of Economics to march against the Vietnam War and then setting up a modernist art cooperative that revolutionized LP cover art and British furniture design.

For millions of teenagers in the 1960s, the grooviest thing that happened to them was leaving school at fifteen and then getting a boring low-paid job in a factory. 'I'll never forget the mind-blowing experience of that summer of 1967, man. It was like, I was going down this tunnel, and then, like wow, there were all these lights at the end, like bobbing about on people's heads, and that's when I realized I had got a job as a coal miner and I was going to spend the rest of my life down the pit.'

One of the general rules of history is that if you hear about some golden age when everyone was swept along by crazy hedonistic euphoria, you can be sure it was just a privileged minority who were drinking cocktails and dancing the Charleston in the 1920s or freaking out at free festivals in the 1960s. The same rule, however, does not apply to the bad times. 'So, this Great War that has just started, with all these trenches, gas attacks and mass slaughter? I suppose this only applies to the middle-class London elite as well, does it?'

'Er, no, that's one bit of history you get to experience first-hand.'

The white heat of the scientific revolution (closed for essential maintenance)

The dawn of the 1960s saw a sense of great excitement about the birth of the space age. The Russians had put a man into space, the Americans had had a man orbit the Earth, and the British, well, the British had got a man several inches off the ground in a hovercraft. The wonderful thing about all these new technological advances, computers and labour-saving devices is that soon the people would be free to enjoy hours and hours of time away from the workplace. Visions of the futuristic life awaiting us in the twenty-first century generally depicted contented-looking families in space suits filling their working day with self-improving leisure activities, playing sports or reading novels. No one quite worked out that once we had portable computers and mobile communicators, the bastards would just make us work even harder. 'Do those figures on your laptop on the way into work, make those extra calls on the way home from work and then when you're home, plug your datastick into your home computer and finish that presentation before Monday.' *I have seen the future. And it's work, work, work.*

The supersonic zeitgeist appealed to Labour's new leader, Harold Wilson, who was determined to make his party look modern. 'How about calling the party *New Labour*, that might do it?' 'No, we're not that desperate.' After three successive election defeats, each worse than the last, Labour had begun to fear that their old support base was narrowing so rapidly that they might never win power again. In the age of television sets and indoor toilets, voting Labour might seem to belong to a disappearing era of class struggle and flat caps and trying to keep the whippets out of the pigeon shed.

And so Wilson rebranded the Labour Party as the political wing of the scientific revolution. The problems of the future would be solved not by political strife or prudent management of the economy, but by modern technology, and computers and atomic power and men in white coats holding clipboards. On 1 October 1963, Harold Wilson gave the speech that captured the public imagination and set the tone for the coming general election, casting the grammar-school technocrat as the champion of all that was modern and new.

At the climax of his conference speech in the futuristic setting of Scarborough, Wilson eulogized about the 'Britain that is to be forged in the white heat of this revolution'. The leader of the opposition was a rocket scientist, he was Dan Dare, he was a computer designer; he was definitely not some old toff on a grouse moor struggling to understand the instruction manual for Britain's atomic power stations. One commentator wrote that in his speech Wilson had brought the Labour Party forward 'fifty years in fifty minutes'.

The Conservatives thought they had better look interested in all this newfangled science business, and so Sir Alec

Douglas-Home appointed a new Minister for Science: Quintin Hogg QC, an old Etonian Latin scholar. An admission by Sir Alec that he tried to understand economic statistics by counting out matchsticks did not exactly help his cause.

Wilson's focus on the so-called 'scientific revolution' was a nifty bit of side-stepping for the leader of a party previously so consumed with divisions over nationalization, nuclear weapons and which pub to go to after ward meetings. Nobody could be ideologically *against* technology or scientific advancement after all, even if it was a bit of a meaningless smokescreen. But in an age of space satellites and Formica kitchen tops, he really did seem to be offering something new. With his talk of youthful dynamism, Wilson was consciously seeking to come across as another John F. Kennedy. His manifesto commitments didn't actually outline any plans for a botched invasion of Cuba or having it off with Marilyn Monroe but people got the general idea.

The leader of the opposition was a younger man when suddenly youth was important. Because 1963 wasn't just the year of Harold Wilson; the MP for Liverpool Huyton had to surrender centre stage to four young men who as struggling musicians had played many times in his constituency.

'Rattle your jewellery'

Liverpool, 1962. Four working-class lads, a little rough round the edges but full of enthusiasm and ready Scouse wit, settled on the line-up they hoped might make their little rock-and-roll outfit finally click. Their modest ambition: to make it as a beat group, perhaps to get a song or two in the charts. The reality was to be very different. Because, unfortunately, Ricky Thunder and the Typhoons were utter rubbish and so they were never heard of again. However, playing in the club down the road was another group called The Beatles, and they were much, much more successful.

Judging by the number of Liverpudlians who later claimed to have seen The Quarrymen, or the Silver Beetles,* they must have been playing to audiences of 100,000 seven nights a week before they finally made it. Legend tells how Paul McCartney first bumped into John Lennon at the St Peter's church fair in July 1957. Always something of a hard-headed businessman, Paul was looking ahead fifty years and wondering how on earth he was going to find the £24 million he'd need to pay the divorce settlement from a one-legged former escort and soft porn actress. John suggested that the solution might be to form the world's most successful pop group and so The Beatles were born.

What tends to be forgotten about the music scene immediately prior to the breakthrough of The Beatles is that by the early 1960s it looked as if the rock-and-roll bubble had burst. The singles charts were full of tame Elvis wannabes crooning middle-of-the-road ballads, while album sales were dominated by the soundtracks of musicals and comedy recordings.† In Britain, jazz musicians were confident that their moment had finally come; surely soon everyone would be sporting black polonecks and little goatee beards? So nobody could have guessed that the group that got to number 17 with their first hit in October 1962 were about to transform the music scene, youth culture and the key area of male hair fashion. Over the course of the next twelve to fifteen months they had such an enormous cultural impact that they

---

* The band went through various names before they settled on 'The Beatles'. Their original bassist Stuart Sutcliffe had suggested 'The Beetles' as a tribute to Buddy Holly and the Crickets.

† George Martin was mainly producing comedy records for Parlophone when he signed The Beatles, and he conceded that it was their sense of humour that won him over when he was wondering whether to sign them. The laughter on the title track of *Sgt Pepper's Lonely Hearts Club Band* is taken from George Martin's recording of *Beyond the Fringe*.

would come to define and represent Britain even more than the royal family or the government.

And nothing like this had ever happened before. In two thousand years of British history, no working-class person had ever been more popular or feted than their supposed superiors in the ruling class, and many in the British establishment were appalled and alarmed by this apparent revolution.* 'Those in the cheap seats clap; the rest of you rattle your jewellery,' quipped John Lennon to the glittering audience at the *Royal Variety Performance* in November 1963. 'The rest of you' included Her Majesty the Queen Mother, who wasn't used to being told to take off her tiara and shake it like a tambourine. When The Beatles were awarded MBEs eighteen months later, two other holders sent their own medals back.

In fact, part of the appeal of The Beatles was how unthreatening they were. They had been persuaded to forgo the greasy hair and leather jackets that were part of the usual rock-and-roll uniform, and were dressed in matching suits and ties. They didn't smoke or swear on stage, but bowed together at the end of each song. This rebranding of the rough-and-ready band that had played the clubs of Liverpool and Hamburg was the work of their manager Brian Epstein, whom the Conservative newspapers variously described as 'a canny marketing man' (= 'Jew'), 'a very clever entrepreneur' (= 'Jew'), 'an ambitious businessman' (= 'Jew') and 'yet, despite all his success, still somehow one of society's outsiders' (= 'homosexual Jew').

By the end of 1963 The Beatles held the number one and two spots in both the British album and singles charts, but Epstein was even more ambitious for them and had booked a tour of the United States. The Beatles' music was completely unknown in the

---

* It wasn't just the stuffy old establishment that took against these upstarts. There was no shortage of voices on the left that were hostile to what they saw as crass commercialism and the Americanization of British culture.

birthplace of rock and roll, and most American music executives were decidedly sniffy about them. Yet by April 1964, The Beatles occupied the top five positions in the American Billboard Chart. Their conquest of the States was even more dramatic than their sudden arrival on the English music scene. When they appeared on *The Ed Sullivan Show*, seventy-three million viewers tuned in to what became the biggest audience in the history of American television. This was fame at a new level, and the hype and excitement was so intense it seemed completely unsustainable. And yet by being endlessly creative, innovative and original, The Beatles remained at the pinnacle of musical and critical success throughout the 1960s. Little could those naive young musicians from Liverpool have known that their stratospheric journey was destined to end in tragedy two decades later, when Paul McCartney would record 'The Frog Chorus'.

'Let's go with Labour' (just don't ask where)

At the end of 1963, *That Was The Week That Was* had summarized the choice before the electorate as 'Dull Alec versus Smart Alec', but the option was not put before the country until the following autumn. Home delayed the election to the latest possible point in an effort to give his party the best chance of recovering its position, and so polling day was set for 15 October 1964, more than five years since the previous election and therefore barely constitutional. Sir Alec Douglas-Home had the misfortune to become Prime Minister at a time when physical appearance began to matter like never before, and polling was revealing that having 'a face that looked like a skull' was a definite disadvantage. One TV make-up lady was quite frank with him about the similarity, and Home replied, 'Does not everybody have a head like a skull?' Her reply was an unapologetic 'No'.

Wilson, on the other hand, came across well on television, pausing to take a puff on his pipe whenever he was asked a tricky question (in private he actually smoked cigars), in the days when it was perfectly normal for TV interviews to be conducted through a fug of tobacco smoke. Unlike Home, he coped well with hecklers at public meetings, and he was a witty and engaging speaker. But of all the political rallies and TV appearances, none were worth half so much as one picture taken at the Variety Club Awards, when the leader of the opposition managed to get himself photographed with The Beatles. Sir Alec Douglas-Home's own attempts to identify himself with The Beatles went badly wrong when his speechwriters tried to get him to quote from 'She Loves You' in a speech, but the old duffer clearly did not get the reference and stuttered, 'And you know, er, that can't be too bad' to the utter bemusement of his audience.*

Everything seemed to point to a Labour victory after thirteen years of Tory government. In fact, the result was even closer than the two parties' policies. For all his slick presentational style and youthful vigour, Harold Wilson actually got fewer votes than old Hugh Gaitskell had managed in 1959. Instead, the Tories lost votes to the Liberals. Labour squeezed in with a tiny majority of just four seats, and any number of minor factors could have easily swung the result the other way and kept the Conservatives in power.†

Worried that Labour voters would rather stay in and watch their favourite television comedy than go out and vote, Harold Wilson managed to persuade the BBC to postpone the hugely

---

* Edward Heath also did his utmost to praise The Beatles, saying they could be the saviours of the British corduroy industry.
† The overconfident Conservative MP for Brighton Kemptown failed to insist that his local association cancel a trip to Boulogne for 200 Conservative ladies that had been set for election day. He lost his seat by seven votes. But on the plus side, they did bring back some lovely cheeses.

popular *Steptoe and Son* till polling had closed. Asked what he would suggest broadcasting in its place, he suggested a Greek tragedy. News of two other major world events came after the polls had closed, and might well have sent the voters scuttling to the safety of the party of government had the stories broken a few hours earlier. As Britain was waiting to see who would lead them into the next phase of the Cold War, Khrushchev was toppled in Moscow and the Chinese tested their first atomic bomb.

Events in Britain were a little less dramatic, even if the 1964 election is seen as a watershed in British political history. But on the giant screen at Trafalgar Square, every Labour gain was cheered as if it was a new dawn. So what if the screen was so dark you couldn't really see anything and the sound system was virtually non-existent. *The Times* described the scene as more like a bank holiday at a south coast resort, given the numbers of 'Mods, Rockers, Beatniks and other species of youngsters'.

By lunchtime on the Friday, it became clear that Labour would have an absolute majority and the leader of the Labour Party was summoned to Buckingham Palace. They hadn't been expecting him to bring his wife and kids with him, but that's the Labour Party for you: no sense of protocol.

I can see for miles and miles (but not quite the nearest shop)

It was an excited meeting of urban planners, council officers and modernist architects who gazed upon the scale model of Urine Towers in Whitechapel, the exciting new high-rise housing project designed to bring together all the best of 1960s architecture and modernist design.

'This giant forty-storey block will be constructed in crumbling pre-cast concrete with a mildew finish and painted in obscene graffiti by local artists,' boasted the architect. 'The residents arrive here, passing the broken lift, and proceed to carry their crying toddlers, double buggy and bags of shopping up the forty flights of stairs to the top floor.'

'It's like a gym outside their own house . . .!'

'Exactly – so we'll be housing mainly pensioners and young families at the very top. The apartment interiors are finished in lethal asbestos and wafer-thin plasterboard giving residents an extra sense of community as they listen to their neighbours fighting, sobbing or having sexual intercourse.'

'I see you've left a whole side of the model exposed for us to see the interior . . .'

'No, that's what it will actually look like after it's been blown open by a gas explosion.'*

'Of course, yes. What's the dark area under the stairwell?'

'Well spotted. We wanted somewhere dark and dank to provide the right ambience for intravenous drug use. The rubbish chute blocked with fermenting disposable nappies will add to the charm of the setting . . .'

'Marvellous – you really have thought of everything!'

'Why is this little figure climbing over her balcony railings?'

'She's an elderly widow relocated from a terraced street ten miles away. The buildings are designed to be so alienating and depressing that residents regularly take advantage of the three-hundred-foot drop right outside their living room, thus providing a regular turnover of available apartments.'

---

* In May 1968, an old lady lit the gas hob in her eighteenth-floor council flat in the block that had been opened two months earlier. The resulting explosion took away not only her flat, but every single corner flat in the storeys above and below, as the building gave way like a pack of cards. Ronan Point became synonymous with the disenchantment with 1960s modernism, and Councillor Ronan began to wish they'd called the block something else.

And another brilliantly innovative idea was welcomed with a smattering of light applause as they passed round the sandwiches and the envelopes stuffed with cash for members of the Housing Committee.*

The image of the arrogant and hypocritical urban planners of the 1960s seems too clichéd and reactionary to be true. But in fact there was a fantastically patronizing attitude to architecture and public housing that made bold futuristic statements about 'streets in the sky' without ever taking the trouble to talk to any of the people who might have to live in them. When the staff of *Architectural Review* were planning a special issue on modern housing, one naive young staff member had the idea of finding out the sort of homes people actually wanted. 'But we *know* . . .' replied the dismissive editor. Whole town centres were ripped out and rebuilt in concrete. Birmingham believed it was going to be one of the most modern cities in Europe, with its ring roads, Bull Ring, Rotunda and 24,000 high-rise flats. And sure enough today, architects talk of Birmingham in the same sentence as Florence and Venice. As in: 'You should see Florence or Venice, but just don't go to Birmingham.' The city of Glasgow prided itself on the tallest blocks of flats in Europe, nearly all bolted together in pre-cast concrete, while London saw hundreds of thousands of people rehoused in tower blocks that rose up out of the slum clearance and bomb damage of the East End. But did they ever stop to ask John Betjeman what he thought of it all?

With rural railway stations closing down as Beeching's† cuts

* The leader of Newcastle City Council T. Dan Smith was found guilty of taking bribes from the architect John Poulson. The Poulson scandal would also bring down the Conservative Home Secretary Reginald Maudling.
† Dr Richard Beeching was appointed chairman of British Railways by Macmillan's government with a brief to stop the loss-making railways haemorrhaging public money. His infamous axing of branch lines and rural stations removed 4,000 miles from the rail network and changed the country for ever. The British public condemned his brutal attack on the railways in about the same numbers as they had bought motor cars so they wouldn't have to take the train.

started to bite, and motorways being carved through the English countryside, it was not hard to feel that some of what made olde England special was being bulldozed in the questionable name of 'progress'.

You knew the modernist architects must be baddies when among the most famous was a character named Erno Goldfinger. This Hampstead-dwelling Marxist and designer of such eyesores as Metro Central Heights at Elephant and Castle so infuriated his near-neighbour Ian Fleming that the James Bond creator named one of his nastiest characters after him.* Fortunately his high-rise flats did not swivel open to reveal a secret nuclear missile silo. They just looked horrible and then got sick building syndrome.

To be fair to the housing committees of the 1960s, at the time of building, many working-class families were delighted to be getting new homes with an indoor toilet, a bathroom and fitted kitchen; these homes were a huge improvement on the slums where they had lived before. 'We thought we'd moved into Buckingham Palace!' said one elderly Battersea resident. And the decision to go upwards rather than outwards spared much of the Green Belt around Britain's cities from being swallowed up by urban sprawl. But less than a generation later it was pretty clear that families did not want to live in towering, cheaply built blocks of concrete flats with no back yard or sense of community. They gazed nostalgically upon their old Victorian terraced houses, which had now been done up by yuppies, and wondered how long they would have to work there as a cleaner before they could afford to move back.

---

* Goldfinger consulted his lawyers about this and Fleming threatened to rename the character 'Goldprick', which might have made for some interesting lyrics for Shirley Bassey.

Wilson moves in to find last tenants trashed the place

Few cabinets have been as well documented as those of the Labour governments of the 1960s. Tony Benn was keeping a diary, Barbara Castle was keeping a diary, Richard Crossman was keeping a diary; thanks to all of them we know what was really happening inside the Wilson government. Nothing – they were all too busy writing their diaries.

The day after the general election, James Callaghan, the new Chancellor of the Exchequer, entered Number 11 Downing Street. His Tory predecessor Reginald Maudling was still collecting his things and casually commented, 'Sorry to leave such a mess, old cock . . .'

'That's strange,' thought Callaghan walking into his new office, 'because the desk actually seems quite tidy. And the floor is clean and the shelves have been dusted.' The civil servants were just marking the latest financial figures on the graph on the wall. Then they got off the floor and welcomed him to the job.

Great Britain was virtually bankrupt. Maudling had spent the last few million quid engineering a pre-election boom and the rest of it had been blown during the previous decade on giving the neighbours the impression that Great Britain was still a major world power. Reserves had been spent keeping the pound artificially high, while millions a year were committed to keeping armies stationed in the outposts of an empire that no longer brought in any revenue.

The UK owed so much money to various creditors that Mrs Wilson was thinking of talking to that dodgy loan shark who hung around outside the bookies. The deep-seated reasons for Britain's economic stagnation were not easily remedied; indeed, many of them dated back to before the First World War. Once the 'work-shop of the world', Britain now imported far more than it exported. The country was plagued with poor industrial relations, it had a workforce with out-of-date skills, management that generally had contempt for the first-hand experience of those on the shop floor, and a poor record of recruiting leadership from the lower ranks.

The Conservatives may have left the economy in a terrible state in 1964, but that's not to say that Labour made the right decisions once they took over. Perhaps the key mistake of the Wilson government was made that very first weekend as they were still filling the Downing Street fridge with beer and sandwiches. Without consulting cabinet or the House of Commons, Wilson and Callaghan decided against the idea of devaluing sterling. Being lefty public-sector types, they did not have much of a grasp of how the City of London and world markets actually worked. 'So buying and selling currencies then, let's try our hand at this . . . Right, I'm going to sell you these hundred-pound notes . . .'

'All right, I'll give you ninety quid each for them.'

'No way – I'm ten quid down on the deal. How about £110?'

'Hmm, tell you what: meet you halfway – two fifties, cash in yer hand. You can't say fairer than that, can you?'

'Done!'*

What they did understand, however, was that it might be political suicide for Labour's first act to be the devaluation of sterling, and a death blow to the international standing of Great Britain Ltd. But the decision was taken for party political rather than economic reasons; with a parliamentary majority of only four, the campaign for the next general election had already begun and Labour's opening move was certainly not going to be to announce to the electorate that they were bankrupt. Instead James Callaghan stuck a surcharge on imports into Britain (unthinkable today) and then wondered how

---

*.James Callaghan later admitted that it took him several years of being Chancellor of the Exchequer before he understood how the City worked. Labour ministers had to rely on the advice of Treasury officials, who were inherently conservative.

much he might raise if he took all of George Brown's empties back to the off-licence.

The rest of the decade is the story of trying to stave off the inevitable: spending reserves to prop up the pound, negotiating with the American government to get them to keep supporting the pound, until the money and the support eventually ran out and Wilson's central economic policy was blown to pieces in November 1967. It would have been so much less painful to get it over with the day after the 1964 general election and say it was all the other lot's fault. But expecting Harold Wilson to put the long-term interests of the country ahead of short-term political expediency would be like hoping the Kray brothers would be happy with an IOU note.*

The Ministry of Silly Ideas

When the writers of *Yes Minister* wanted to create the most point-less and self-defeating government department in which to place their embattled cabinet minister, they invented a ministry called the Department of Administrative Affairs. Their inspiration had been Harold Wilson's hobby horse, the Department for Economic Affairs, a new ministry that was intended to curb the power of the Treasury, and so was completely neutralized by the Treasury. Poor George Brown would go in there every day with a terrible hang-over, and focus on the important business of rebending the unbent paperclips until the pubs opened at lunchtime.

There was also a Ministry of Technology, or 'MinTech', created to see through Wilson's promised vision of a Brave New

---

* Reggie and Ronnie Kray were the best known of the gangsters operating in London in the 1960s and gained a certain amount of celebrity status before they were finally sentenced to prison in 1969, having been found guilty of inspiring a load of dodgy airport paperbacks.

World of scientific socialism. But one of the problems with the perennially optimistic Harold Wilson is that he had started to believe his own propaganda. He really did think that technological advancement might come to the rescue of Britain's desperate economic situation. 'Fear not, for the scientists will soon invent the patented PSBR Reducer, using atomic energy and invisible gamma rays to magically shrink the Public Sector Borrowing Requirement.'

One of the icons of this modern age was the newly built Post Office Tower, the tallest building in Britain, with its communication hub and famous revolving restaurant. Keen to be associated with this soaring symbol of scientific Britain, Harold Wilson visited the tower in 1965, travelling to the very top to survey the modern metropolis that was leading his technological revolution. The fog was so bad there was no view at all.

Another symbol of this scientific socialism was to be a supersonic passenger jet aircraft to be built in cooperation with the French. The plane was to be called 'Concord', to symbolize this historic agreement and scientific cooperation. 'Non, non, it eez *Concorde*, avec un *e*,' said the French insistently, and the rest of the decade was wasted arguing over the spelling.

'I believe in yesterday'

As if to symbolize the passing of another age, Sir Winston Churchill died at the beginning of 1965. He had first become an MP during the reign of Queen Victoria, but had only left the Commons at the 1964 election. In the years since the end of the war he had become a national icon like no other and 300,000 people queued to file past his coffin as it lay in state at Westminster Hall. In the only state funeral accorded to a Prime Minister during the twentieth century, crowds openly wept and threw garage flowers at the passing hearse as Elton John played 'Candle in the Wind' – no, hang on, that all comes later. Churchill's funeral was a genuinely dignified shared national experience; the cranes along the river were lowered as his body passed on a Thames launch before his coffin was placed on a train at Waterloo station.*

But Richard Crossman's diaries commented on the sight of the assembled ageing establishment, the lords and admirals and medal-laden generals shuffling out of St Paul's cathedral in old military uniforms or feathered hats symbolizing lost authority in some far-flung part of a disappearing empire. 'What a faded, declining establishment surrounded me,' he wrote. 'It felt like the end of an epoch, possibly the end of a nation.'

Perhaps the funeral served to highlight the contrast between the great Winston Churchill and the second-rate aristocrats now running the Conservative Party. With the new Labour government looking youthful and vigorous, pressure increased on Sir Alec Douglas-Home to surrender the leadership of the Conservative Party to someone who might look like he hadn't actually died several decades earlier. Now there would be no magic circle of old Etonians making their secret selection; following the scandal that surrounded his own appointment, Sir Alec ensured that his replacement would be chosen by a straight vote of Conservative Members of Parliament. Thus Edward Heath became the first commoner to lead the Conservatives; now the next election would be between two grammar-school boys. Sir Alec stayed in right-wing politics by becoming president of the MCC the following year. When travelling back to Scotland around this time, he was told by a man who leant across the first-class compartment to speak to him, 'My wife and I think it a great shame that you were never Prime Minister.'

* The story goes that Churchill had wanted to incorporate Waterloo into the proceedings just to annoy President de Gaulle.

Ready steady go!

In 1955 British teenagers bought 4 million singles a year. By 1963 they were buying 61 million. BBC radio had been too slow to respond to the huge appetite for popular music and so it was left to pirate radio stations to fill the gap. These were only 'pirate' in the sense that they were breaking broadcasting regulations; they weren't boarded by Somali warlords demanding massive ransoms for all the Dave Clark Five singles. Radio Caroline* began transmitting from a ship off the Suffolk coast in 1964, with cheery DJs like Simon Dee and Tony Blackburn interspersing upbeat pop and cheeky chatter, and then dashing to the rail to throw up into the heaving North Sea. Radio Luxembourg shifted from family-oriented programmes to targeting teenagers listening to radios in their bedrooms. They had to take everyone's word for it that the music was great; it was hard to tell with the long-wave signal fading in and out as the cheap transistor radios crackled and hissed. But more illegal radio stations sprang up, until finally the government acted, passing legislation which made it much harder for the pirate stations to collect advertising revenue, while the BBC were encouraged to launch a pop music station of their own. Radio 1 began transmitting in September 1967. It is commonly believed that the first song played on Radio 1 was 'Flowers in the Rain'† by The Move. In fact, anyone listening to that frequency at 5.30 a.m. on launch day would have heard simultaneous broadcast of Radio 2, and so, rather wonderfully, the first song ever heard by listeners tuning in to 'the

---

* Radio Caroline was named after President Kennedy's daughter.
† The manager of The Move promoted this song with a cheeky postcard showing a naked Harold Wilson with his political assistant Marcia Williams. Wilson sued, and stipulated that all royalties from the record be given to charity. Over the decades the joke postcard stunt has cost Roy Wood and the rest of the band perhaps up to £1 million in royalties.

exciting new sound of Radio 1' was 'The Sound of Music' by Julie Andrews.

The breakthrough of The Beatles also opened up America and the rest of the world to other British groups. The Rolling Stones, The Who and The Kinks all toured America, although The Kinks were blacklisted from performing in the USA for four vital years after a punch-up with a Los Angeles Musicians Union official who had called Ray Davies a 'commie wimp' and 'talentless fuck', which he clearly wasn't (talentless, that is). Cliff Richard never quite made the breakthrough, and so some degree of British post-war dignity was maintained.

It was The Rolling Stones who opened the first ever edition of *Top of the Pops*, an experimental pop music chart show that was originally only intended to run for a few programmes. The first show ended with a performance from the band that was number one, inevitably The Beatles, singing 'I Want to Hold Your Hand'. The London area already had *Ready Steady Go!* over on ITV, and suddenly the whole country had a window to the 'swinging scene' about which they had heard so much. *Top of the Pops* ran for another forty-two years, with the last ever programme presented by the man who had introduced the very first, with the difference that the young girls standing either side of Sir Jimmy Savile looked a little less comfortable now that they had seen him on a Louis Theroux programme.

If you were a young person at the beginning of the 1960s, you were automatically a second-class citizen: you were a lowly paid apprentice, or a silly hot-headed student or a naive debutante not to be trusted with a front-door key, let alone a vote, until you came of age at twenty-one. But over the course of the next two decades, being young went from being a social impediment to becoming the look and the voice that society most coveted. Somewhere in the middle of all of this was a demographic that missed out on both fronts. Told to keep quiet and wait for their time during the

1940s and 1950s, a whole generation entered middle age exactly at the point when nobody was interested in what they thought. Suddenly it was the young people that were lionized, not square bread-head Dad with his pipe and his boring opinions about the value of sterling. People didn't have plastic surgery in 1960 to look younger. When a young Harold Wilson was first in the cabinet, he grew a moustache to make himself look older.* But the next Labour leader after Wilson to win a general election would wear jeans and pose with an electric guitar.

Labour wins hearts and loses mind

When it opened in 1981, the Humber Suspension Bridge was the longest single-span bridge in the world. The bridge cuts the road distance from Hull to Grimsby by 50 miles, but that presumes that anyone would want to go to either. The reasons for the existence of this massive piece of engineering originate in Harold Wilson's wafer-thin majority in early 1966. Facing a by-election in North Hull, the fragile government promised this hugely ambitious bridge to the local voters and the by-election was comfortably won. Wilson immediately declared a general election and gained a majority of 97 seats. Perhaps all the other constituencies thought that they too would get their own longest bridge in the world.

The 1966 election saw a large influx of fresh Labour MPs, many of them middle class and university educated. When the predominantly working-class Labour MPs had first arrived in the House of Commons at the beginning of the century, they had

---

* Roy Jenkins had a rather extraordinary theory that Harold Wilson might have forged his birth certificate and was ten years older than he let on. Hence the precocious talent becoming such a young cabinet minister, and the Prime Minister finally retiring so much earlier than was expected.

been visibly shorter than their well-nourished upper-class adversaries. Now the Labour Party could literally look the Tories in the eye. Labour began to be talked about as 'the natural party of government'.

Labour's second ever landslide, in 1966, should have been the moment for a radical programme to bring greater equality, opportunity and social justice, but Wilson had set his heart on disenchantment instead, and all things considered, made a fantastic job of lowering everyone's expectations and then failing to meet even those. Wilson wasn't just going to devalue the pound, he was going to devalue the Labour Movement and the whole business of politics. 'What we really need is a Minister for Disappointment to institute a National Plan for Disillusionment, a whole government department dedicated to making an entire generation feel bitter and cynical about mainstream politics.'

Perhaps the greatest tragedy of the 1960s is that at a time of enormous social change, when progressive winds were blowing around the world, Britain was led by someone who turned out to possess no long-term vision or burning desire to right the injustices of society. Harold Wilson wanted to be in government so that he could be in government. Once in office, his overriding concern was remaining in office. When Barbara Castle told him that one of his policies was a messy middle-of-the-road muddle, he was quite indignant that this should be a criticism. 'I'm at my best in a messy middle-of-the-road muddle,' he told her.

Wilson trusted no other politician, working most closely with his political secretary Marcia Williams, who was also rumoured (probably falsely) to be his mistress. The atmosphere within the cabinet became increasingly paranoid and suspicious as the Prime Minister attempted to play each potential rival off against the other. Harold Wilson was the political equivalent of a manipulative thirteen-year-old girl who clings on to her position as Queen Bee of Year 9 by lying to her friends about what complete cows all their other friends are. 'God, Roy, I like totally can't believe George Brown didn't invite you to his sleep-over, he is like such a total bitch, because he told me he was going to text you when I spoke to him at Jim Callaghan's birthday pyjama party – oh-my-god, I wasn't supposed to tell you about that!'

And now in glorious Technicolor . . .

Up until the end of the 1950s, of course, the British Isles had only been visible in black and white. Grey-haired politicians in dark suits might be spotted occasionally between dense columns of inky newsprint, grimy cars pootled their way through smoggy streets, while huge black trains poured out smoke, steam and specks of soot onto the whey-faced population shuffling along in grey overcoats, hats and headscarves.

Then in 1966, the new Labour government legalized life in colour. Following this controversial widening of the colour spectrum, Carnaby Street was suddenly swinging with girls in purple and yellow mini skirts; the England football team pulled on red shirts and won the World Cup, and Sunday newspapers printed shiny colour supplements advertising Habitat furniture in bold reds, yellows and blues. Television executives finally came out of a long lunch the following year and noticed this change, and BBC2 introduced colour TV in 1967. As a little scheduling joke, the first ever programme broadcast in colour was *The Black and White Minstrel Show*.

Life became more colourful in the philosophical sense as well, after an English gentleman explorer, wandering far from previously charted territory, stumbled upon a mysterious region that he named 'the Clitoris'. He claimed the province for the British Empire and then promptly forgot about it again. *Sexual intercourse began in nineteen sixty-three*, wrote Philip Larkin, *Between the end of the Chatterley ban, And The Beatles' first LP*. Prior to the summer of the Profumo scandal, the purely reproductive act of sex obviously occurred only in the dark, between married couples who kept their pyjamas on. *Playboy* magazine would show their models topless but no more: inexplicable micro-climates would throw up a mist across the lower half of a model's body, or else the area between a woman's legs would be a flesh-coloured nothingness, so that teenage boys would have it confirmed that female private parts were exactly as portrayed on their sisters' Barbie dolls.

The BBC still kept a long proscriptive list about what were and weren't acceptable subjects for broadcast; and comedians were forbidden from making suggestive remarks about travelling sales-men calling on lonely housewives or any reference to ladies' underwear. 'Winter draws on' was given as an example of a pun that crossed the line of decency. So it was a bit of a shock when during a live late-night discussion programme the critic Kenneth Tynan became the first person to say 'fuck' on British television, prompting a formal apology from the BBC, three separate Commons motions and a suggestion from Mary Whitehouse that he 'should have his bottom smacked'. It later turned out that Tynan was into flagellation, so that wouldn't have been much of a disincentive.

Over the course of the decade, Britain's buttoned-up Victorian prudery and censorship were gradually loosened, and a string of liberal reforms helped create an atmosphere of tolerance and honesty that finally acknowledged that, yes, people had sex out of marriage, that some people were homosexual, that others might like to see naked people on stage or choose to read literature that others might deem obscene, that some people liked to keep Polaroids of themselves performing fellatio on Douglas Fairbanks Jnr and Conservative Minister Duncan Sandys – oh, that last one was just the Duchess of Argyll apparently.*

Roy Jenkins – a reformer with a capital 'W'

The reforms were not achieved without a certain amount of political dexterity by the Home Secretary Roy Jenkins. With the governing Labour Party far from united on matters such as homosexuality, censorship and abortion, he developed a strategy to see through reform without splitting the cabinet and the parliamentary party. Jenkins singled out backbenchers to introduce Private Members' Bills and then ensured there was enough time for the matters to be debated and passed onto the statute books. Perhaps the most controversial was the Abortion Act of 1967. Before this landmark act, legal abortions could be secured if you had the money to go to Harley Street and pay a doctor to say that the patient's well-being would be harmed by the continuation of the pregnancy. But for working-class women, an illegal backstreet abortion was the only alternative. It is estimated that well over a hundred thousand women a year were risking their lives through this horrific practice (some claimed it was as high as a quarter of a million), but what was known for certain was that around 35,000 a year were being treated on the NHS after illegal amateur abortions had gone badly wrong.

The young Liberal MP David Steel was encouraged to introduce a bill widening the availability of abortions and Jenkins

* The divorce of the Duke and Duchess of Argyll was the other great upper-class sex scandal of the 1960s but was rather upstaged by the Profumo affair. The infamous Polaroid photos were used as evidence in the couple's divorce case. Before the divorce reforms of 1969, a couple could not divorce unless there was proof of adultery by one or both parties. Thousands of people were trapped in failed marriages because they didn't possess saucy Polaroids like the Duchess of Argyll.

ensured that the bill got all the support that he could provide short of a three-line whip.

A free vote was also allowed on the Sexual Offences Bill in 1967 that legalized homosexuality in England and Wales. The terms of the debate surrounding this act seem ludicrous and offensive today; even the supporters of rights for homosexuals talked of them as poor diseased individuals who already had this terrible burden to suffer without being criminalized as well. Most members of the Conservative Party were appalled at the suggestion that homosexuality be made available to all, when they'd always had to pay good money to send their sons to exclusive boarding schools to experience it.

Modern-day campaigners have criticized the timidity of this milestone act that set the homosexual age of consent at twenty-one (five years older than for heterosexuals) and actually increased the potential for police to harass homosexuals. But it is hard to understand just how extreme the prejudice was a mere forty years ago, and even with tireless lobbying and major concessions, the bill was passed by only one vote, thanks mainly to the work of Leo Abse MP.

The word 'gay' had started to be used by more politicized homosexual campaigners, but 'queer' was still the more usual adjective/noun, even among educated liberals. As the word 'gay' gained widespread currency in the late 1960s and early 1970s, indignant right-wingers would publish the same tiresome article about every three weeks in the *Daily Mail* and the *Spectator*, lamenting the hijacking of *this happy, joyful English word, which has come to mean something so disgusting, so vile, filthy and depraved, I mean when I think about it . . . excuse me, I must break off from this angry tirade to take a brisk walk on Hampstead Heath . . .*

For his liberal approach to social issues, Home Secretary Roy Jenkins became a bogey figure for the Conservative right and for policemen or prison officers. They were shocked at this namby-pamby liberal who refused to authorize the birching of prisoners, and were appalled when capital punishment was suspended for five years in 1965* (before being abolished in 1969). The ending of stage censorship was just another example of how the country was going to the dogs, and before long shows like *Oh Calcutta!* and *Hair* would make the most of the chance to incorporate gratuitous nudity that needed to be checked out to see just how gratuitous it really was.

Sex, violence and Mary Whitehouse

Mary Whitehouse was the leading figure campaigning against the apparent moral collapse of Victorian Britain. Her 'Clean Up TV' crusade held its first public meeting in Birmingham in April 1965 and claimed to have attracted over two thousand people. A co-ordinated letter-writing campaign became a logistical nightmare for the BBC, while the civil servants at Downing Street later admitted to having pretended to lose her letters to avoid having to respond to them. She often complained about the content of pro-grammes she had not actually seen, although with the advent of video recorders she would then tape suspicious-sounding pro-grammes and fast-forward through them, looking for any sex or violence to which she might object. According to her homespun amateur psychology, exposure to such images and ideas would prompt viewers to commit copycat violent or degrading sexual acts themselves. But since she was clearly watching more sex and violence than anyone else, we can only presume she spent the rest of her spare time driving around in a Ford Anglia committing drive-by shootings or engaging in casual sex with pimps and drug dealers. Mrs Whitehouse was awarded a CBE soon after

* The last hangings in Britain were on 14 August 1964.

Mrs Thatcher came to power, and as a tribute to her tireless efforts one publisher named a pornographic magazine after her.

But the 'Permissive Society' seemed all pervasive and soon the entire nation was convinced that just about everyone else was having endless, instant, uncomplicated sex. Young men were able to say to attractive women that celibacy and monogamy 'and all that shit' were just social constructs, man, chicks should just sleep with guys all the time, 'especially you two Scandinavian twins, I personally volunteer to liberate you from the fascist patriarchy that tells you that you shouldn't have sex with me whenever I suggest it'.

Perhaps most significant of all was the contraceptive pill, which became available at the beginning of the decade but was only widely taken up by the mid-1960s. Without wishing to suggest that every reader born before 1965 was an unwanted accident, the baby boom peaks at exactly the point when use of the Pill becomes widespread; once women were in charge of preventing pregnancy, the line on the graph rapidly declines. The generation born in the early 1960s remains by far the largest demographic age group; now this bulge in the population is gradually heading towards old age and retirement without having thought too much about savings or pensions, and frankly we're sort of counting on the rest of you to keep us all in enormous comfort when we retire.

First among egos

Looking back at the disappointing Labour governments of the 1960s, it is Roy Jenkins' achievements as Home Secretary that stand out. However, despite his effectiveness as a minister and his determination to make a difference, he was never cut out for the top office. A fondness for claret and society women, coupled with an inability to pronounce the letter R, made him a figure of fun for lazy humorists, who liked to get a cheap laugh out of what was an unfortunate impediment. But it was worth asking him if he'd describe himself as a really radical reformer just to see if everyone could suppress the giggles.

There were many other formidable politicians in the cabinet. Being female and a redhead, Barbara Castle was generally dubbed 'fiery' or the 'firebrand little left-winger'. Labour's greatest ever female politician was the first ever Minister for Overseas Development before becoming a controversial Minister for Transport. To the horror of saloon bar bores holding forth in country taverns, this *woman*, who couldn't even drive herself, introduced the breathalyser to undermine the quaint rural tradition of going to the pub and then driving home pissed out of your head.* Despite never having been to university, James Callaghan would become the only British politician to occupy all four great offices of state: Chancellor, Home Secretary, Foreign Secretary and eventually Prime Minister. Prolific diarist Anthony Wedgwood Benn had started out as a speechwriter for Harold Wilson but rose to become Minister of Technology, though his diaries reveal him becoming increasingly disillusioned with Wilson's leadership as Benn himself moved to the left. Wilson famously said of Tony Benn that he 'immatures with age'. It was the disillusionment caused by Wilson's leadership, and the radical response to it from people like Tony Benn, that would later cause the party to split. The 1966 landslide might have made Labour seem unassailable, but it wouldn't win a workable majority again for over thirty years.

* In the three months after the introduction of the breathalyser, road deaths dropped by just under a quarter. But it took at least another decade before the majority of the population considered drinking and driving to be morally wrong.

'Have you noticed how we only win the World Cup under a Labour government?'

One of the best-kept secrets of post-war British history is that in 1966 the final of the football World Cup was won by England. You would think with all today's tabloid flag-waving and the over-wrought obsession with football that someone might like to point out this interesting historical fact, but you have to search through the archives to find any mention of an apparent hat-trick by some-body called 'Geoff Hurst', and another association football player called 'Bobby Moore', who it turns out was the captain of the victorious England team.

What is slightly depressing about England's footballing success in 1966 is that we care more about it now than we did then. When the host nation kicked off their opening game, there were thousands of tickets left unsold. One of the games in England's group had to be relocated from Wembley to White City Stadium because it was on a Friday night, and they weren't cancelling the greyhound racing for this World Cup thingy. Yet to read about it now, you would imagine the entire nation was on tenterhooks, with everyone from Twiggy to Noel Coward filling out their wall charts and grabbing the best armchair in front of the black and white television set hours before each match. But England's early progress was uninspiring, and England were lucky that Brazil and Italy were unexpectedly knocked out early on, and that the hosts played against ten men in their games with France and Argentina. Only when England reached the final did the nation sit up and start the flag-waving (although it was the red, white and blue of the Union Jack that adorned the terraces of Wembley – it was not until 1996 that soccer fans discovered England had its own flag).

Now the excitement really started to spread. Harold Wilson offered himself to comment on the match at half-time, while Scotland's Denis Law played a round of golf. The most famous game of football in English history was to be played against West Germany in front of 98,000 fans including the Queen. Swearing and smelling strongly of beer, Her Majesty staggered through the turnstiles in a replica shirt and draped in the national flag, before it was explained that, actually, she was supposed to be supporting England. It is worth noting that although memories of the Second World War were still fresh, the final against our former enemies provoked no depressingly jingoistic references to D-Day or Adolf Hitler in the English press. It's only more recently that we have felt the need to reach way back to military victories to make up for underachievement in the sporting arena. That said, our British Tommies certainly were heroic against the onslaught of the Bundesleague Blitzkreig, but then, suddenly, Achtung! Achtung! the Huns went one–nil up, and not for the first time in her history Britain stood alone. But showing true Dunkirk spirit Sir Winston Charlton doggedly refused to surrender and Bomber Hurst destroyed the German defences, scoring three direct hits as the dam burst, and with the Russian linesman coming into the war on our side towards the end, England's finest hour was assured.

Geoff Hurst remains the only person to score a hat-trick in a World Cup final, even if his second goal didn't actually cross the line. But England were the better side on the day, and just in case those people who were on the pitch were in any doubt as to whether or not it was in fact all over, England's fourth goal made it clear that *it was then*.

The Germans have been in eleven major finals since that 4–2 defeat; England have been in none. But any neutral will tell you that 1966 is the only one that counts. The following year, England lost to Scotland, who then declared themselves to be world champions. '*One* year of hurt,' sang an English football fan. 'Hmm, doesn't really work yet . . .'

Deutschmark 4 Sterling 2 (after extra time)

Having beaten both Germany and France at football, Wilson decided this might be the moment to reapply for membership of the European Economic Community. Wilson had gradually come to the conclusion that Britain's future lay in Europe, rather than as an American satellite or imperial power in her own right. Labour under Gaitskell had always been against joining the Common Market, but being the wily party fixer he was, Wilson managed to prevent a single resignation from the cabinet when he decided that Britain should now apply for entry. To show what good Europeans we were, it was announced that Britain would be going metric, and the first decimal coins were introduced a couple of years later.

However, Harold Wilson was rather disappointed to discover that his application for membership of the Common Market did not immediately result in a grateful thank-you letter, a welcome pack and a little enamel badge he could wear on his blazer. The submission had been handled by a French bureaucrat called Charles de Gaulle, who seemed particularly unhelpful when Wilson rang up to find out when the first meeting was. Apparently the British Prime Minister had overlooked a line in the small print on the back of the form, Paragraph 17, subsection b): *The executive is unable to consider applications for membership from any country that is better than France.*

Such was the pattern of so many of Wilson's attempts to play the international statesman. When Rhodesia (modern-day Zimbabwe) had unilaterally declared independence, Wilson had held high-profile talks with the rebel white nationalist leader Ian Smith, incorrectly predicting the government would fall after the imposition of sanctions, but he was actually powerless to prevent the former colony pursuing a policy of white minority rule. Wilson attempted to remain on the best of terms with the White

House, but in the end gained little, while losing an enormous amount of domestic credibility with his words of support for American actions in Vietnam.

He was not helped in international affairs by having his irascible deputy George Brown as Foreign Secretary. In an area that requires clear thinking and level-headed diplomacy, Britain had a man who regularly got very drunk and was then extremely rude to people. At every official reception or overseas function, his officials were constantly trying to steer him away from waiters with trays of wine. At a reception in honour of the Belgian government, the British Foreign Secretary made an impromptu speech to all the assembled dignitaries, declaring: 'While you have all been wining and dining here tonight, who's been defending Europe? I'll tell you ... the British army. And where, you may ask, are the soldiers of the Belgian army tonight? ... They're in the brothels of Brussels!'

The best-known story of his excesses, almost certainly apocryphal but still recounted in the Foreign Office today, involved a trip to Latin America when, at a lavish reception, George Brown spotted a striking figure in a flowing crimson gown and, as the band struck up, he rushed up and asked for this dance. 'There are three reasons, Mr Brown, why I will not dance with you. The first, I fear, is that you have had a little too much to drink. The second is that this is not a waltz the orchestra is play-ing, but the Peruvian national anthem ... And the third reason why we may not dance, Mr Brown, is that I am the Cardinal Archbishop of Lima.'

Brown was constantly threatening to quit Wilson's govern-ment, but when he finally did so, it was done in a drunken fit of pique, so that nobody was very sure whether he had meant it or not.* His decline was actually a great loss to the Labour

---

* Brown lost his seat in the 1970 general election, and wrote his memoirs entitled *In My Way*, which Wilson quipped is where George Brown had always been.

government because, on most of the issues, George Brown turned out to be right: Vietnam, devaluation, the Common Market, 'East of Suez' – even if it was hard to remember exactly how after seven pints of light and bitter.

Apocalypse then

One of the greatest international challenges facing the cabinet was that Britain clearly could not afford to continue funding its extended military presence 'East of Suez', but that Britain's financial guarantor, the United States, did not want its ally abandoning various parts of Asia to their fate. America was becoming increasingly bogged down in the Vietnam War and not only wanted Britain to keep its troops in Singapore, Hong Kong and Malaya, but was desperate for those soldiers to fight alongside theirs in South-east Asia.

'Just two brigades and all your financial problems will be over . . .' Lyndon Johnson told the British Prime Minister. For the American President, the propaganda value of just a marching band from the Royal Marines in Saigon would have been immense: he could have portrayed the Vietnam War as a principled stand by Western democracies against the spread of totalitarianism. It must have seemed an attractive instant solution to all of Wilson's financial problems, but despite enormous pressure from Washington, the best thing Wilson ever did as Prime Minister was something he did not do.

And so no soldier of the British army was deployed in Vietnam. Unlike Tony Blair forty years later, Wilson judged that the relationship with America was not so precious that we were obliged to follow them into a faraway war that seemed to have no prospect of ending. Wilson's motives were always pragmatic rather than moral, and he probably judged that involvement in

Vietnam would split the Labour Party and cost him the next election. Or perhaps he really did think that if Britain sent British troops to Vietnam the consequences would be too awful to contemplate. Where the Americans would go on to produce a stream of chilling Vietnam movies, like *Hamburger Hill*, *Platoon* and *Full Metal Jacket*, the British film industry might exorcise the national trauma with *Carry On in Vietnam* starring Sid James and Kenneth Williams. 'Ohhh, I say, those Yanks do have enormous choppers!' 'Oh, Major, he's gone and napalmed my Privates!' It was too terrible a scenario to contemplate, and Wilson refused all the pleas from Washington, limiting himself to a failed peace mission instead.

Without British support on the battlefield, the Americans were no longer prepared to underwrite Britain's currency. The national humiliation of devaluation in November 1967 was partly a consequence of sparing the country the trauma of British involvement in Vietnam. But because he was not prepared to 'kick our creditors in the balls', as he eloquently put it, Wilson refused to condemn American action in South-east Asia, and earned himself the vilification of the British left along the way.

'This will not affect the pound in your pocket'

At the beginning of the century, £1 had been worth $4.87. By 1967 it was set at $2.80, but was clearly overvalued even at that level. But when the British Chancellor went to the Bureau de Change, the lady behind the glass explained that the British economy could not sustain its currency at this level.

'I'm afraid you need to make your exports cheaper and imports less attractive to domestic consumers . . .'

'Look, can I just have my holiday money please?'

'And you have no reserves left to keep buying sterling anyway, what with your public-spending commitments and government debts . . .'

'Is there anyone else I can speak to?'

'I tell you what – I can give you $2.40 to the pound, how about that?'

The devaluation of sterling that was forced upon the British government was the defining moment of Wilson's administration. His entire economic policy was blown away and all the spending cutbacks, austerity measures and wage freezes had failed to achieve their goal.* Ebullient as ever, the Prime Minister went on television to announce that 'that does not mean of course that the pound here in Britain, in your pocket or purse or in your bank, has been devalued' – although of course within a short time it clearly would, and howls of derision greeted this ridiculous assertion.

Not only was it a calamity for Britain. Many countries, such as those in the Commonwealth, held their national reserves in sterling, and overnight they were 14 per cent poorer. Callaghan was compelled to resign as Chancellor, and the government's poll ratings sank faster than the pound.

Hey, hey, LBJ: how many kids d'yer kill today?

The impression of a country descending into chaos was not helped by the violent scenes witnessed on the streets of London as anger grew about America's role in the Vietnam War and Britain's perceived collaboration. In fact, most ordinary people in the United Kingdom were completely indifferent to the Vietnam War, while many in the chattering classes supported what America

---

* Particularly embarrassing was the decision to increase prescription charges, since resignation over the issue of NHS charges is what had first brought Harold Wilson to public attention in 1951.

was doing.* The violence outside the American Embassy in 1968 did not symbolize the tip of the iceberg in terms of angry British opinion in the way that the anti–poll tax riot did in 1990. Instead, the famous Grosvenor Square demonstrations were another bit of Americanization. The protestors had seen the angry anti-war protests in the United States and decided that they too ought to do a bit more than just march. Perhaps getting themselves beaten up by the police in the name of peace might do the trick. The shouts of 'Pigs!' and 'Fascists!' directed at the British police were a new insult, directly imported from the America they purported to despise.

But for hundreds of well-intentioned middle-class protestors, the random violence of the police was a shocking eye–opener. Many peaceful protestors were set upon by mounted police or later charged with invented assaults. The very idea that British policemen would lie just to get a conviction against someone they didn't like would have been a truly scandalous suggestion back in 1968, so shocking it was dismissed as impossible by those who heard it. But in a tumultuous year around the world, from the near revolution in France, to Russian tanks in the streets of Prague, 1968 showed once again that the majority of British people were not inclined towards revolutionary politics. More people were humming along to 'Congratulations' by Cliff Richard† than 'Street Fighting Man' by the Rolling Stones.

* For example, in Martin Amis's memoir *Experience*, he recalls arguing with his father Kingsley, who was in favour of the American action. Such a pro-Vietnam War position from a moderate or mainstream Conservative spokesman would be unthinkable today, now that history has judged the Vietnam War to have been an unqualified disaster for America.

† Cliff cemented his super-cool image by representing the United Kingdom in the Eurovision Song Contest in 1968. According to the official history of the competition, Cliff Richard was cheated out of victory when General Franco rigged the Spanish jury to ensure victory for Spain. The Spanish entry 'La la la' beat our Cliff by one vote. This time Franco had gone too far.

'Back Britain, not Black Britain'

Indeed the political movement that really caught the public imagination was the 'I'm Backing Britain' campaign, which, like so many of the world's great political crusades, began in Surbiton. Five typists resolved to work an extra half an hour a day for free, as their bit for the embattled British economy. This patriotic stand was seized on by Fleet Street and before long there were Union Jack badges and window posters everywhere saying 'I'm Backing Britain'. It's a shame that the T-shirts were made in Portugal, but apparently they were just much, much cheaper.

Although there was no direct link between this movement and what happened later in 1968, a surge in flag-waving patriotism always risks inviting in its ugly cousin xenophobia, and the issue of racism exploded onto the scene just a few months later. Labour had passed two major pieces of race relations legislation since it had come to power, but this was followed by the shameful Commonwealth Immigration Act, which broke a promise made earlier to Kenyan Asians, who were now denied entry to Britain. The newspapers were full of images of people with dark skin arriving in Britain, and even though the law had been changed to deny immigrants the right to settle here, Conservative frontbencher Enoch Powell chose this moment to go nuclear. His infamous 'rivers of blood' speech forecast that in twenty years 'the black man will have the whip hand over the white man' and he talked of 'wide-grinning piccaninnies' unable to speak English and negroes who had persecuted an old lady by stuffing excrement through her letterbox (a claim that was later found to be completely unsubstantiated).

The speech was timed for early in the evening so as to have maximum impact on the nightly news, and came less than three weeks after the assassination of Martin Luther King and the subsequent race riots across the United States. Although the audience in the room just listened and clapped politely at the end, in the wider political arena it created a huge storm. The next day Edward Heath spoke to Powell on the telephone in order to sack him from the shadow cabinet, and the two men never had another conversation. But later in the week, on St George's Day, thousands of London dockers marched to Parliament in support of what Powell had said. 'Back Britain, not Black Britain' said their banners as tens of thousands of letters of support poured into Powell's office.

Who knows how many more racist attacks occurred because disaffected white youths felt they had been given legitimacy by one of the leading politicians of the day? How many other invisible acts of discrimination occurred because Powell had given people permission to be racist? It says a great deal about the entrenched moderation of British politics that Powell never held a front-bench post again.*

Conservatives gain Stalingrad South

But the political situation continued to feel volatile, with extremists on both sides wondering if this might be their moment. The newspaper proprietor Cecil King hatched a nutty plot that Lord

---

* In the 1964 election the Tories had infamously gained Smethwick against the national swing with the help of the slogan: *If you want a nigger for a neighbour, vote Liberal or Labour.* The episode achieved such notoriety that the new Prime Minister declared the victorious Peter Griffiths 'a parliamentary leper' while Malcolm X felt moved to visit the town, giving his last television interview before he was assassinated. Peter Griffiths was not finally ousted from the House of Commons until the Labour landslide of 1997.

Mountbatten might head an emergency government after a coup against the Prime Minister. Wilson became increasingly paranoid and distrustful of everyone from the security services to the media to his own cabinet, not to mention all those little laughing men who lived in his radiator.

The discredited Labour government continued to lose by-elections in a spectacular fashion, while in Scotland and Wales opposition to the government began to be expressed through nationalist politics. Up till now the Scottish and Welsh nationalists had been tiny pressure groups who routinely lost their deposits, but now they started to win by-elections, establishing a permanent presence at Westminster. Amazingly the investiture of Prince Charles as the Prince of Wales in 1969 didn't seem to mollify them at all. Politics in Northern Ireland was turning ugly, and by the early 1970s Ulster would become perhaps the biggest challenge facing the government. As well as rioting in the streets of Derry, the television seemed to be showing a general upsurge in violent confrontations across the whole country, whether it was clashes between police and squatters, police horses and demonstrators, or Chelsea Shed End versus Arsenal's North Bank. It all added to the general sense of a nation in deep crisis.

Five years earlier, the fresh and dynamic Wilson had seemed the solution to everything that was wrong with British society; now the politics of protest looked beyond Westminster for solutions. Students developed direct action as a means of protest, organizing mass sit-ins to protest about how embarrassing these images of them would look thirty years later when they were New Labour MPs. The feminist movement, or Women's Lib as it was known, began to make its voice heard, at a time when it was still legal to pay men and women different amounts for the same work. It was not uncommon for pubs to refuse admission to women, while the Stock Exchange and Lloyd's did not admit women until the early 1970s.

The trade-union movement did not shy away from confronting a Labour government at a time of wage freezes and government cutbacks. Barbara Castle was given the unenviable task of drawing up government proposals to curb the power of the unions. Her White Paper *In Place of Strife* split the cabinet, some of whom were cautious about attacking the very organizations that funded the Labour Party, and the idea ended up as just another failure to add to the government's long list, while moving the issue of union power up the national agenda to the political advantage of the Conservatives.

With many activists giving up on the Labour Party, the 'New Left' sought to synthesize a revolutionary socialist theoretical position of a humanist, post-colonial Marxism, departing from, but informed by, orthodox Marxist theory. But unfortunately nobody came to the meeting. The hippy movement rejected war and guns, putting their faith in love, flowers and hallucinogenic drugs, but thankfully this uneven contest was never seriously tested on the battlefield. There were those who advocated the alternative reality offered by drugs as some sort of consciousness-expanding panacea to the ills of society. The use of 'pot' and LSD exploded in the 1960s, and it was discovered that by using the mind-altering powers of cannabis on a regular basis you could become really, really boring.

I blame the 1960s

It is not hard to see why conservative traditionalists look back to the 1960s as the time when all the problems of modern society began. Callers to late-night local radio phone-ins often point the finger at this tumultuous decade as the period when the rot set in: *Hello, Ken? Well, I blame the 1960s with all those*

Open University* sociologists on the telly preaching their permissive attitudes to the immigrants with their long hair and big lapels I mean that Dr Beeching cutting all the pound in half like that no wonder we've lost the Empire I blame the unions closing down the car factories so that Britain could produce homosexuals I mean high-rise housing no wonder we can't afford to keep the Empire it's all the fault of these pop stars and long-haired footballers kissing each other after every goal no wonder the British motorcycle industry went down the pan what with all these socialist town planners letting the Russians put their satellites over England they should bring back hanging I blame all those Austin Mini skirts and dangerous new drugs like crimpolene and LSE but that's burn-the-bra women's lib for you I saw Ipi Tombi twelve times absolutely disgusting but ethnic nudity is different they should bring back National Service instead of fashionable child-centred learning and comprehensive Arndale Centres I mean I BLAME THE SIXTIES!!

You'd think Prince Charles would have better things to do.

It was a time when society seemed to lose a lot of its cohesion, but that is partly because prior to the freedoms gained during the decade, many people had been only pretending to conform. There weren't more homosexuals after it ceased to be illegal; there weren't more unhappy marriages after a no-fault divorce could be granted. Britain became a more honest, open society but part of this integrity was facing up to its diminished status. Denied a role in Europe, cast adrift by the Americans and with the

---

* The establishment of the Open University in 1969 was the achievement of which Wilson said he was most proud. It provided distance learning and previous academic achievements were not a requirement for most courses. The lectures were broadcast on BBC2 in the early hours of the morning, and were endlessly repeated years after the lecturers' brightly coloured tank tops and extreme facial hair had gone out of fashion. In the years before all-night programming and multi-channel television, late-night entertainment involved staggering in from the pub with nothing to watch but a bearded 1970s maths lecturer in a tank top explaining the negative value of x.

Commonwealth looking increasingly pointless, the British didn't even have the consolation of looking after their own interests very well. Few expected Harold Wilson to recover from the depths of unpopularity that his government suffered during the late 1960s. And yet as the country entered the 1970s, the economic situation seemed to be picking up and the government's poll record improved.

As the summer of 1970 approached, the Prime Minister had every reason to feel optimistic. England set off to defend their status as world champions with an even better side than in 1966, The Beatles were releasing a new album and Labour were finally ahead in the polls and defending a huge majority at the forthcoming general election. Sometimes everything goes wrong all at the same time.

4

The 1970s

How strikes, soccer hooligans and ludicrous hairstyles made Britain seem like the sick man of Europe

The World Cup quarter-finals, 1970. Fourteenth of June: England are playing West Germany and are two–nil up with less than half an hour to go. The holders are favourites to win. In the dug-out, tight-lipped manager Harold Wilson is watching with a degree of satisfaction as he aims to repeat his triumph of 1966. But then the boss makes what proves to be a disastrous tactical switch, taking off Bobby Charlton and putting Roy Jenkins into central midfield instead. England are already a little nervous without Gordon Banks in goal; little redhead Barbara Castle was something of a surprise substitution. Now Beckenbauer picks up the ball, dribbles round a rather wobbly George Brown, shrugs off a frankly ineffectual challenge from Shirley Williams and blasts the ball into the back of the net.

There are those who think that the world champions' shock exit from the World Cup four days before polling day is what cost Labour the 1970 general election. Wilson had certainly been counting on a feel-good factor as England progressed to the semi-finals. But a rather more sinister factor in the Conservatives' unexpected win was the intervention of the maverick right-winger Enoch Powell. 1970 was the only general election in British history in which the subject of race played a significant part. Although Powell was not even in the shadow cabinet, the Press Association allocated two reporters to follow him throughout the campaign, while the Prime Minister and the leader of the opposition only got one hack each. Tory meetings were peppered with home-made 'Enoch' banners, as Tory frontbenchers were constantly asked whether they agreed with Mr Powell. Aware that criticizing the popular racist might backfire, Harold Wilson instructed his team to avoid all mention of him (so Tony Benn helpfully referred to the member for Wolverhampton South in terms of Dachau and Belsen). Powell was like the embarrassing relative at Christmas, sitting in the corner saying, 'I don't like the blacks,' as everyone tried to pretend they hadn't heard him. 'They breed, you know. And the babies come out smelling of curry . . .' 'Yes, all right, Grandpa, shut up now.'

But the Conservatives had trailed badly in the polls throughout the campaign when Powell had been noticeably silent; when he finally felt compelled to urge people to vote Conservative, Heath was swept into Downing Street. One academic study reckoned that Powell had gained the Conservatives 2.5 million votes, easily enough to make the difference.

Perhaps to pin Heath's surprise victory on a maverick racist and the West German football team does a disservice to the British electorate. Other factors might have been a particularly bad set of trading figures, or, as Barbara Castle had speculated in her diary, that the silent majority were revealing nothing to the pollsters but would come out in large numbers to vote Conservative on election day. It was Barbara Castle's failure to put some limits on trade-union power that would have enormous repercussions the following decade. The battle with the unions would finish off two prime ministers in the 1970s and become the political raison d'être for the woman who would enter 10 Downing Street at the decade's end.

The strike-bound 1970s, which began with a rather surprised-looking Ted Heath waving on the steps of Downing Street and ended with Margaret Thatcher 'quoting' St Francis of Assisi, saw the dis-United Kingdom at what many consider to be its lowest point in modern times. Dubbed 'the sick man of Europe', Britain staggered from crisis to crisis as power cuts reduced housewives to shopping by candlelight or, worse, going to bed and actually having sex with their husbands.* Since the amount of sex is not one of the indices taken into account, Britons' standard of living was judged to have fallen behind those of their European neighbours.† The television news seemed to transmit an un-remitting tale of woe: inflation and unemployment up as the pound sank lower, IRA bombs exploding from Belfast to Birmingham, strikers and soccer hooligans, mass walkouts and angry demon-strations; and all carried out with the worst fashion sense ever seen. Today you watch the 1970s news footage of an eyewitness describ-ing some IRA outrage, and you think, 'God, that's awful. Bushy sideburns brushing up against jumbo collars protruding out of a tartan tank top. Truly that was a terrible decade.'

The England football team obligingly pursued the sporting metaphor of Britain's decline by failing even to qualify for the next two World Cup finals.‡ That infamous 'election-deciding' football game was the last World Cup match England would play in the decade. But interestingly those finals are a good example of how history gets distorted as people's memories are replaced by subsequent retrospectives. We all remember watching the yellow

---

* There was a marked increase in the birth rate nine months after the power cuts.
† The Italian press heralded this historic milestone with the headline *Il Surpasso!*
‡ To make things even worse for England fans, Scotland qualified for both the 1974 and 1978 finals, generally pulling off impressive results against the big teams and then going out on goal difference by failing to thrash some useless team like Narnia.

Brazil shirts weaving around the Italian azzuris in 1970, when in fact nearly everyone watched the original final in black and white. But if you repeatedly present something a certain way years after the event, people will swear blind that is how they originally witnessed it. The same is true for the two major political crises of the 1970s. Heath's three-day week and official state of emergency were far more disruptive and alarming than Jim Callaghan's 'winter of discontent', and yet the national folk memory has made the winter of 1978/79 into Britain's low point because that is how it has been served up ever since.

Edward Heath – the 54-year-old virgin?

Ted Heath grew up in Broadstairs, so he was always more likely to join the Conservative Party than the Popular Front for the Liberation of Palestine. He gained a music scholarship to Oxford, where contemporaries remember him as a rather serious and naive young man. Denis Healey's memoirs recall the shock expressed by young Ted that a couple of students were sleeping together,* and Heath was never particularly comfortable with the opposite sex, remaining a bachelor all his life. This led many to speculate that the new Prime Minister was gay, but it seems that he just never had a relationship with anyone of either sex. Perhaps this is why the country went through such trauma during his time in office, because its Prime Minister was trying to negotiate with the unions whilst almost exploding with sexual frustration. His two great loves were sailing and music; and so cartoonists portrayed him alternately as the conductor of an orchestra all playing different tunes or the captain of a sinking ship. The impressionist Mike

* Healey recalls Heath saying, 'Good heavens, I can't imagine anyone in the Conservative Association doing that.'

Yarwood just did the voice and lampooned the way his shoulders went up and down when he laughed. Political satire was a little gentler back then.

His first cabinet contained some of the leading figures of the last Conservative government, including Sir Alec Douglas-Home as Foreign Secretary. Perhaps the most able politician was Iain Macleod, a widely respected political thinker who combined experience with vision, which he rather spoilt by failing to stay alive for more than a month after the election. Heath later also lost his Home Secretary Reginald Maudling, who was forced to resign when his name became linked to a corruption scandal.* It was suggested to Heath that he ought to have a woman in his cabinet, and the new Prime Minister probably blushed at the mention of the opposite sex. It was agreed that Margaret Thatcher was by far the most able, and so his future assassin was admitted into the fray.

All the history books say the same thing about Edward Heath, that he has had a very bad press in recent years, that history has not been kind to him, that perhaps we need to revisit his tarnished reputation. And then by the end of their analysis they are pulling their hair out about what an utter disaster his government was: seeking confrontation in battles he could not win; making bold policy announcements about an end to supporting lame-duck industries or vowing never to agree to wage demands above his strict predetermined level, and then making humiliating U-turns that showed his government to be completely without purpose or direction and utterly driven by events. No wonder he rarely

* The award for the most unfortunate resignation of this government goes to Lord Jellicoe, who was the Conservatives' leader in the House of Lords. After a call-girl scandal forced the resignation of junior defence minister Lord Lambton, the name 'Jellicoe' was found in the prostitute's notebook and Lord Jellicoe admitted that, yes, he had used call girls from Mayfair Escorts. It turned out that 'Jellicoe' was only written down as a meeting place, probably the Jellicoe Pub in Chelsea. Bad luck, your lordship.

played the piano in public: his right hand never knew what the left hand was doing.

'You can't get me; I'm part of the union'*

A major piece of Ted Heath's domestic programme was his Industrial Relations Bill, which was intended to tackle the increasing problem of strikes, but immediately had the opposite effect as unions struck in protest against it. But Heath's tactic of confrontation also increased the number and length of strikes, and in 1970 the number of working days lost was the highest since 1926, the year of the General Strike. By 1972 it would be 24 million days, ten times the level of Wilson's first year in office.

You would think with Britain's disastrous balance-of-payments deficit that a dockers' strike might have been just the thing to give the economy a bit of a break, but Heath declared a state of national emergency. This makes the situation sound quite desperate, but Heath ended up declaring more national emergencies than any British government in history and the effect becomes rather diminished after you learn a national emergency has been declared because the Prime Minister can't find his conductor's baton.

The dockers were followed by the so-called 'dirty jobs strike', which saw dustmen and sewerage workers withdrawing their labour. Bags of rubbish were piled up in the streets, splitting open and spilling stinking refuse everywhere; it was the national equivalent of what happens to your front garden if you fail to give the dustmen a tip at Christmas. Just as it would again at the end of the decade, Leicester Square became a temporary rubbish tip and rats

* This was the title of a hit song by English folk-rock band The Strawbs. Despite its sarcastic anti-union lyrics, it was nevertheless adopted by trade unionists as an unofficial anthem.

could be seen scuttling around one of London's most famous landmarks, watching the silver robot mime artist for a bit and then getting bored and moving on before they were embarrassed into giving him any money.* Untreated raw sewage was poured into the rivers, killing thousands of fish. Local news reporters were lumbered with the job of picking rotting carp out of the stinking brown water to illustrate their earnest report about the terrible consequences of the strike, while the TV audience at home thought, 'Well, they're only fish, it's not like they're anything cute like baby rabbits.'

One significant difference between the strikes that consumed the Heath government and the battles Margaret Thatcher would have with the unions in the 1980s is that public opinion was much less hostile to the concept of trades unions before a decade of closures, work-to-rules and power cuts completely exhausted everyone's patience. Major union figures were national celebrities affectionately impersonated on TV comedy shows; in the early 1970s people felt sympathy with those in low-paid jobs and with Britain's miners in particular. So when in 1972 the National Union of Mineworkers began their first nationwide strike since 1926, there was a general sense that they were deserving of a few extra quid a week for the grim and dangerous work they did. The government was poorly prepared, and the miners were disciplined and well organized. They succeeded in preventing the movement of coal around the country, and at Satley coke depot in the West Midlands, around 6,000 flying pickets† led by a young firebrand

---

* In fact, the street performers of Leicester Square and Covent Garden came later; back in the 1970s, the piled-up rubbish was spoiling a West End that was a maze of sex shops and XXX cinemas.

† Flying pickets were a relatively new development in industrial disputes, and the following year saw the jailing of the 'Shrewsbury Two', a couple of union activists from the construction industry who became a *cause célèbre* after they were charged with 'conspiracy'. One of them would go on to find fame of another sort as the actor Ricky Tomlinson.

by the name of Arthur Scargill succeeded in preventing the delivery of supplies. When the police officer in charge decided it would no longer be safe to try and get the lorries through, Scargill suggested that the policeman lend him his tannoy in order to inform the pickets to withdraw. The officer duly did so, only to stand there feeling rather foolish as he listened to Scargill give an extended speech on the power of organized labour and this great victory for socialism.*

Power cuts began to bite, Big Ben and Piccadilly Circus were in darkness and even a cabinet meeting was held in candlelight. Desperate for a way out, the government appointed the independent Lord Wilberforce to examine the miners' claim, who quickly decided that the miners should get an increase well in excess of 20 per cent, and the miners eventually settled for three times what had been offered by the National Coal Board. It was an utter humiliation for the government and the miners became acutely aware of their industrial muscle.

Northern Ireland tourist board seeks smaller office

If the early 1970s were a low point for Britain, they were even grimmer for the forgotten corner of the United Kingdom across the Irish Sea. Most people in Britain knew very little about the north of Ireland except that their accents weren't as nice. But the six counties had been quietly self-governing since 1921 with their own Parliament and Prime Minister, all undemocratically elected under outrageously gerrymandered boundaries to stop

---

* Patrick Hannan's book *When Arthur Met Maggie* recalls that when Scargill was ringing around trying to recruit union support for the mass picket, he called the Welsh miners' leader Dai Francis, who said 'But, Arthur, Wales are playing Scotland at Cardiff Arms Park tomorrow.' To which Scargill replied, 'But, Dai, the Working Class are playing the Ruling Class at Satley tomorrow.'

Catholics being fairly represented. But in the late 1960s, inspired by the civil rights movement in the southern United States, the minority Catholic population began to march for an end to discrimination in politics, housing and employment. Their peaceful protests met with premeditated violence from sections of the Loyalist community, supported by the infamous 'B Specials', a sort of cross between a volunteer police force and vigilante lynch mob.

In the summer of 1969 predominantly Nationalist* Derry saw two days of rioting in which six people were killed and three hundred Catholic homes were burnt out, while the Protestant Royal Ulster Constabulary patently did little to protect the minority Catholic population. 'IRA = I Ran Away' was the graffiti on the streets of Derry, as some frustrated Catholics wondered who could possibly protect them. The civil rights movement was a very moderate organization and had certainly not been demanding the reunification of the island. But as the violence escalated, the semi-dormant Irish Republican Army was given fresh impetus and the crisis widened to focus on the continued British presence in Ireland. The decision to send in British troops was taken by Harold Wilson, who interrupted his holiday in the Isles of Scilly† to consult with his Home Secretary.

'Can't it wait, dear?' complained Mary Wilson. 'We're supposed to be visiting the botanical gardens this morning.'

---

* The descriptions 'Catholic' and 'Nationalist' tend to be used as if they are interchangeable and synonymous but of course they are not. Not all Catholics wanted a united Ireland and not all Protestants were against it. Some people would refuse to be defined as either, although Belfast was almost unique in Britain's major cities in lacking a significant black or Asian population. A sprinkling of Buddhists or fundamentalist Muslims might have really made things interesting.

† Harold Wilson always took his holidays in the Isles of Scilly despite the fact that the islands were technically still at war with the Netherlands. The 300-year 'conflict' emerged out of the English Civil Wars when the Isles of Scilly were a last Royalist stronghold. The Dutch forgot to make peace until this anomaly was finally rectified in 1986.

'Sorry, dear, it's just that civil war is breaking out in Ulster . . .'

'Honestly, it's always something, isn't it?'

In 1969 the IRA split, with those in favour of pursuing a policy of violence calling themselves the 'Provisional IRA'. It was the 'Provos' that began the seemingly indiscriminate bombing campaign that was to cost thousands of lives over the next thirty years. Loyalist terror groups responded with the random murder of Catholics, and a depressing spiral of violence turned one corner of the United Kingdom into a war zone. In such an atmosphere there was no place for the moderates who rule Ulster today. Martin McGuinness, for example, obviously spent the early 1970s driving disabled children to the seaside and doing a little flower arranging for his local church. On the other side emerged the Reverend Ian Paisley (or Dr Ian Paisley if you count the 'doctorate' he was given by the outlawed American 'Pioneer Theological Seminary'). Many witnesses insist that Paisley was among the cudgel-wielding mob that had ambushed the peaceful civil rights marchers, and now he emerged as a spokesman for hard-line unionism on the grounds that he had the loudest voice.

With the situation rapidly deteriorating, the powers that be sat around trying to think of the worst possible policy to apply to the explosive situation. 'I know. Why don't we round up hundreds of innocent Catholics, then lock them up for no good reason other than the prejudice of the local Protestant security forces?'

'Yes, that's a great idea, because it would fill previously peaceful Nationalists and their families with a burning sense of resentment and anger . . .'

'And while they are locked up, they will meet the handful of highly politicized and persuasive terrorists that we did manage to net.'

'Good point – we must make sure there are lots of application forms available to join the IRA . . .'

The Northern Irish government's policy of 'internment' in

August 1971 was the biggest boost the IRA recruiting sergeants could have hoped for. Nationalist opinion hardened further after Bloody Sunday the following year when twelve innocent marchers were shot dead by British troops on the streets of Derry. The British Embassy in Dublin was burnt to the ground, and the IRA was gaining support from both North and South. In March 1972, the British government imposed direct rule from Westminster, and brought the Northern Irish parliament at Stormont to an end after fifty years. With everything else so under control, solving the problems of Northern Ireland would at least give Ted Heath's cabinet something to do.

Soon the violence would spread to the British mainland. Bombs in Birmingham, Guildford and Aldershot would see a resurgence of anti-Irish prejudice; police pressure to secure arrests generally resulted in them finding the nearest convenient Irish suspects who could have confessions beaten out of them (and even those statements were secretly tampered with) so they could be locked up for twenty years despite being completely innocent.

Still, there were some positives to take from the troubles. Street art got a shot in the arm; nothing brightens up a blighted community like a nice big mural, even if it is of some masked gunmen shooting AK-47s over a coffin. 'Oh, when we gave permission for an end-of-terrace mural,' said the man from the council, 'we were sort of hoping for a colourful picture of a local carnival, maybe? You know, children laughing at circus performers, under a great big rainbow with doves flying about, maybe?' And then he notices a couple of guys in balaclavas looking menacing at the back of the crowd. 'But no, "UVF kill Fenian scum" has a certain gritty topicality to it. And that big red hand certainly brightens up what was a very grey wall.'

Back in Britain there were those on the far left and even a few in the Labour Party who attempted to justify IRA violence on the grounds of eight hundred years of British oppression, of which

Bloody Sunday was just the latest chapter. There's no doubt that the human rights of the Catholics had been ignored by Westminster and further abuses were committed during this dark period. But when it comes to human rights, being randomly blown up for going to a Birmingham pub, or having your kneecaps shot off because someone said you were an informer, is not exactly a grey area either. The IRA's punishment beatings, doorstep assassinations and racketeering added up to a far more brutal oppression of the Irish than modern British rule ever managed. Just don't say it very loudly in a pub on the Falls Road.

The IRA was not just a nationalist terrorist organization; its revolutionary violence was also based on an extreme Marxist doctrine that was shared by terror groups across Europe and beyond. Italy had the Brigate Rosse, Germany had the Baader-Meinhof gang, but, once again, England was lagging behind with the frankly rather pathetic Angry Brigade. While European urban guerrillas were hijacking planes or kidnapping government ministers, the Angry Brigade planted a small home-made bomb in a fashion boutique. So very cross were the Angry Brigade about people going shopping all the time that they wanted to symbolically destroy Biba; icon of the swinging sixties but clearly guilty of fashion crimes against humanity. Other bombs were planted outside the home of a government minister and other senior establishment figures, not to mention those very cross letters to the local paper. Fortunately no one had been killed by the time the Angry Brigade were arrested and imprisoned, and today the ageing former members of the Angry Brigade tend to be more irritated by things like litter and inconsiderate parking.*

* In fact, one of the so-called Stoke Newington Eight who were charged in connection with the explosions has since been awarded an OBE.

'Time for bed,' said Zebedee

With the evening news so unremittingly grim, the BBC decided that the British public needed their brains anaesthetizing before-hand with five minutes of spaced-out druggy animation like *The Magic Mushroom Roundabout* or *The Herb Garden*. And so prior to being exposed to distressing images of violent picket lines or soccer hooligans, every family was drugged up by a trip to some hallucinogenic alternative reality. By the time they had witnessed the kinky ménage à trois between a dog, a cat and a frog that was *Hector's House*, or the Clangers making weird noises to the Soup Dragon, Ted Heath's decision to bring in a three-day week and reduce the national speed limit to 50mph would seem quite sane and rational.

The only time the five-minute animation was suspended was for a series called *Decimal Five* in 1971, which every day would explain the intricate complexities of the crazy new monetary system. Over cheap animated images of the new coins (most of which had been in circulation for three years anyway), a posh BBC announcer explained repeatedly how the new money would work. 'Yeah, we get it!' everyone would scream at the TV. 'There are one hundred pennies in a pound. It's not that complicated!'

'Under the decimal system . . . Ten New Pence is equivalent to two old shillings . . .'

'Yes, for God's sake, that's why 10p is the same size as the two-bob bit, and we have been using it for that value since 1968!'

'But the old shilling will disappear,' he said speaking clearly and slowly, as if to a senile relative at Christmas, 'to be replaced by the new five-pence coin. The coins are the same size, and have exactly the same value,' said the government Head of Patronizing Everyone, except no one was fooled for a minute, because all the retailers had been saving up their price rises for this moment and used Decimalization Day, 15 February 1971, to hike up the cost of just about everything.

The shilling and the half-crown might have gone, the penny might have changed its value but, we were assured, the value of the pound would remain constant. Except it didn't; the following year, sterling finally ceased to be a global reserve currency after President Nixon abandoned some post-war convertibility agreement that no one understood any more anyway, and the pound was allowed to 'float' (in much the same way that the *Titanic* had 'floated').

There'll always be a Rutland . . .

It wasn't just the loss of farthings and threepenny bits and the creeping advance of metric weights and measures that made the decade a disorienting one for older generations who had grown up when Britain was still the world's major military and economic power. Apart from the idea of begging to be allowed to join a European club of countries we thought we had rescued or defeated thirty years earlier, there were countless small but symbolic examples of Britain seeming to lose its identity.

The shops in the high street were closing and making way for American-style supermarkets where you could stand all day and still the shopkeeper wouldn't serve you. Whole town centres were being enclosed into shopping precincts or Arndale Centres; dual carriageways cut through communities with badly lit pedestrian subways provided underneath to help Britain's burgeoning mugging industry. If anyone was unsure what to do with any section of road, the default solution was to stick in a roundabout. Thousands of roundabouts mysteriously appeared like concrete corn circles; you'd turn your back for five minutes and suddenly the lane near your house had three roundabouts all linking together and leading off to other roundabouts. Even when they ran out of money they didn't let up; at one blue-sky ideas meeting one of the guys turned a sheet on the notice-board and announced to gasps around the room: 'Gentlemen, I give you the *mini*-roundabout!'

With so much of the country being covered in tarmac, they realized they were going to have to get rid of a few counties to make room, and so the Local Government Act abolished some of the ancient Anglo-Saxon shires such as Rutland and Huntingdonshire while new counties like Avon and Cleveland were invented. Borders between surviving shires were wildly and rather insensitively redrawn, though putting a bit of Yorkshire into Lancashire was probably worth it just as a wind-up.

Although Britain had managed to hang on to the traditional pint measure in its pubs, the keg beer in the glass was now a sterilized fizzy impression of the real ale that had traditionally been enjoyed.* The first McDonald's restaurants began to appear, displacing the traditional British health foods that had been served up in Wimpy for so long. The grammar schools were being replaced by comprehensives (Mrs Thatcher oversaw the abolition of more grammar schools than any other Education Secretary). German, French and Japanese cars became increasingly popular despite patriotic calls to 'Buy British', calls that did nothing to save the domestic motorcycle industry, which became the default symbol of British manufacturing decline. 'Elm Avenue' became 'Elm Stump Avenue' as millions of trees were killed by Dutch Elm Disease; ancient regiments such as the Scottish Greys† were

---

* The insidious spread of keg beer led to the formation of the Campaign for Real Ale in 1971, which stands as one of the most successful consumer movements ever. However, there has been no equivalent campaign for a return to the traditional pub food of pickled eggs and curled-up cheese sandwiches.

† The regiment was merged with the Royal Scots Dragoon Guards who recorded a special album, *Farewell to the Greys*. From this came the surprise bagpipe disco sensation 'Amazing Grace', which was number one for five weeks.

being abolished; they stopped playing the national anthem in the cinema because half the audience were dashing out to catch last orders, and to cap it all the man from the Royal Automobile Club didn't even bother to salute any more when he arrived on his motorbike.

Do you wanna be in my gang?

It seemed to some as if all the traditional British values and institutions were being undermined. Thank God there were still a few singers with a good old-fashioned sense of fun and family entertainment, like Gary Glitter and Jonathan King. Much of the music in the charts seemed to confirm that this was a deeply naff period of music and fashion. The 1960s had The Beatles, the 1970s had Wings. The charts were particularly backward-looking, featuring rock-and-roll tribute bands like Mud and The Rubettes, while the most successful pop group of 1974 was actually The Wombles.* Their meteoric rise to rock superstardom ended in tragedy when Great Uncle Bulgaria overdosed on amphetamines and bourbon and choked on his own vomit. Some of the more intelligent bands such as Pink Floyd and Led Zeppelin pretty well ignored the singles charts altogether, while David Bowie at least managed to rise above the crass and tacky exhibitionism of 'glam rock'. Probably the most influential musician of the decade, Bowie changed his image and style so regularly that rock journalists struggled to find a way to describe him. 'He's a man of ch-ch-ch-charity work?' 'No.' 'Ch-ch-ch-chequered trousers?' 'We'll get there in the end.'

* The Wombles had four albums go gold. For one appearance on *Top of the Pops*, the Womble costumes were occupied by Steeleye Span. The man behind the Wombles pop group was a fervent Conservative supporter and later wrote a Tory campaign song.

Television, too, seemed to be rather backward-looking, as millions tuned in to watch *Dad's Army* or *Upstairs Downstairs*. Although it was a particularly fine decade for the situation comedy, the entertainers who had emerged after the war still dominated the comedy schedules, and jokes based on racial stereotypes or fat mothers-in-law still got the laughs. Bigger budgets were given to entertainment shows that included music, so comedy sketch shows would be going perfectly well and then Ronnie Barker would turn to camera and say, 'Ladies and gentlemen – The Young Generation,' and then a load of coiffured ponces in white flares with Farrah Fawcett haircuts would prance around the studio in a pointless dance interlude before it cut back to the comedy. And at no point did anyone say, 'Hang on a minute, what the bloody hell have they got to do with anything? I was enjoying Morecambe and Wise,* thank you very much. Why did Ernie suddenly have to say, "Ladies and gentlemen – Barbara Dickson"?' This jarring change of mood and genre didn't happen in other walks of life. In Prime Minister's Questions, Enoch Powell didn't reach a climax of angry accusations about the betrayal of Ulster Unionists before suddenly turning to the public gallery and saying, 'Ladies and gentlemen – Elkie Brooks.'

The economy finally dies after a long illness

In earlier times governments generally had to make the difficult choice between inflation and unemployment. Full employment seemed to make prices rise; holding down prices tended to put people out of work. The Heath government managed to break out

---

* Morecambe and Wise dominated the ratings in the 1970s in a way that just wouldn't be possible today. The innocence of the age is demonstrated by the fact that they regularly appeared sitting up in their double bed, and nobody thought there was anything slightly gay about this.

of this impossible dichotomy and oversaw spiralling joblessness *and* rampant inflation. Dubbed 'stagflation', this syndrome was not just an abstract economic curiosity; it meant that the poorest in society suffered on two fronts. In 1971 unemployment passed the one-million mark for the first time since the 1930s, prompting Dennis Skinner to shake his fist at the Prime Minister, declaring that he should be ashamed of himself. Inflation was running at around 15 per cent, with wage settlements generally exceeding this. The government did not, of course, have control of all the levers that affected the economy, and so they focused on the issue of public-sector pay settlements, which seems to have taken an inordinate amount of cabinet time, according to the thrilling memoirs of Douglas Hurd.

In November 1972 the government announced a compulsory 90-day freeze on wages and prices, which is roughly the solution to inflation you come up with when you are nine years old: 'They should like, just make it illegal to put up prices, right?' Enoch Powell asked the Prime Minister, 'Have you taken leave of your senses?' When you are being asked if you have gone mad by a nutter like Powell, you perhaps need to ask yourself whether things have now gone seriously wrong.

Raging inflation of course meant that one year's wage increase was worth significantly less twelve months later, although only the well-organized labour forces in the key industries had the strength to make sure they did not fall behind. Most powerful of all after their victory in 1972 were the miners. Ted Heath's humiliation by the NUM had fed his paranoia that it had been taken over by communists intent on using their industrial muscle to bring down the democratically elected government of the day. This was completely false, deluded and paranoid; only some of the NUM felt like that. After winning his spurs at Satley coke depot, Arthur Scargill had been elected leader of the Yorkshire miners and the executive of the NUM shifted significantly leftwards. The communist leader of the Scottish miners, Mick McGahey, was a particular bogey figure for the Conservative Party and right-wing press, and allegedly told Heath that it was their intention to bring down the government, with the seditious revolutionary declaration: 'Of course I want to change the government, but I want to do it by democratic means.' The leader of the miners was Joe Gormley, a moderate who later said that the strike was completely avoidable. The ordinary miners just wanted better pay for dangerous and gruelling work. Forty thousand were suffering from incurable pneumoconiosis and three separate accidents in 1973 had seen over thirty miners killed.

But Heath's obsession about the revolutionary intentions of the miners made him more confrontational than he needed to be, and bizarrely his paranoid conviction that the miners were trying to oust his government became a self-fulfilling prophecy. Buoyed by their success in the first strike, the miners prepared a sequel. *The Godfather II* had just gone on release across the nation's cinemas, breaking the long-held view that sequels are never as powerful as the original. Now Ted Heath made the miners a pay offer they definitely could refuse.

Arabs invade Israel in solidarity with British miners

The year had begun with a stock market crash, it had continued with worsening economic news and near civil war in Northern Ireland, and now the miners were working to rule and running down the coal stocks. By the autumn of 1973, Ted Heath must have wondered if anything else could possibly go wrong. And then on 6 October he turned on his telly to see that Egypt and Syria had gone to war against Israel, and that a major world oil crisis was about to unfold. The price of oil rose four-fold and the West was plunged further into economic crisis.

With shortages of both coal and oil, the government tried to invoke a wartime spirit of national sacrifice and endurance, but by now the exasperated population felt more inclined to reverse the V-for-victory sign. Saucy tabloid suggestions included sharing a bath with your partner, which looked like a rather sexier proposition in the helpful illustrative photo in the *Sun* than the freezing cold reality for most spouses squeezing into their poky little bath with their overweight partner. 'SOS!' declared the posters, doing their best to whip up a sense of panic: 'Switch off Something!' Always keen to help, Ugandan dictator Idi Amin launched a 'Save Britain Campaign', to which he personally made the first donation.

But even this was not enough, and with the threat of an all-out miners' strike growing ever stronger, more stringent measures were required, and so Heath went on the television and told people the terrible news. The nation was to be put on a three-day working week. No such desperate step had ever been attempted before and Heath's grave manner confirmed what very bad news this was. Office workers shook their heads in utter despondency at the prospect of a four-day weekend. British Leyland factory workers wept at the prospect of missing two whole days of sitting in front of a conveyor belt trying to feel good about making crappy Morris Marinas and Austin Allegros.

'Well, it's six o'clock on Thursday, Ted; we're off to the countryside,' said all Heath's ministers. 'We'll see you on Tuesday . . .'

'What are you talking about? Where are you going?'

'It's the three-day week. We thought we'd better set an example . . . We can't have one rule for the politicians and another rule for everyone else. Now, where's my Diners' Club card . . .'

The crisis saw football floodlights being banned (and so for the first time professional matches were allowed to be played on Sundays). The national speed limit was reduced to 50mph.

Television was to end at 10.30 p.m. (until they realized that this would result in the entire nation switching on their kettles at 10.31, thus overloading the national grid, and so the BBC and ITV alternated between 10 and 10.30). All around the country families sat staring at a blank screen trying to remember what they used to do in the days before television. 'Merry Xmas Everybody' sang Slade, until another power cut stopped the music halfway through, and anyway Christmas lights weren't supposed to be switched on in the first place. On 4 February 1974, the miners voted for an all-out strike and Heath played the only card left to him. He called a general election on the theme 'Who Governs Britain?' And the answer he got was: 'Anyone but you.'

Elections 1974 – buy one, get one free

Heath had dithered over whether to go to the country in the early months of 1974 and it is thought by some that his three-week delay may have cost him the election. His government had been ahead in the polls as public support for the miners slipped. But the longer the crisis dragged on, the less patient the electorate became. Heath was not helped by Enoch Powell announcing that he had already used his postal ballot to vote Labour, citing their promise to hold a referendum on Britain's membership of the Common Market. Although the oil crisis was clearly an international one,* disastrous trade figures during the campaign confirmed that many of Britain's economic woes were of her own making.

The election was intended to give a clear mandate to a new government that could then deal with the current crisis. And so

---

* The USA reduced the speed limit to 55mph (at which it remained for years), while West Germany banned driving on Sundays.

the British electorate responded by saying, 'Well, you're *both* right. You know, I mean, there're arguments on both sides.' No party achieved an overall majority; Labour had slightly more seats, while Heath had got slightly more votes, but gains for the Nationalists and the Liberals had resulted in an infuriating draw.

Heath attempted to woo the Liberals into a coalition, but they could not agree terms. Events in Northern Ireland had left the Conservatives unable to rely on their traditional Unionist allies. And so after four days of failed negotiations, Heath resigned, and the nation watched the removal men manoeuvring his grand piano out of 10 Downing Street. A few months later his beloved yacht *Morning Cloud* was destroyed in a gale in the English channel and then he lost another election and then his home was attacked by IRA bombers. Apart from that he had quite a good year.

Harold Wilson II: 'This time he can barely be bothered'

And so Harold Wilson was asked by the Queen to form the first minority government since 1929. As the Labour leader walked up to the doors of Number 10 to a mixture of cheers and boos, a heckler could clearly be heard shouting, 'It's Joe Gormley come to take office!' Wilson duly agreed to the miners' pay demand, and the state of emergency was lifted.

Despite attempts to claim that the miners were a special case, a succession of increasingly high wage demands were eventually met by the Labour government after protracted negotiating sessions between ministers and various union leaders. 'Beer and sandwiches at Number 10' became the taunt for what the Tories portrayed as the back-slapping matey chit-chats round at Harold's place; and even Tony Blair felt compelled to assure voters that there would be no return to 'beer and sandwiches' under New

Labour. It would be 'chablis and wholegrain focaccia', obviously.

The minority government repealed the now thoroughly discredited Industrial Relations Bill (which had managed to earn the scorn of both the TUC and the CBI) and replaced it with the Trades Unions and Industrial Relations Act, which would fail to deal with the industrial unrest in an entirely different way. But with the government being defeated twenty-nine times during June and July, it was clear another election was going to have to come soon. Jumping the gun rather in August, the ostentatious Liberal leader Jeremy Thorpe launched his campaign on a hovercraft, which was promptly wrecked by a large wave on a Devon beach. In September Parliament was dissolved and all the kids in schools that were used as polling stations could look forward to yet another day off on 10 October. With schools being closed for lack of oil for heating, or due to industrial action or power cuts, or classrooms being used as polling stations in February and October, plus another day off for Princess Anne's wedding, there weren't many days when any lessons actually took place.

The election was another tight contest, but Labour gained eighteen seats, leaving it with a majority of just three. The sight of Harold Wilson waving on the steps of 10 Downing Street masked the wider picture: that Labour's vote was declining. In both the 1974 polls Wilson had won under 40 per cent of the popular vote – far less than Labour had achieved in all the elections it had lost since the war (although far more than it was to manage for another twenty-three years). Wilson said he believed it would be enough to govern with for two or three years. Little did people know that this was his private timetable for his own retirement from politics.

He had been surprised to find himself back in Downing Street in 1974, and he was now a different sort of politician. Previously Harold Wilson's overarching priority as Prime Minister had been that Harold Wilson remain Prime Minister; all government policies and initiatives were judged according to this lofty ideal. Now secretly planning to step down, 'the Walter Mitty of politics' was no longer so obsessed about plots to oust him or damage his standing. But the hunger for power had also been what motivated him and now his drive was noticeably diminished.

One of the clues that Harold Wilson was already planning his retirement was his announcement that all former prime ministers should have a government car and chauffeur for life. Tony Benn's diaries reveal how the drivers in the government car service jumped straight to the conclusion that the PM was going to step down soon. Whether Wilson also suggested that former prime ministers should get a life supply of pipe tobacco, a free season ticket to Huddersfield Town and a holiday cottage in the Scilly Isles is not recorded. None of his cabinet had any inkling they were the runners in a looming leadership race.

Heath vs Thatcher: 'Whoever wins, there'll be no hard feelings'

A more immediate leadership contest faced the loser of the election, when former Education Secretary Margaret Thatcher put herself forward as a candidate for the right wing of the party. No one expected this surprise novelty challenger to win the Conservative leadership title; the outcome was supposedly predetermined, like the Saturday afternoon wrestling on ITV's *World of Sport*. But this bout would be different: one of the combatants hadn't read the script. 'In the red corner, Ted "The Grocer" Heath!' declared the moustached announcer in his flared suit, and the gruff old fighter barely acknowledged the scripted cheers as he ran his thumbs under his leotard and adjusted his trademark sailor cap. 'In the blue corner, the challenger, Maggie "Milk Snatcher" Thatcher!' and she stepped in between the ropes, clutching her trademark handbag and smiling at the boos coming from the crowd.

Everyone understood that she was just there for show, that they had to put someone up against the old champ; even the old ladies in the front row who shouted and jeered knew deep down that the bouts were fixed. But then before the referee had even stepped out of the ring, Giant Thatch swung at Grocer Heath with her handbag and knocked him flat onto the canvas. With him lying there groaning, she continued to whack him around the head and body as everyone looked on in confused disbelief. The referee attempted to stop her, pointing out that the rules didn't allow for the use of a handbag, let alone one with a large brick inside it, but seconds later he too was scrambling out of the ring, clutching a bleeding nose and a large swelling above his right eye.

Because Margaret Thatcher went on to become such a major political figure, people tend to presume that her rise to the leadership of the Conservative Party was inevitable. But her election in 1975 was an accident. Health and Safety regulations were far less stringent in the mid-1970s, otherwise someone might have spotted the dangerous structural weakness in the Conservative Party rules and had the thing made safe again. There had been a good degree of grumbling on the Tory benches about Ted Heath's leadership, and the most likely challenger from the right was the arch-monetarist Keith Joseph, of whom Mrs Thatcher was a loyal and junior follower. But then he made an embarrassing ill-judged speech about working-class mothers, seeming to suggest that a bit of enforced sterilization might not be such a bad idea, thus destroying his credibility in one evening (even if half the leader-writers affecting shock and offence secretly agreed with him). The leading right-winger of the day Enoch Powell had rather damaged his chances by resigning from the Conservative Party and telling people to vote Labour, and so Margaret Thatcher went to see Ted Heath and told him she was going to challenge him for the leadership. 'Very well,' he said. 'You'll lose.'

They both understood the plan. Margaret would be the stalking horse candidate who would so damage Heath that he would be forced to resign, allowing some loyal heavyweight like Willie Whitelaw or Geoffrey Howe to step into the job. So many Conservative backbenchers thought this was an excellent plan that they all went and voted for the stalking horse. Instead of merely damaging Heath in the first round, she beat him outright. By the time Heath had resigned she was too far ahead for anyone else to stand a chance. Many Conservatives were alarmed at what they had gone and done. She wasn't just inexperienced, brash and provincial; she was a woman, for God's sake.

Labour supporters were openly delighted with this accidental result, that the leader of the opposition was a brassy, haughty, almost ludicrous figure. She was like the posh neighbour played by Penelope Keith in *The Good Life*. In one episode broadcast around this time, Margot Leadbetter summons a workman to her drawing room and makes him stand on some newspaper while she berates him. 'You can't talk to me like that,' objects the worker. 'I can because I pay your wages, and get off my carpet!' and he steps back onto the newspaper. And all the trade union members watching back at home thought, 'Thank God I'll never have to deal with anyone like that!'

Heath had lost the leadership of the Tory Party in much the same way that he had lost the Premiership: misjudging the strength of feeling against him and failing to consider the possibility that he might lose. He was not the luckiest politician ever to enter Downing Street. But despite the considerable achievement of a lower-middle-class grammar-school boy rising to the top of an upper-class Tory Party, and then beating Harold Wilson in 1970 when everyone was sure he would lose, it is still hard to feel sorry for him because he lacked a key weapon in the armoury of any top politician: he was completely without charm. Other leaders might do far worse things than Ted Heath, but they would pat their outraged ministers on the back, open a bottle of whisky and have a laugh about it. Heath was just a cold fish who found that he hadn't taken the trouble to make many friends when he suddenly needed them.

Ted Heath took his defeat very sportingly, apart from sulking and sniping for the next thirty years. Occasionally Mrs Thatcher would be briefly damaged by former Tory grandees such as Harold Macmillan expressing mild disquiet about the social costs of some of her policies, and the papers would splash it all over their front pages. But Ted Heath's vitriolic attacks were so regular and predictable that the papers barely bothered reporting them any more, or they just gave them their own little column, like the Court Circular or the racing results.

An end to European wars (by letting the Germans run everything after all)

The one thing that Ted Heath does generally get some credit for is negotiating Britain's entry into the Common Market. This particular episode of *Jeux Sans Frontières* saw a British diplomatic team desperate to get to the finishing line where their predecessors had always fallen flat on their faces, publicly humiliated by a French team throwing wet sponges and tipping them off the giant wobbly negotiating table. 'What madcap embarrassing things would they be made to do this time?' wondered the viewers of *International It's A Knockout*. 'Ha ha ha, and now the British team have to clamber up the slippery butter mountain, trying not to fall off into the wine lake and then pour as many pound notes as they can into the swill bucket of the giant cartoon French farmer,' laughed Stuart Hall. 'And ha ha ha, oh dear, and the

Belgians and the Germans are allowed to try and kick them up the backside, remember, and I wonder if the British team are regretting playing their joker on this one, ha ha ha . . .'

The difference this time, of course, was the absence of the French captain, President 'Non' de Gaulle. His successor President Pompidou was keen to distinguish himself from the giant figure of post-war French politics and wondered if the catchphrase 'Oui' might just do it. Like so many of his generation, Ted Heath had seen the ravages of the war in Europe first-hand, and was desperate to secure Britain's entry where others before him had failed. And so the terms of Britain's entry were greatly advantageous to the existing members, as Britain paid in millions more than it got back. In return, the Europeans would have to listen to Ted Heath's French accent, which some would argue was not worth any amount of EEC contributions.*

Taking Britain into Europe was clearly his proudest achievement as Prime Minister (which is not very surprising when you consider what an unmitigated disaster everything else was). In fact, Heath was only following up on an original application made by Labour before he came to power, but there is no doubting that he was the keener European of the two party leaders.

The Labour front bench had always been divided on the issue, and gradually Wilson had become persuaded by Tony Benn that the political solution to this problem was to promise the British people a referendum on whether or not Britain should stay in the Common Market.† This was duly held in June 1975, and remains the only time a national single-issue vote has been held right

---

* Pompidou warned Heath that Britain would have to accept that the first language of Europe was French. Yeah, right.

† The political fall-out from Labour's decision to hold a referendum would be felt years later. Roy Jenkins, always a passionate pro-European, resigned the deputy leadership of the Labour Party on this issue. The Social Democratic Party was conceived the moment Jenkins psychologically gave up on ever leading the Labour Party.

across the United Kingdom, unless you count the massive turnout for the crucial constitutional decision, 'Should Will Young be the winner of this year's *Pop Idol*?'

It was an uneven contest from the start. The 'No' campaign had a fraction of the funds of the business-backed 'Yes' campaign that wanted Britain to remain in the EEC. All the major party leaders were publicly in favour of staying;* Margaret Thatcher even sported a hand-knitted jumper featuring all the flags of the member states that one presumes is no longer at the front of her wardrobe. But the debate tended to centre on the cost of baked beans and fish fingers rather than any lofty ideas of sovereignty and nationhood, and Britain decided by two to one that it could live with German umlauts and French accents on its Alphabetti Spaghetti.

The EEC later became the EC. No one is quite sure what happened to the extra 'E'; some think it might have been accidentally lost by incompetent Brussels bureaucrats, others that it was taken by the French to stick on the end of 'Concorde'. Either way, the community became about much more than just trade barriers, but at no point in the 1970s did the politicians actually stand up and warn the British public: 'These Brussels bureaucrats, you know, they want to do away with the Westminster Parliament and ban British women from shaving their armpits.' Well, one or two did, but unfortunately it tended to be the likes of Enoch Powell or Tony Benn, which left most of the British people convinced that their dire warnings of the ending of a thousand years of British history was as nutty as everything else those loonies generally ranted on about. It's the same today, of course. You see the list of sovereign rights being surrendered by Westminster and feel unsure that you are entirely comfortable

---

* No one actually knows what Harold Wilson voted, but both his wife and his political secretary Marcia Williams voted against, which probably tells us something.

with this. And then you see the people campaigning most vigorously against Europe, the Thatcherite relics of the Tory Party or the wild-eyed bigots of UKIP, and you think, 'Blimey, there's no way I'm being seen to agree with that lot; sure, abolish the House of Commons, swap the pound for the euro. I'll agree to anything rather than be associated with Norman Tebbit and Robert Kilroy-Silk.'

But by the mid-1970s Britons were doing their best to be open-minded about mainland Europe. Millions of people had independently come to the same conclusion that a beach in Spain was a more attractive holiday destination than Butlins in Skegness, and they came back from mainland Europe with a taste for sangria and spaghetti bolognaise (which was almost a proper meal as long as you served it up with a huge portion of chips). 'Continental quilts' replaced traditional sheets and blankets, hotel guests were offered a 'continental breakfast' (which was a euphemism for 'no breakfast') and in April 1974 the United Kingdom offered to host the Eurovision Song Contest (to help out Luxembourg who couldn't afford to). The contest was won by an exciting new Swedish group who had been trialled as 'The Abba'. With the British still rather worried about European integration, 'Waterloo' seemed like an appropriate winner. The Portuguese entry came fourteenth, but had the consolation of being the secret signal for the beginning of the 'Carnation Revolution' that over-threw the fascist Estado Novo regime that had ruled Portugal since the 1920s. 'Portugal, can we have your votes please?' asked the host in Brighton. 'Oh, they seem to be having some technical difficulties. A lot of gunfire and explosions in Lisbon there . . .'

Our finest hour?

With British international status so diminished by the falling pound, images of strikes and football hooligans, the country badly needed a unifying national struggle to rekindle the Dunkirk spirit and remind us of our great imperial past. Britain had defeated Nazism in the 1940s; it had stood firm against Soviet totalitarianism in the 1950s; now in the naff 1970s the great moral stand would be on the principle of fish. The so-called 'Cod Wars' were never really up there with the epic military struggles of the twentieth century and there was little enthusiasm for the idea of Laurence Olivier narrating a twenty-part TV series called *The World at Cod War*. There had been similar disputes over fishing rights in 1958 and 1972 when Iceland had extended its territorial waters, but now it declared that no one else was allowed to fish within two hundred miles of Iceland, particularly the British who turned all the cod into frozen Findus dinosaur-shapes anyway.

But in 1975 things turned nasty as Icelandic ships cut the lines of British trawlers and Royal Navy frigates and Icelandic coastguard vessels were involved in hotly disputed ramming incidents. Captain Birdseye went grey from all the stress. When Iceland threatened to close its NATO base, thus annoying the Americans, Britain backed down and a negotiated settlement was reached in which Britain recognized the extended territorial waters in return for a limited allowable catch. Peace was inevitable when they realized there were no more cod left anyway. It didn't matter because the Icelanders had already decided that sea fishing was a miserable, cold and smelly job and that they should throw all their energy into banking and financial services: that promised a much more secure future.

Love thy neighbour

Two of the most notable achievements of Harold Wilson's fourth term in office were bills aimed at tackling discrimination which showed that, despite the cynicism of its leader, the Labour Party still had a little bit of reforming zeal left in it. Essentially the Sex Discrimination Act of 1975 made it illegal to pay women less for the same work as men, but it also outlawed discrimination in other areas such as training and recruitment. One of the most commented upon aspects of the bill was the ban on discriminatory job advertisements; bosses were no longer able to specify that they were looking for 'pretty' secretaries. Now they just put 'include recent photo with application'. Some felt that the sex discrimination bill didn't go far enough, that it should have outlawed 'not asking what I've been doing' and 'sitting with your legs wide apart on tube trains'.

Predictably, the setting up of the Equal Opportunities Commission prompted the spreading of all sorts of urban myths, such as, 'apparently they're not allowed to sell gingerbread men any more', which people thought was 'political correctness gone . . . too far?', no, 'over the top?', no . . . they were still working on the right metaphor. One unintended consequence of the act was that a secondary school in Newcastle announced it would now beat girl students with the strap, which had previously only been used on the boys. You can't stop social progress.

The change in law was long overdue; indeed the 'Women's Lib' movement had long since evolved into a broader and more analytical feminism that sought more than just legal equality; radical feminists demanded an end to oppressive patriarchal structures in male-dominated androcentric society or something, something . . . I'd stopped listening, to be honest. Germaine Greer's landmark book *The Female Eunuch* had been published in 1970 and two years later the magazine *Spare Rib* was launched, although WHSmith declined to stock it. But they did take *Cosmopolitan*, launched the same year, so that was some consolation. It is hard to convey just how different attitudes to women were just four decades ago; how openly men would patronize, put down or sexually harass women. Of course, all these things have continued to happen, but increasingly less brazenly. By the end of the century it would not be considered acceptable behaviour to pat a lady's bottom (unless you were Bill Clinton or Boris Yeltsin). This was an age when Wimpy bars would not allow unaccompanied women into their restaurants after midnight on the assumption that any woman out on her own at such an hour must be a prostitute. Cynics often claim that passing laws never changes anything, but ever since the 1960s social attitudes have tangibly changed as governments have sent clear messages that intolerance and bigotry on the basis of sex, race or sexual orientation is not acceptable. Of course prejudice and injustice don't disappear overnight, but millions of lives have been improved by the law clearly stating that you may not discriminate against those who happen to be different. Now such prejudice is socially unacceptable, and everyone just laughs at chavs instead.

A government attempting to legislate against sexism was at least spared the worry that improving the rights of 50 per cent of the population might be electoral suicide. But the same could not be confidently asserted about the matter of race. Perhaps this issue above all others saw the widest gap between the metropolitan liberals such as Home Secretary Roy Jenkins and the government's traditional working-class Labour voters. Many felt threatened by the arrival of foreigners from the Caribbean or the Indian subcontinent, believing tabloid inventions of immigrants being given priority in employment and housing. And these Asians didn't even have any idea how to make a proper curry; there was not a sultana or sliced banana in sight.

The 1976 Race Relations Act set up the Commission for Racial Equality, which was established to annoy Enoch Powell and stamp out discrimination in the workplace. To get things off on the right footing, its first chairman was a white old Etonian former Conservative MP. Although the door had been locked to most Commonwealth immigrants in 1968, there were still occasions which provided grist to the racist's mill. In 1972 Idi Amin expelled the so-called 'Ugandan Asians' after Allah had told him to do so in a dream. Not wishing to question such a high-level diktat, the British government duly took in around 30,000 British-passport holders. The media reaction was little short of hysterical; images of Gujaratis coming off the plane with their few belongings were printed alongside articles demanding, 'How many more?' Leicester Council put an advert in the Ugandan press asking them not to come to Leicester (which the rest of the country had always managed without need of an advert). In fact, the Ugandan Asians proved to be a bonus to the local economy of wherever they settled; Amin had expelled them because they were visibly successful, and this was not without reason. But you try explaining this sort of thing to insane, murderous, polygamous military dictators; they just don't listen.

Racism reared its shaven head again in 1976 when riots followed the Notting Hill Carnival. Seeing images of violence by black people on the television gave some white racists the excuse they were waiting for to commit violence against ethnic minorities. (Although as their name suggests, so-called 'Paki-bashers' generally picked on Asians, rather than Afro-Caribbean victims.) The Notting Hill riots were a shock to the Metropolitan Police, who had never imagined that if you openly persecuted and insulted one minority group over many years, then one day their frustration might boil over. The vision of policemen amateurishly defending themselves with milk crates and dustbin lids actually helped win public sympathy for the Met. (But did they put the dustbin lids back on the right bin? That's the question the inquiry never answered.) In subsequent years the Notting Hill Riot was far better organized, with both sides coming fully prepared with missiles and truncheons, and today of course you can't wear a political badge in Parliament Square without the police turning up with riot shields.

Black people barely featured on the media in the mid-1970s, although an exception was made when it was footage of black youths hurling bricks at policemen. With only these negative images of Britain's immigrant community available, with urban myths spreading that the Commission for Racial Equality was forcing unsuitable immigrant candidates onto powerless employers, the idea that it was the white Britons who were being discriminated against gained wider currency.

Fascists and anti-fascists 'agree to disagree'

The National Front had been formed in 1967 out of various nutty groups such as the League of Empire Loyalists and the Racial Preservation Society, although its founders decided to refuse to incorporate any of the overtly pro-Nazi fringe groups. It's one of those grey areas, isn't it; pro- or anti-Nazi? 'What about letting in the Waffen-SS Retired Concentration Camp Guard Aryan Purity Association?' 'Well, all right, as long as they play down their pro-Nazi side.' In the end the excluded groups joined the party as individuals and promptly took it over. The NF called for compulsory repatriation of coloured immigrants, an end to 'multiculturalism' and then bowled a googly to the far left by declaring its support for the Palestine Liberation Organization. It fared alarmingly well in a few by-elections in the 1970s, although more dangerous still were its provocative marches through areas with large immigrant populations. Phalanxes of Union-flag-carrying social misfits strutted (they definitely strutted) alongside Blackshirt veterans, disillusioned Conservatives, skinheads and Chelsea supporters. Some minor members of the royal family were said to be most upset, but their advisors insisted it might look bad for them to join in.

Anti-fascists organized counter-demonstrations and violence

inevitably flared, though the anti-fascists couldn't help suspecting that the police were rather more sympathetic to those doing the racist chanting, especially when they said, 'See you at cross-burning on Sunday, Ken.' (Eventually the police were banned from joining the National Front, as were prison officers, which obviously had very little impact on their membership totals as prison staff were much more interested in the Woodcraft Folk.) The Union flag was hijacked by the National Front as a result of these high-profile demonstrations; for a couple of decades moderate patriots felt uncomfortable waving the national flag for fear of being tainted with fascism.

One novel reaction to the rise of the far right was the formation of Rock Against Racism, an organization that staged concerts with a clear political agenda. In the mid- to late-1970s, thousands of young people would see musicians taking a stand against racism, and many must have been less tempted by the simplistic nonsense of the National Front. But important though the stands of the musicians and the activists of the Anti-Nazi League were, they were not what finished off the NF. The neo-fascist party had originally been formed in response to the Conservative Party's dismal performance in the 1966 general election. Its founders had believed that if the Tories had been more overtly anti-immigrant, they could have won. And when this advice was finally taken, it virtually destroyed the National Front overnight. In January 1978 Mrs Thatcher gave an interview in which she said, 'People are really rather afraid that this country might be rather swamped by people of a different culture.' The furore about the use of the pejorative word 'swamped' dramatically boosted Mrs Thatcher's poll rating and she received 10,000 letters of support. The National Front never really recovered, while, as is well known, Mrs Thatcher went on to annexe the Sudetenland and declare herself Reichs-Chancellor.

Wilson confuses everyone with honest explanation

Enoch Powell is credited with having said that 'all political careers end in failure', and this is quoted* so regularly that it's become generally accepted as true. But not all political careers end in failure; some end in a dignified retirement, like Sir Winston Churchill; other political careers end for different reasons, like that Tory MP who accidentally killed himself attempting auto-erotic asphyxiation. But rarely does a politician leave of their own volition, long before everyone was expecting them to. So when Harold Wilson announced he was stepping down as Prime Minister because he had always planned to retire from frontline politics at sixty, everyone was certain that he must be running from a web of dark secrets, threats of blackmail or that he was about to defect to Moscow. But it seems that the rather disappointing truth is that on this one occasion Harold Wilson was being completely honest and sincere. His wife hated life in the spotlight, and Wilson said his successor would need time to make his mark before the next general election. He had lost the hunger and energy required to keep the Labour Party together; it was time to make way for an older man.

Jim Callaghan had been the only minister warned of Wilson's impending departure, and so the PM's favoured successor was given extra time to be nice to backbenchers, remember their birthdays and offer them his last Rolo.† Denis Healey's memoirs reveal that he was told in the Downing Street toilets just before the rest of the cabinet. It's always hard to find something to say when

* As so often the famous quotation has been paraphrased. What he actually wrote in his biography of Joseph Chamberlain was: 'All political lives, unless they are cut off in midstream at a happy juncture, end in failure, because that is the nature of politics and of human affairs.'

† The Queen had been told the big secret back at Christmas and for three months must have been impossible to live with, giving little knowing giggles and goading the family by chanting, 'I know something you don't know.'

you're standing next to a work colleague at the urinals. Callaghan's reputation had grown in the previous couple of years in government. He actually came second in the first ballot of MPs, when Michael Foot emerged as a surprisingly strong candidate of the left, but by the time of the third ballot that was required for a candidate to get over 50 per cent of the votes, the old union fixer from Portsmouth emerged as the new leader of the Labour Party and thus Prime Minister.

Jim'll fix it

'Now then, now then, guys and girls,' said the silver-haired man in the big chair. 'As it happens, I have a letter here from a Mr Jack Jones from the Transport and General Workers Union, who says, "Dear Jim, Can you fix it for my members to get a 27 per cent pay award?" How's about that then?' Jim Callaghan was not dealt the easiest of hands as Prime Minister and will for ever be associated with the way his term in office fell apart in chaos following a winter of strikes, power cuts and, if you believed the tabloids, bin liners full of unburied dead bodies piled up in Leicester Square. But for most of his term in office he was actually a very skilled leader of a divided Labour Party that had not been expected to survive without an overall majority in the House of Commons. He had moved to the right during his years in government and was illiberal on issues such as immigration and homosexuality, but after years of the duplicitous Harold Wilson, ministers and civil servants found him refreshingly straightforward.

Callaghan did things the other way round from Richard III. He ended with a 'winter of discontent' but began with 'glorious summer'. In 1976 months of uninterrupted sunshine dried up rivers, reservoirs and the journalists' supply of weather adjectives. In fact, for the whole summer the main item of news seemed to be that attractive girls were enjoying the extended heatwave in their bikinis. Callaghan did not shirk from his first crisis of 'lots of nice weather', and appointed a Minister of Drought. Denis Howell must go down as the most successful minister in British political history, as by the autumn the country was suffering from floods and he was put in charge of dealing with that instead. Back then whenever there was an intractable problem, the simple solution was to create a Minister of Intractable Problem and hope that would sort it. 'Prime Minister, people are complaining that Concorde is too noisy.' 'All right, I shall appoint a Minister for Making Concorde Less Noisy.'

In fact, the cabinet member most closely associated with the Anglo-French supersonic passenger jet was Tony Benn, who had been Minister for Technology during its development and whose Bristol constituency was close to where the giant Airfix kit was glued together. There is something rather perverse about the most tangible achievement of the hero of the left being to champion an incredibly expensive plane so that the super-rich could whiz across to New York to go shopping. Although Callaghan had sacked the veteran left-winger Barbara Castle, the increasingly radical Tony Benn remained in the cabinet as Energy Secretary, despite being at variance with just about everything the government did. Benn became a bogey figure of the right-wing press, the red under the bed who plotted to bring Soviet-style socialism to Britain. His policies apparently included forcing everyone to wear little furry hats as they harvested the glorious people's beetroot crop in workers' collectives. Despite being a Minister of the Crown, he was spied upon by MI5, but if Tony Benn was a secret agent for anyone, it was more likely to be the Tories, since they would be the ultimate beneficiaries of his divisive tactics.

Roy Jenkins, humiliated in the leadership election, now left the House of Commons to become President of the European Commission. In his farewell speech to the Parliamentary Labour

Party he proclaimed, 'I leave this party without rancour,' which was not the best choice of word for someone who pronounced the letter 'r' as a 'w'.* Over the water the rather grand new arrival whom the French dubbed 'Le Roi Jean Quinze' would now reflect upon how he might become Britain's Prime Minister without the help of the Labour Party. Anthony Crosland, another veteran right-winger and intellectual, was lost when he died suddenly aged only fifty-eight. Bryan Ferry lookalike David Owen became Crosland's replacement as Foreign Secretary aged only thirty-eight and was immediately hailed as 'dashing', 'high-flying' and 'a future Prime Minister'. 'Goodness, I must make sure all this praise and adulation doesn't go to my head,' he thought. 'It would be awful if I became a vain and pompous unprincipled back-stabber.' Another future SDP founder who was promoted by Callaghan was Shirley Williams, who became Education Secretary. Although a prominent government minister, she famously stood on the picket line during the notorious and pro-tracted strike at the Grunwick film-processing plant. This was before it became the scene of regular picket-line violence, which was lucky for the police because they'd never have stood a chance once Shirley Williams got stuck in.

Things fall apart, the centre cannot hold

But perhaps the biggest personality in the Callaghan government was Denis Healey. The one-time Communist Party member miraculously managed to remain a popular figure with the public throughout these turbulent years of economic crisis despite being Chancellor of the Exchequer. His bushy eyebrows made him a

* At this Dennis Skinner heckled, 'I thought you were taking Marquand with you!' referring to David Marquand, the close ally of Jenkins who was resigning at the same time.

favourite of lazy cartoonists and, despite never having said the words, he was landed with the bizarre catchphrase 'Silly Billy' by impressionist Mike Yarwood, which the Chancellor subsequently adopted as his own.

Although supposedly on the right of the Labour Party, he eventually set the top rate of tax at 98 per cent on unearned income, which frankly is still too low. Noddy Holder of Slade was paying 84 per cent on his earnings. 'Whither the incentives for risk-takers and entrepreneurs?' argued the *Financial Times*. 'Under such punitive tax levels Slade will feel compelled to fall back on rehashing their old soft metal/pub-rock foot-stompers when glam rock is so clearly dead, man.'

Healey had inherited an economy in some disarray. Inflation was at 24 per cent, wages were rising at an average of 27 per cent while productivity had fallen. The oil crisis of 1973 had hit Britain badly and strikes and high levels of government borrowing caused the people who understood these things to decide that the pound was overvalued. (Everyone else reckoned that it was still worth a pound.) The sterling crisis reached a crescendo on 27 September 1976. Healey was supposed to be flying to a finance ministers' conference, but as the economic news worsened he decided he couldn't possibly leave. So with the TV news cameras recording every dramatic minute, his car turned round at Heathrow Airport and he rushed back to Downing Street. It was a humiliating episode, not helped by Healey's decision then to rush up to the Labour Party conference to be booed while he told everyone about all the drastic cuts that would be needed.*

With so much of Britain's reserves having been spent trying to prop up the ailing pound, Healey looked at the figures and the forecasts and realized that Britain was now broke. It was soon after

---

* There were cheers as well as boos, and much of the press portrayed Healey as a brave pugilist who had won the conference over with his straight-talking.

this that a leaflet was posted through the door of 11 Downing Street. 'Why not consolidate all your various debts into one easy low rate loan? Bad debt history no problem! Free quote with no obligation! Contact the International Monetary Fund – call 0800 SCAM.' This was the infamous moment when Britain went 'cap in hand to the IMF', although Healey's memoirs don't make any mention of whether he was wearing any headgear which he then took off to hold out in the hope of some loose change from the American bankers. Britain was in a very weak negotiating position up against the right-wing financiers of the IMF, who demanded massive cuts in public spending before they would write out the cheque. In fact, Healey and Callaghan put up a fairly decent fight, and managed to settle on a much smaller passage of cuts than many had feared, but there was no escaping that it was a political watershed in post-war British political history. Thirty years of Keynesian economics, it seemed, had failed. Jim Callaghan virtually said as much at the Labour Party conference. The election of Margaret Thatcher in 1979 is usually seen as the turning point in post-war history, but in fact things fell apart in 1976. Indeed, some of the money needed by Denis Healey was raised by selling BP shares; privatization was already under way long before Maggie was asking how much she might raise if she sold Scotland.

The crisis was an international humiliation for Britain, who were now hoping that Ethiopia might launch a campaign to cancel First World Debt. The wrench widened the divisions in Labour, and encouraged those who sought a more radically socialist party. The episode paved the way for Mrs Thatcher and the brutally monetarist policies she would pursue.

And the funniest thing was that it was all a big accounting mistake anyway! 'You'll never guess what we've gone and done,' giggled the number crunchers at the Treasury, as Healey wiped the blood from his nose. 'We've only gone and completely miscalculated Britain's gross domestic product! It turns out the economy is much sounder than we thought and we didn't need to borrow that five billion after all!' and they burst out laughing again, though noticing that Healey wasn't really joining in. Healey was later quite magnanimous about the wildly incorrect Treasury projections that had caused this entire crisis. 'At least it means that the money can be paid back in full before the general election,' he mused, 'so the next Labour government won't have to worry about that!' And then everyone went rather quiet and embarrassed.

Anarchy in the UK?

Despite the sense of almost inevitable political and cultural decline and the endless rehashing of the same old ideas, as the decade passed its midpoint there seemed to be a lazy acceptance that nothing would ever change, that the song would remain the same. But then viewers of a teatime current affairs programme hosted by Bill Grundy were woken from their sleepy complacency by a blonde punk dressed in a gaudy blue outfit spouting her offensive anti-society philosophy of confrontation and monetarism.

'It's what?' goaded Bill Grundy.

'Nothing, a rude word. Next question?'

'No, no, what was the rude word?'

'Monetarism.'

'Was it? Good heavens, you frighten me to death . . .'

There were gasps off camera, but Grundy didn't stop her.

'A man who finds himself riding the bus to work at the age of twenty-six can consider himself a failure . . .'

Grundy appeared indifferent to the offensive language pouring from her mouth; he almost seemed to encourage it.

'Go on, you've got another five seconds. Say something outrageous.'

'There is no such thing as society. There are individual men and women and there are families.'

By now the switchboards were jammed, as thousands of appalled viewers demanded that Grundy be sacked and that dreadful woman never be allowed on television again.*

There is something rather prescient about Mrs Thatcher turning up at the same time as punk rock. And like The Sex Pistols and The Damned she was generally regarded as something of a bad joke; she was so grating and awful, it was clear that this ludicrous fad would be forgotten about in a couple of years. In fact, both Maggie Thatcher and Johnny Rotten were a reaction to a general sense of despair that everything was just rubbish. 'Anarchy in the UK,' said one. 'I just can't bear Britain in decline,' said the other.

Punk rock and patriotism clashed directly in 1977 with the advent of the Queen's Silver Jubilee. Because all the people making documentaries today were teenagers in 1977, the impact of punk has been rather exaggerated, as if the two were approximate equals in the amount of interest they generated amongst the British people. The Jubilee was a massive shared national experience; punk rock was just the latest minor craze for the tabloids to be outraged about. Not everyone was pogoing at the Marquee and gobbing at The Buzzcocks; in fact, not even most young music fans cared for punk rock very much, despite what they pretend now that they are in their forties and listening to The Ramones on their iPhones. The moment a Sex Pistols record was put on the turntable at the village hall was the moment the dance floor cleared. You could go and leap about to it if you wanted, but you understood that if you did all those bikers watching from the bar would beat you up. So it was the more traditional arrangement of

* The infamous Sex Pistols interview effectively destroyed Bill Grundy's broadcasting career. The Sex Pistols had only got the booking as last-minute replacements for Queen, who had cancelled.

'God Save the Queen' that was heard around the country on the twenty-fifth anniversary of Elizabeth II's accession to the throne, however much the teenage Prince Edward wanted to sing 'The fascist regime!' as he stood in the thanksgiving service at St Paul's. The climax came in June as hundreds of bonfires were lit across the country 'in the exact same place as the bonfires that had warned of the Spanish Armada', which seems bad luck for anyone who lived in a bungalow that happened to have been built on that spot in the intervening four centuries. The street parties may have felt a little contrived, and the patriotism a little superficial (this was the first year that Britons bought more foreign cars than British) but it confirmed that most Britons were essentially supportive of the royal family and the Queen herself in particular. To round off the perfect year she got her first grandchild, and Charles met a lovely young lady called Diana who might make him the perfect wife.

But not all patriotism was expressed in terms of the United Kingdom. One of the thorniest questions for Callaghan's government was the issue of devolution. Scottish and Welsh nationalism had risen dramatically over the previous decade, with fourteen Nationalist MPs adding up to a considerable voting bloc in a House of Commons in which no party now had an outright majority. (It would be this issue that finally brought down Jim Callaghan's government.) In Scotland in particular the discovery of oil in the North Sea had increased resentment that once again England's gain would be Scotland's loss. It had been bad enough losing Kenny Dalglish. As a sop to the nationalists, referendums were to be held in both Scotland and Wales to test whether the Celtic nations really wanted their own assemblies. With this prospect on the agenda, the Callaghan government managed to keep a level of parliamentary support from the Nationalists, and the hope that it might help quell the uglier expressions of Celtic nationalism, such as the burning of English holiday homes or the fashion sense of the Bay City Rollers.

Millions spill onto street to celebrate historic 'Lib-Lab pact'

But with his government regularly losing by-elections to the Conservatives, Callaghan needed something more solid to sustain him. On this front he was lucky that the Liberal Party was now under new management following one of the more bizarre scandals of the decade. Jeremy Thorpe had been a very 'flamboyant' leader of the party, a 'theatrical personality' as the newspapers had unsubtly put it. The British public might have forgiven him for his alleged homosexuality, but he was doomed the moment his name was dragged into the murder of a dog. Norman Scott, the 'former male model' who publicly claimed to have been Thorpe's lover, was confronted by a gunman on Exmoor who shot the Great Dane he was taking for a walk. The gun was then pointed at Scott but failed to go off. Scott claimed this was an attempt to silence him over his affair with Thorpe. There were allegations of blackmail; Scott certainly would have needed the money because by the look of him he can't have been making too much as a male model any more. Eventually Thorpe was charged with conspiracy to murder, with the trial due to take place right in the middle of the 1979 election campaign. He managed to get it put back till after polling day when he was found not guilty, after a summing up so biased it was difficult not to conclude that Thorpe's new lover was the judge.* But Thorpe's political career was in ruins; indeed, he lost his seat, not helped by Auberon Waugh standing against him on behalf of the Dog Lovers' Party.

The new leader of the Liberal Party was David Steel, the young Scottish member who had made his name introducing the

* The judge's bizarre pro-establishment summing up was brilliantly parodied by Peter Cook in a monologue entitled 'Entirely a Matter for You'.

Abortion Bill to the House of Commons in 1967. Steel was aware that his party had been badly damaged by the Thorpe scandal; indeed, for a brief period the noun 'liberal' was a jokey slang word for homosexual. He was as keen as Callaghan to avoid a general election; and so a public deal was made.

And who does not remember where they were when they first heard the newsflash about the Lib-Lab pact? Centre-left supporters of cross-party cooperation danced in the streets at the news that the minority Labour government had come to a constitutional arrangement with the Liberal Party in return for consultation on government legislation. 'I'm so happy,' wept one idealist in Parliament Square. 'This could mean a degree of parliamentary stability for up to eighteen months . . .' In reality Labour got more out of the Lib-Lab pact than the Liberals, who did not get a seat in the cabinet or a promise of their hallowed prize of electoral reform. But Steel was showing that he was open to cooperation, which might have been the first step to a coalition if the next election produced a hung parliament. As it turned out, he would end up joining forces with many of these Labour cabinet ministers. They just wouldn't be in the Labour Party any more.

Election dysfunction

By 1978 it seemed as if the government had possibly turned the corner on the economy. Inflation had fallen and the balance of payments was improving as the benefits of North Sea oil began to be felt. Mrs Thatcher still seemed an unlikely Prime Minister (not least because many men could not envisage a woman PM) and Jim Callaghan's poll rating was looking healthy. Everyone in the cabinet and Fleet Street was certain that Callaghan would call the expected general election in October. Two dates had even been pencilled in, although bizarrely 13 October had been ruled out because it was Mrs Thatcher's birthday.

At September's Trades Union Conference, Callaghan responded to this fevered speculation by singing an old music hall song: 'Can't get away to marry you today, My wife won't let me!' And everyone laughed and nodded and then said, 'Well, what the bloody hell does that mean?' In the end he had to go on television to talk directly to the British people. In an era that boasted such television greats as *I Claudius*, *Monty Python's Flying Circus*, *Pennies From Heaven* and *Fawlty Towers*, Jim Callaghan announcing that there wasn't going to be an election was not the most thrilling night's viewing of the decade. But his decision was to go down as one of the greatest miscalculations in modern political history.*

Part of the reason Labour had won power in 1974 was a belief that they would be able to work with the trades unions where the Conservatives clearly could not. Wilson had made much of his 'Social Contract', in which he had repealed the Conservatives' Industrial Relations Act in return for trades union leaders sort of agreeing to maybe do their best to urge voluntary wage restraint. The problem was that asking people to volunteer to have less money never seems to have many takers. With inflation still high, the unions were not all asking for massive increases in their standards of living; they were often trying just to keep up. Most homes still did not have central heating, a telephone or a car parked outside. But Labour ministers argued that the very poorest were not represented by a powerful union that could negotiate regular pay rises, and inflation would hit them the hardest.

Denis Healey had even shocked some union leaders by the degree to which he was involving them in the financial decisions

---

* In his diaries Tony Benn postulated that the reason Callaghan didn't call an election was simply that he liked being Prime Minister and wanted to carry on for as long as he could, which has a certain ring of truth to it.

taken to try and defeat inflation. In one poll taken at this time, the public named the union leader Jack Jones as the most powerful man in the country, although one suspects that the question was probably phrased along the lines of: 'You do think that union baron Jack Jones is the most powerful man in the country, don't you?' Although they were later painted as militant extremists, most of the major union leaders of the 1970s were pretty moderate and often infuriated their rank and file with the way they cooperated with the government. The lowest paid had repeatedly accepted wage settlements below the rate of inflation (in other words, a pay cut) but they could not endure this for much longer. When Callaghan imposed a 5 per cent limit on public-sector pay to set an example to the private sector, hardly anybody thought that this wildly ambitious target could be met. It's not clear how Callaghan came up with this figure; when the cabinet papers were released for 1979, political historians were disappointed not to find a fag packet with 5 per cent scribbled on the back.

The winter of discontent: the *Sun* quotes Shakespeare

Within weeks strikes were beginning to dominate the news once again. The reporting generally followed the same pattern: images of some pickets with moustaches and flat caps huddled round a brazier on a frosty morning outside the factory gates, a lorry driver being persuaded to turn around, and then an interview with a union leader whose Scottish or Geordie accent was so strong that the BBC interviewer didn't have the faintest idea what he was saying: 'I shell be consultin' wi' me exec'tif com'tee, ta poot it ta members, tha' this ladest off is oonaccet'le.' Apart from *Z Cars*, *The Likely Lads* and John Noakes on *Blue Peter*, listening to strike leaders on the news was about the only time you heard northern accents on the BBC.

In November Ford workers settled at 17 per cent (slightly less than the 80 per cent rise awarded to Ford's chairman) and other British car workers soon sought comparable rises, since they were making similarly crappy cars. Lorry drivers indicated that they might strike, which is about the only time in history lorry drivers ever indicated anything. Sewerage workers withdrew their labour, and people tried not to think too hard about what that would actually involve. With food and fuel deliveries at a standstill and oil refineries and docks closed down, the army were put on standby amid a sense of mounting chaos.

The news was bad, the weather was worse. And so Jim Callaghan thought this might be the time to be photographed swimming on a beach in the Caribbean. His media advisors had thought long and hard about how the embattled voters back at home might like to see their PM. They had rejected 'working at a desk', 'shaking hands with world leaders' and had agreed that 'swimming in the clear tropical waters of a sun-kissed Caribbean island' would be the best image to cheer everyone up. Callaghan returned from an international summit in Guadeloupe rather surprised at the gloomy mood that had gripped Britain and said to a reporter, 'I promise you that if you look at it from outside, and perhaps you're taking rather a parochial view at the moment, I don't think that other people in the world would share the view that there is mounting chaos.'

'Crisis, what crisis?' screamed the *Sun*, with the result that millions of people came to believe that this is what the Prime Minister had actually said. Indeed it was the editor of the *Sun* who had dubbed the unrest 'the winter of discontent'. British politics shifted significantly to the right during the late 1970s and 1980s, and one factor was surely the influence of the *Sun* on working-class voters (and the handful of Oxbridge students who bought it ironically). It was a bitter pill for the British left that the once socialist *Daily Herald* had failed and been relaunched as the *Sun*, which once it was rebranded under the ownership of Rupert Murdoch gradually shifted to the right during the 1970s until it finally came out for the Conservatives in 1979.*

The road-haulage dispute was settled with an almost total victory for the lorry drivers; now there was no way that the more lowly paid public-sector workers were going to settle for the government's limit. A day of action in January 1979 saw the greatest number of workers down tools since the General Strike of 1926. Various separate yet related disputes continued; schools were closed for lack of caretakers and cooks, and journalists tried but failed to find any kids who were distressed about this. Refuse collections were halted, and in the single most iconic image of the winter of discontent, Leicester Square once again became a public dump, attracting rats and tabloid photographers in roughly equal numbers. In Liverpool grave-diggers were on strike and, well, could you bury the dead? Apparently not. 'Excuse me, I'd like to bury the dead, please.' 'Sorry, mate, the gravediggers are on strike.' 'You mean to say you can't even bury the dead? Wait till Mrs Thatcher hears about this . . .'

Although the winter of discontent was not as calamitous as the crises of the early 1970s, it was far more significant politically speaking. It destroyed the impression that Labour was the best party to negotiate with the unions, and played into Mrs Thatcher's hands by putting the idea of curbing union power at the top of the agenda. On a deeper level, closures of schools and hospitals seriously damaged Beveridge's post-war ideal of

---

* A decade earlier, on the historic day that Murdoch's very first edition was to be printed, he suggested that his wife set the presses rolling. Mrs Murdoch was about to press the button when the printers objected. She couldn't possibly do a task normally done by a printer if she wasn't a member of the print union. So Anna Murdoch duly joined the union and then pressed the button, while her husband must have been thinking, 'I'm going to make a few changes around here . . .'

collective provision. By giving public-service workers no choice but to strike, Callaghan undermined the very concept of public service. Increasingly in the 1980s those who could afford to pay for health care would do so (except die-hard middle-class lefties whose neighbours couldn't understand why they didn't just join BUPA). 1979 was a watershed year in Britain in many ways, as *The Times* would have recorded if it hadn't been out of production for most of the year due to industrial action.

Wake up, Maggie

In March the results of the devolution referendums in Scotland and Wales brought more bad news for the government. The Celtic electors had not voted in sufficient numbers to support the government's plans for separate assemblies and now the support of the Nationalist MPs was lost. A motion of no confidence was tabled for 28 March. Desperate attempts were made to win the support of the various minor parties or maverick MPs.* Both sides knew that it was going to be close but even so the Labour side decided against bringing in a dying MP who had been keen to do his duty. And so at the end of a long and dramatic night, the Labour tellers approached the Speaker and a victorious roar of delight went up from the Labour benches. One of the Labour whips had given his front bench a gleeful thumbs-up: the government appeared to have survived by one vote! Mrs Thatcher was incandescent with rage. But the Labour whip had forgotten to count the two Tory tellers, and for the first time in over half a century a government had lost a confidence vote in the House of

* Roy Hattersley recalls how he was approached by Enoch Powell who offered Unionist MPs' support if the government promised an oil pipeline to Northern Ireland. Callaghan rejected this offer flat. It seems the great union negotiator and deal maker was now just grimly resigned to his fate.

Commons. Now it was the Tories who were cheering, despite the defiant singing of 'The Red Flag' by many of the Labour MPs. The socialist anthem had been sung from the Labour benches in 1945 as a victory song. Now it was a lament for the death of the last old Labour government. They couldn't have sung the current number one. It was 'I Will Survive'.

'Where there is discord . . .'

Long before the 1979 election campaign had even begun, the Conservatives had been employing the expertise of the advertising agency Saatchi & Saatchi, who ran cinema ads and poster campaigns attacking the government's record. The most famous image was of a long line queuing at the Job Centre under the strapline 'Labour Isn't Working'. The figures in the queue weren't real unemployed people, obviously; they were actually members of Hendon Young Conservatives. Labour strategists sat around and wondered which aspect of their record they should now emphasize. 'Should we concentrate on the economy and talk about the collapse of sterling, and high unemployment and inflation? Or maybe we should concentrate on industrial relations and talk about our special understanding with the unions?' Unsurprisingly Labour was on the defensive from the outset. Mrs Thatcher worked the media well with photo opportunities that guaranteed her front pages even of the papers that didn't support her (which by now were very few).

It was not an election without violence; the day after it was declared, her close ally Sir Airey Neave was killed by a terrorist*

---

* There are a number of mad conspiracy theories about the death of Airey Neave: that his murder was an 'inside job' by the British security services. Enoch Powell believed that the Americans killed him, along with Lord Mountbatten and probably Bambi's mother as well.

bomb as he drove his car out of the Palace of Westminster car park. And at a National Front meeting in Southall, an Anti-Nazi League protestor called Blair Peach was killed by police allegedly using illegal lead-filled truncheons. The National Front virtually bankrupted itself in the election following its decision to put up over three hundred candidates, losing every single deposit and splitting soon after. Callaghan tried to play the experienced elder statesman, but all that experience had just taught him that the country was undergoing the sort of sea change that only occurs once every thirty years or so, as he put it. The days before Beveridge were now such a distant memory that voters presumed the welfare state was just part of the furniture.

The polls consistently put Margaret Thatcher ahead, but the result on 3 May was a bigger swing to the Conservatives than many had expected. Robin Day in the BBC election studio puffed away on a cigar while he reported the Tory gains in the south and in the Midlands. The Tories won a majority of forty-four seats, and for the first time since 1935 there was a gap of more than two million votes between the two parties. The Nationalists who had actually forced the election saw their House of Commons representation drop from fourteen to four. The next day, dressed in Tory blue, Mrs Thatcher arrived in Downing Street and on the threshold of Number 10 famously quoted St Francis of Assisi. 'Where there is discord, may we bring harmony; where there is error, may we bring truth, where there is any manufacturing industry, may we bring a derelict wasteland full of smackheads and drunks. Hang on – who's been tampering with my notes?'

And then she went inside to begin the most controversial premiership in modern political history. It wasn't one difficult winter that had helped Mrs Thatcher come to power, but an entire *decade* of discontent, perhaps even twenty or thirty years of economic decline, strikes and mismanagement that she would now attempt to put right. Few would dispute that the body politic of

Great Britain was in need of some very judicious surgery. The trouble was that they had just employed a mad axewoman to do the job.

5

1979–1990

How one woman made the rich richer, the poor poorer and everyone in the middle feel briefly guilty about stepping over the homeless on the way to cash in their Telecom shares

It's amazing there's never been a West End musical about her. A major song and dance spectacular depicting the rise and fall of the plucky girl from the corner shop who rose to lead her country at its darkest hour, who saw off the enemies without and within, and then was cruelly despatched by her disloyal lieutenants. Cameron Mackintosh presents *Thatcha!* written by Andrew Lloyd Webber and Ben Elton.

No modern politician ever dominated a decade like Mrs Thatcher bestrode the 1980s. Her victory was the triumph of the individual over community, when the first person plural was replaced by the first person singular. Just look at the treatment meted out to the Elephant Man as soon as she came to power. Jeering Victorian mobs laughing at his hideous disfigurement; and all because Thatcher had cut the DHSS head-sack allowance for claimants who 'looked a bit like an elephant'.

Margaret Thatcher was a non-conformist in every sense of the word. There was Methodism in her madness. She was a lower-middle-class outsider in a Tory Party of upper-class men. As a woman she was never going to be accepted as a member of the club, so unlike Heath she didn't even bother trying. Although she sold herself as the daughter of a humble grocer, it was being the wife of a millionaire that gave her the freedom to pursue her political career. She had produced the statutory one son and one daughter in the form of twins, which in terms of a children-to-sex ratio was typical Thatcherite efficiency. The fact that she was a woman meant the bewildered chaps in the cabinet had no idea how to deal with her. Products of traditional all-male bastions like the top boarding schools and famous regiments, they had no experience in working with a female superior and were at a complete loss as to how one took her aside for a quiet word of criticism. One or two of them attempted it from time to time. Their bodies were later discovered when the Docklands were dredged.

Mrs Thatcher's position was not strong enough in her first term to surround herself with those also on the right of the party. She felt obliged to appoint consensus politicians of the sort who had served in the despised Heath government. There was some speculation that Ted Heath himself might be offered the key post of Foreign Secretary, but instead he was invited to leave Britain and Westminster politics altogether when Thatcher offered him the British Embassy in Washington. Heath declined the job of ambassador (though she was probably talking about the vacancy for janitor).

Her first Home Secretary and Deputy Prime Minister was William Whitelaw, who throughout her first two terms remained a loyal and trusted advisor, often tempering her more aggressive and impatient instincts. 'Every Prime Minister needs a Willie!' the first female Prime Minister famously declared when he retired, not understanding why everyone was giggling. Other upper-class patricians included Lord Carrington, Lord Soames, the ruddy-faced James Prior and Sir George Younger. Eventually Mrs

Thatcher would find ministers from more modest, aspirant backgrounds like herself, and cabinet get-togethers would involve fewer pheasant shoots and more Sunday evenings sitting around watching *Antiques Roadshow*.

Corner shop economics

Mrs Thatcher had made much of her humble origins and how she had learned the importance of thrift and sound economics in her father's grocery store. Now she boasted that she would apply those simple shopkeeper's principles to the British economy. Many was the time when Alderman Roberts would report, 'The shop had a good day today, young Margaret. We have reduced the public sector borrowing requirement as a proportion of gross domestic product, raising confidence in the markets, which strengthened sterling against a basket of currencies. Oh, and we sold a quarter of lemon bonbons as well.' In fact, the image of the British shop had evolved somewhat since Margaret's childhood, and so when she talked about 'corner shop economics', it presented an image of Britain making all its money from fags, porn mags and the business cards of 'intimate masseurs' in the window.

In truth, her economic thinking was more influenced by her political guru, the slightly alarming wide-eyed right-winger Keith Joseph, who had studied the economic theories of Friedrich Hayek and Milton Friedman and persuaded his protégée of the merits of monetarism. The only previous government to have pursued such a monetarist economic policy was the fascist dictatorship of General Pinochet in Chile, so it came highly recommended. Monetarism was the economic theory that elevated control of the money supply above all else; it maintained that inflation must be tackled by reducing the amount of cash in the economy, which would in turn sort out all the other problems such as unemployment, balance of payments or your Trade and Industry Minister getting his secretary pregnant.* When you played Mrs Thatcher at Monopoly, *she charged you* £200 for passing 'Go!' and then sold off the utilities and train stations you thought had belonged to you.

To push through these unconventional policies she appointed Sir Geoffrey Howe as Chancellor of the Exchequer, who agreed that this was a job far more suited to his talents than joining Alexei Sayle and Ben Elton on the nascent alternative comedy circuit. It was a brilliant tactical move by the Prime Minister; to sneak through a controversial economic experiment under the cover of a chancellor so mind-numbingly dull that no one could have possibly remained conscious five minutes into his ministerial briefing. 'So everyone happy with that fiscal policy?' she could say at the end of one of Geoffrey's monologues, and everyone would jolt awake and go, 'What! Oh, er, yes, very good, Sir Geoffrey . . . Yup, that all, er, sounds fine . . .'

Labour had recently done a good job in reducing the amount of money in the economy by taxing the super-rich so much that they all moved to Switzerland. But now in his first budget, Howe cut the top rate of tax from 83 per cent to 60 per cent,† VAT virtually doubled to 15 per cent and he initiated a massive cut in public expenditure as wealth was shifted from the poor to the rich. 'I was thinking of doing her as Robin Hood,' the cartoonists would say to their editors, 'only, like the other way round? Maybe? Does that work?' Sky-high interest rates contributed to the record numbers of bankruptcies and liquidations as manufacturing output fell by 16 per cent more than it had done in the great slump before the

* Thatcher lost one of her favourite ministers, Cecil Parkinson, when it was revealed that his former secretary was bearing his child.
† The top rate of tax remained at 60 per cent for most of Mrs Thatcher's time in Downing Street, way above the 40 per cent paid by the very rich throughout Tony Blair's premiership.

war. A hundred thousand people a month were being put out of work; very rapidly it looked as if what Denis Healey called 'sado-monetarism' was an unmitigated disaster. There were calls for a U-turn, but at the Conservative Party conference Mrs Thatcher declared, 'You turn if you want to. The lady's not for turning!'

Her government's plan was to make things worse before they got better, and the first part was working marvellously. By 1981 unemployment was heading towards three million and there were riots in Brixton, Southall and Liverpool, prompting police to use CS gas for the first time on the British mainland. Mrs Thatcher visited Liverpool and was at a loss to understand the psychology of the rioters, commenting that if so many of these young people were unemployed, then you'd think they might have the time to pick up all that dreadful litter.

A letter from 364 economists was published in *The Times* calling for this brutal monetarist experiment to be abandoned, and even one or two cabinet ministers were making coded speeches criticizing the government's economic policy. In fact, the so-called 'wets' were in a majority in the cabinet, and had they been more courageous and organized they could have easily ousted Mrs Thatcher. But they never did because they were so, well, wet.

Instead she picked the faint hearts off one by one, either sacking them outright like Sir Ian Gilmour or, even crueller, making them Minister for Northern Ireland like Jim Prior. When Nicholas Soames was dismissed from the cabinet, Thatcher said he couldn't have taken it worse if he had been sacked by his housemaid. The mistake the wets made was that they argued about the risks of high unemployment *as if it were a bad thing*. Thatcher realized that high unemployment would cut inflation by reducing demand, and above all else high unemployment would fatally weaken the unions. So adding one or two critical ministers to the jobless total was the least she could do.

Labour pains

With Mrs Thatcher's hard-line policies going so disastrously wrong, pollsters might have expected the Labour Party to be racing ahead in the polls. However, the Labour Party was more focused on internal battles than fighting a government destroying the jobs of Labour's natural supporters. Central to this struggle on the left was the controversial figure of Tony Benn.

Benn had been surrounded by politicians from an early age, as he would reluctantly tell interviewers if they pushed him hard enough: 'So, Tony – I don't suppose you ever met any prime ministers when you were a child . . .'

'Actually, yes, I've met a hundred and twenty-seven British prime ministers; I remember when I was a little boy, Sir Robert Walpole sat me on his knee and said, "Tony, we've got to have democratic socialism, and that means a fundamental and irreversible shift of power towards working people and their families." And of course Gladstone was a family friend and used to give me sixpence and a pat on the head and say, "Compulsory reselection of MPs – that's the way forward, young Tony" . . .'

Benn's own political journey from reluctant peer to socialist bogey man is chronicled in one of the most comprehensive sets of political diaries ever published. From Volume One, *Rather Pleased With Myself*, right through to Volume Eight, *Still Quite Pleased With Myself*, he describes the inexplicable implosion of the Labour Party from one of the best vantage points possible: as the person who was responsible for so much of it.

He had been on the Labour front bench for a decade and a half, but when the Tories took power in 1979, he quit the shadow cabinet in order to give himself greater freedom to speak his mind. This was the raising of the flag at the beginning of a conflict that would keep Labour out of power for a generation. It was such a complex and protracted civil war that these days there are special war-gaming clubs that restage the Labour Party conference of 1980. You can buy little 6mm scale models of the Conference Arrangements Committee and marvel at the detail on the hand-painted Denis Healey eyebrows. 'Now I move the Benn figure to the podium for him to propose the mandatory reselection of MPs by their constituency parties,' declares the spotty teen in the Warhammer T-shirt. 'But you haven't moved your massed ranks of the Union Block Vote to the left of the hall,' argues the balding man in the anorak.

Many of the activists and trade unionists were frustrated that years of endless political compromise had not kept even a right-wing Labour Party in power. Not only was the wider party moving to the left, but a number of constituency associations had also been targeted by a Trotskyist entry group, the so-called Militant Tendency.* The gap between the shadow cabinet on the podium and the angry delegates could not have been wider as Jim Callaghan was humiliated and defeated on just about every issue. The Blackpool conference passed resolutions in favour of unilateral disarmament and abolishing the House of Lords, promising that 'the next Labour government will take Britain out of the EEC' or 'the next Labour government will close all US bases in Britain'. Not one of them said, 'The next Labour government will invade Iraq and Afghanistan and bring in 28-day detention without charge.'

Callaghan still had one trick left to play and resigned two weeks later, forcing a leadership election just before the new rules that would hand power to the unions and constituency parties came into effect. To the delight of those who were already planning to leave the Labour Party, Michael Foot beat Denis Healey for the Labour leadership, though he did less well in a separate

* Formerly the 'Revolutionary Socialist League'. *Militant* was also the name of the organization's newspaper, which despite expanding to 16 pages in the late 1970s was still disappointingly short on puzzles and celebrity gossip.

Best-dressed Politician poll. He was nicknamed Worzel Gummidge after a hugely damaging tabloid front-page photo-graph of him wearing a donkey jacket at the cenotaph on Remembrance Sunday (it was actually a perfectly acceptable coat). It wasn't just that Foot looked like a scarecrow; given Labour's incompetence, he wouldn't have even scared a crow. Had Callaghan resigned immediately after the general election it is quite likely that the hugely popular Denis Healey would have won the Labour leadership. But as Chancellor he was tainted with the 'betrayal' of the previous Labour government and now MPs were casting their votes knowing that their constituency parties were watching them. It was not the choice of a party focusing on winning the next election, it was the collective vote of individual MPs frightened of being deselected.

Pass the claret

Not-very-secret plans to set up a separate centre-left party were already well advanced and a handful of right-wing MPs later admitted to deliberately voting for the left-wing Foot in order to make the Labour Party seem less electable when it was time for them to abandon it. In January 1981, as a special party conference established new party rules for losing general elections, four prominent Labour MPs announced the establishment of the Council for Social Democracy. They rather disingenuously described themselves as 'a pressure group within the Labour Party' while feverishly planning the launch of a breakaway party to occupy the apparently deserted centre ground of British politics. And all the while David Steel was shouting, 'Hello? We're already here! Can anybody hear me? There already is a party in the centre ground. We've been here ages ... Is this microphone working?'

In March 1981, the Gang of Four* – Roy Jenkins, David Owen, Shirley Williams and What's-his-name, the other one – formed the Social Democratic Party, taking two dozen Labour MPs with them (and one kamikaze Conservative) to become a significant third force in British politics. Alexei Sayle described the SDP as 'the K-tel of British politics' – after the cheap, heavily advertised record label that just repackaged everyone else's hits. They were a party without a political soul, motivated primarily by the egos and personal ambitions of Jenkins and Owen. It is one of the great tragedies of modern British politics that the greatest Labour Home Secretary should have allowed his vanity to take precedence over his party loyalty and long-term political judgement. In his Dimbleby Lecture in 1979, Jenkins had somehow equated Britain's economic decline with its two-party system and the absence of European-style coalitions. However, given the level of political consensus in the post-war years, it's hard not to agree with Tony Benn who joked that he didn't know what the SDP were moaning about, since they had been in power continuously between 1951 and 1979.

One Conservative advertising hoarding of the period declared 'SDP = Still Deciding Policies' but this didn't seem to bother the voters, who gave the SDP some spectacular by-election victories, electing Shirley Williams in Crosby and then Roy Jenkins at Glasgow Hillhead.† Stratospheric poll ratings in 1981 gave the media darlings of the SDP such massive opinion-poll leads that if they had been translated into parliamentary seats, they would have

* Rather bizarrely they were named the 'Gang of Four' after the Chinese Communist leaders charged with counter-revolutionary treason after the death of Mao Tse Tung. In the late 1970s a rather fine radical post-punk rock band chose the name The Gang of Four, and then found themselves associated with a bunch of middle-class woolly liberals.

† Roy Jenkins eventually lost the seat back to Labour who hoped they'd now found a candidate who represented the very best of the Labour Party in terms of honesty, humility and loyalty. 'Great, what's his name?' 'Er – George Galloway.'

given the SDP 600 seats out of 635. At a time when Thatcher's policies were clearly tearing the party apart and the Labour Party was engaged in a bitter and angry civil war, the voters were probably just relieved to have someone nice to vote for.

Labour's infighting was about to get even nastier when, taking advantage of the new rules, Tony Benn announced he would be challenging Denis Healey for the deputy leadership of the party. Foot had begged Benn not to proceed with such a damaging course of action, but throughout 1981, the bitterest of public battles saw Healey shouted down at meetings and pelted in flour, and left Labour looking all but finished as an effective political party. Healey won 'by a hair of my eyebrow', as he put it – 50.4 per cent to 49.6 per cent – after a crucial abstention by shadow Education Secretary Neil Kinnock and other left-wing members of Labour's Tribune group had pulled Labour back from the brink. Kinnock was physically attacked for his 'betrayal' and then apparently beat up his assailant, leaving 'blood and vomit' all over the walls and floor. Somehow you could never imagine Tony Blair doing that.

We love foreigners (as long as they're American)

International affairs took up a considerable amount of time during Thatcher's first term. Things got off to an excellent start with a negotiated settlement in Rhodesia that saw Robert Mugabe winning the following election and becoming Prime Minister. Although he was to remain in power longer than Mrs Thatcher, he was to have slightly less success in bringing down prices; by 2008 inflation in Zimbabwe was running at 231 million per cent with no sign of it dipping below that psychological 230 million mark.

Thatcher was the first foreign leader invited to the White

House after the inauguration of President Reagan, a fact that pleased her enormously. Much was made of their 'special relationship', although the British peace movement asked what was so special about being made a first-strike target by having America's nuclear arsenal stationed here. When a news story broke that a terrorist had tricked his 'girlfriend' into carrying a bomb onto a plane, which would have killed her along with all the other passengers, the satirical show *Spitting Image* saw a direct parallel. Reagan was portrayed kissing a love-struck Thatcher in the airport terminal before he gave her a very suspicious package to carry on board.

1979 was not just a watershed year in Britain; far more significant in world terms was the Islamic revolution in Iran, which precipitated a second oil crisis and increased tension in the Middle East. A siege in the Iranian Embassy in Kensington was brought to a sudden and dramatic end when masked SAS troops stormed the building and shot dead all the Iranians, before climbing out onto the flaming balcony and telling each other, 'Ooh you were super in there, honeybun! And that balaclava is soo you!' 'Oh thanks, luv, but I must use fabric conditioner on it next time, it was really chafing on my sensitive skin . . .'

Mrs Thatcher probably would have liked to have used stun grenades and assault rifles on the other European leaders as she negotiated Britain's EEC rebate. She exasperated her European counterparts with her rudeness and her xenophobia but was determined to claw back money that she believed was Britain's. The German Chancellor actually pretended to go to sleep, while the French President read a newspaper, but eventually she wore them down and got two-thirds of the money she was demanding.

Although Thatcher did irreparable damage to relations with Britain's European partners, she knew that her anti-European hectoring played well with the British right-wing press and her little Englander supporters back home. 'I bat for Britain,' she once proclaimed, though her advisors told her she shouldn't really swing a cricket bat around in EEC meetings. In truth, Maggie Thatcher did not bat for Britain, she batted for England, and only the comfortable parts of the south at that. She was the Prime Minister of Middle England.

Mrs Thatcher's intransigence (or steadfast courage, depending on your point of view) was demonstrated with a new crisis in Northern Ireland. The pattern of violence and reprisals had continued throughout the 1970s with occasional shocking spectaculars. Soon after Thatcher came to power, the Queen's cousin Lord Louis Mountbatten was killed by the IRA, on the same day as fifteen soldiers; it was the army's worst day since the beginning of the troubles. In 1981 IRA prisoners at Long Kesh (commonly known as H Block) began a hunger strike demanding status as political prisoners, which Thatcher was adamant would not be granted. Their protest involved wearing blankets instead of prison clothes and refusing to slop out. Excrement was dealt with by smearing it on the walls, which was not a look that caught on in many interior design magazines. The leader of the hunger strike was Bobby Sands,* whose supporters took advantage of a by-election in Nationalist Fermanagh and South Tyrone to get him elected as a Member of Parliament.

All things considered, Bobby Sands was not much of a constituency MP. Usually when you criticize the excesses of maverick politicians, the statutory defence is: 'Yes, but apparently he's an excellent constituency MP.' But if you tried writing to Bobby Sands MP at the House of Commons about getting your parking ticket rescinded, while he was starving himself to death

---

* In Tehran the British Embassy used to lie adjacent to Winston Churchill Boulevard, but the Iranian revolutionary government renamed it Bobby Sands Street, a political gesture that was slightly undermined by them spelling it 'Baby Sandez'.

in a cell smeared in excrement, he never even got back to you.

The death of Sands triggered riots in Ulster and brought international condemnation on the British government. A hundred thousand people attended his funeral and another nine prisoners went on to die over the summer of 1981, elevating the terrorists to the status of heroic martyrs around the world and giving Sinn Fein a huge boost as a political party. Once again Mrs Thatcher had made a very public demonstration that she was resolute and strong, even though a discreet early settlement (along the lines of the one that was eventually made anyway) would have avoided the huge boost for the IRA and would have saved many more lives in the long run, including those of several of her own colleagues. It was the 1981 hunger strikes that led the IRA to resolve that they would assassinate Mrs Thatcher, and three years later they came to within an inch of succeeding.

'People getting angry'*

In Britain as well as in Northern Ireland, the 1980s was an acrimonious decade, with intense hatred felt towards political enemies on all sides. Violence on the street was mirrored by enormous bitterness in the House of Commons, in council chambers and public meetings around the country. Strikes and demonstrations had an edge of violence and danger.

Only the royal wedding of Prince Charles to Lady Diana Spencer in July 1981 gave the patriots anything to smile about, although there were those on the far left who convinced themselves that the great flag-waving celebration had been deliberately contrived to provide Mrs Thatcher's government with a feel-good

* From 'Ghost Town' by The Specials; a prescient number one in the middle of the riots. And that doesn't include all the singles looted from blazing record shops.

factor in the depths of her darkest year. Diana seemed like the perfect wife; a pretty, upper-class English girl who would one day make a wonderful queen. There was a mild controversy when it was announced that Diana did not want to promise to 'obey' her husband in her marriage vows. Instead she promised to *Love, honour and then tear the royal family apart with a string of embarrassing revelations after having it off with James Hewitt and Dodi Fayed.*

But not even the hugely popular royal family, 'the gold filling in a mouthful of decay' as John Osborne had described it, could obscure the abyss into which Britain had sunk. Three million unemployed, riots, rampant inflation, record bankruptcies, sky-high interest rates leaving homeowners unable to pay their mortgages, and dire warnings from church leaders and academics. Mrs Thatcher broke all records as the most unpopular Prime Minister since polling began; the Tories were third behind the SDP and the embattled Labour Party; no one could imagine any political scenario in which she could possibly survive. 'I said, *I cannot imagine any political scenario in which she might survive . . .*' repeated her ministers, looking around expectantly. And then, as is traditional, the unimaginable duly happened.

Argentina invades Scotland

For most people, the 'Falkland Islands' was just an unplaceable name they had vaguely overheard with about as much frequency as the Hebrides or the Shetland Islands. So when in the spring of 1982 it was announced that the Falklands had been invaded by Argentina, there were some very alarmed politicians picturing kilted Highlanders forced to speak Spanish and raise llamas. Information was patchy at first, but earliest reports suggested that the Falklands were somewhere in the southern hemisphere, maybe near South America, or somewhere off New Zealand? The first rumbling that an invasion was imminent came on April the first. 'Oh yeah, sure, Argentina to invade the Falkland Islands! And I suppose the government are bringing in decimal clocks, are they? And Brussels has said we have to paint the white cliffs of Dover purple?'

The next day it was clearly no joke. Argentine forces had occupied the long-forgotten colony and the tiny garrison of Royal Marines was photographed being marched off with their hands on their heads. The newspapers reported that the Falklands had now been given their Spanish name – 'the Malvinas, meaning, er, bad . . . wine? Yes, that works . . .' – and that the local British population had been instructed to drive on the right and be cruel to animals. When the story first broke, it seemed like here was the crisis that would finally finish Margaret Thatcher off. For the first time since the war, the House of Commons met on a Saturday and the Prime Minister was pilloried for allowing such a national humiliation to come to pass. It transpired that as part of the government's spending cuts, a Royal Navy patrol vessel had been withdrawn from the area, which Argentina had read as a signal of Britain's waning interest in the colony. Lord Carrington the Foreign Secretary resigned; John Nott the Defence Secretary offered his resignation but it was refused. For the millions who really hated Margaret Thatcher, it was the best weekend of the decade.

But in her House of Commons office Mrs Thatcher met with the navy chief Sir Henry Leach, who told her that it would be militarily possible to retake the islands. Indeed, he told her, she must! The Prime Minister instructed him to proceed with the military plans. And so a rather dumbstruck nation watched the surreal spectacle of the Royal Navy assembling a huge task force of warships, troop carriers and requisitioned liners as it prepared to sail 8,000 miles away towards a group of islands inhabited by 1,800 British ex-pats and 600,000 sheep. Mrs Thatcher was unwavering on the principle at stake here. These were British sheep, and their right to self-determination was non-negotiable.

It took a month for the ships to reach the South Atlantic, while the Americans led attempts to achieve a negotiated settlement. 'This is the table at which Neville Chamberlain decided to sacrifice Czechoslovakia to appease Hitler,' she told the visiting American Secretary of State, wondering if she should take up smoking cigars and wearing a homburg. The new American President Ronald Reagan tried to persuade his Conservative ally into a negotiated settlement over 'that little ice-cold bunch of land down there', as he so expertly referred to it. But crucially, when he saw that she was intent on military action, he resolved that America would support her. With the Labour opposition set upon unilateral disarmament and quitting NATO, it was not in the United States' interests to see Thatcher toppled from power. Neither did it help the Argentine case that when American diplomats attempted to discuss the situation with Argentina's fascist dictator General Galtieri, they concluded that he was drunk.

The impending arrival of the task force had been presented as a negotiating tactic; demonstrating that Britain had the capability of responding with force as a very last resort if an agreement could not be reached. Even those closest to Thatcher, such as the new Foreign Secretary Francis Pym,* believed that war would still be avoided. The fact that Margaret Thatcher was wearing an ARP helmet and putting sandbags in the windows of Number 10 didn't seem to suggest anything to him. For without an unequivocal victory, Mrs Thatcher's premiership was finished. That is not to say that she was determined to see people die simply to keep

---

* For a brief moment Francis Pym looked the most likely person to succeed her if the whole adventure went horribly wrong. Thatcher regretted making him Foreign Secretary almost immediately, considering him a faint heart, and she sacked him after the 1983 general election.

power. But in this crisis, what she perceived as the wider interests of Great Britain and the political interests of Margaret Thatcher became perfectly aligned, and once that happens inside a politician's head, pretty well anything is justifiable.

Gotcha!

The British government had declared a 200-mile exclusion zone around the Falkland Islands, a concept the newspapers managed to convey by printing a map of the Falklands with a great big circle drawn around them. However, the Argentine navy might have been forgiven for feeling confused about this notion when, in the first significant military action of the war, a warship outside the exclusion zone and heading away from the islands was attacked and sunk by a British nuclear submarine. The *General Belgrano*, a former American battleship that had survived Pearl Harbor, went down with the loss of nearly four hundred lives. War was now inevitable.

However, at no point was there any formal declaration of war, and throughout 1982 the television news tactfully referred to the entire episode as 'the Falklands Conflict'. (It is a strange twist of modern linguistics that governments only use the word 'war' when they are not actually at war. So we have the 'War on Drugs' or the 'War on Poverty', but when we send our army or air force into places to blow them up, it is referred to as 'the Serbian Crisis' or 'Operation Iraqi Freedom'.)

The sinking of the *General Belgrano* would develop into something of a political scandal, not least because of the number of lies put out by the government about the course of events that led up to its sinking, and the mysterious disappearance of the logbook of the submarine in question and the attempted cover-up. The episode climaxed in the failed prosecution of a civil servant who had felt moved to leak information to a Labour MP. Tam Dalyell MP doggedly asserted that the ship had been sunk for political reasons rather than military ones – he asserted that Mrs Thatcher gave the order to sink the ship to scupper a new peace plan that had just been hammered out by the President of Peru.

The infamous headline on the first edition of the *Sun* was *Gotcha!*, which some considered perhaps a rather insensitive way to report the death of hundreds of Argentine conscripts. 'The paper that supports our boys', as it described itself, plumbed new depths during the war with jaw-dropping jingoism and racist jibes against 'the Argies'. It helped create an atmosphere in which to criticize the pursuit of war was tantamount to treachery – indeed, it even suggested that there was a legal case for Tony Benn to be charged with treason.

Two days after the *Belgrano* was sunk, the British destroyer HMS *Sheffield* was hit by an Exocet missile, killing twenty British servicemen and eventually causing the ship to sink. The mood in Britain noticeably darkened and the BBC was criticized for showing the extent of British injuries; obviously the government would have preferred them to report that these AM-39 air-launch missiles really, really tickled.* By the end of the war, nine hundred British and Argentine lives would be lost – one for every two islanders being liberated. The vast majority of the British casualties came after troops were landed on the islands on 21 May, although in private the politicians had feared the casualties would be a lot higher. But astonishingly by the middle of June it was all over. The Argentine conscripts, many of whom hated their military government, were demoralized and had little stomach to fight, and to the great relief of the British government the war

---

* The BBC had also been severely criticized by the government during the Suez crisis in 1956. On that occasion, BBC folklore has it that the army had been put on standby to occupy BBC studios, while BBC technicians were ready to destroy their equipment rather than let it be taken over by the military.

ended quickly and suddenly. The recapture of the tiny capital Port Stanley and the surrender of the Argentine troops caused a huge surge in patriotism back home in a country that badly needed something to feel good about. Mrs Thatcher was transformed from the dogmatic destroyer of British jobs and industry to a victorious war leader; a modern-day Churchill or Darth Vader, depending on your point of view. *The Empire Strikes Back* was the headline on the American magazine *Newsweek*, after the latest film in the Star Wars series. Although, rather disappointingly, in this version there was no final twist in the end when General Galtieri discovered that he was Margaret Thatcher's son.

The Conservative Party's fortunes were transformed. Having been third in the polls, they were suddenly in the lead, with Mrs Thatcher's own approval rating now over 50 per cent. The national rejoicing seemed to take longer than the actual war, with the return of the victorious troops staggered over several weeks so that every evening on the news there would be yet more footage of flag-waving patriots and families weeping for joy at the safe return of their young heroes.

The victory was very much the Prime Minister's, to the extent that no members of the royal family were invited to the victory parade to upstage the star of the show. Neither were any injured servicemen permitted to be visible at the celebration. The conflict was served up like an old-fashioned war film, a simplistic battle between good and evil in which all of the heroes emerged victorious but unscathed. Indeed, Mrs Thatcher hoped there might perhaps be a stirring film or West End show made of the war, and invited the likes of David Puttnam and Andrew Lloyd Webber to Chequers, where she told them: 'And this is the chair I was sitting in when I made the decision to sink the *Belgrano*.' Whether Tim Rice ever actually searched for a rhyme for 'Galtieri' is not recorded.

'Nuclear war? No thanks.' (Well, obviously.)

Had the Falklands War come along a few years later, Britain's navy would not have had the capability of mounting such an operation. Rather reasonably, military planning had not centred around the defence of 1,800 sheep farmers off the coast of Argentina. The Soviet Union was still perceived as the big threat, and the Cold War had got distinctly colder at the beginning of the decade when Russia took the rather unwise decision to invade Afghanistan. 'The fools!' said Britain and America at the UN. 'You'll never catch us getting tangled up in terrain like that!' And the word 'Irony' was flashed up on all the delegates' monitors. The deployment of American cruise missiles on British soil had been agreed under the previous Labour government, but now their imminent arrival, combined with the hawkish rhetoric of Ronald Reagan and Margaret Thatcher, gave the peace movement new impetus. Huge CND demonstrations were seen in London and other European capitals, and protestors were quite insistent that one-two-three-four, they did not want a nuclear war, and that five-six-seven-eight, they did not want to radiate.

Outside one of the cruise missile bases at Greenham Common in Berkshire, a women's peace camp was set up, where anti-nuclear protestors endured cold winters, police harassment and tabloid articles about their lack of effort on the make-up front. The women slept under improvised polythene shelters, and occasionally went 'over the wire' into the base, where for some reason their anti-nuclear critique was made by whooping like a Red Indian in a 1950s Western.

'May I ask why the camp is women only? Is this a statement about nuclear weapons being a product of a patriarchal society?'

'Woo-woo-woo-woo-woo-woo-woo-woo-woo-woo!'

'Ah yes, well, I hadn't seen it like that before, thank you. Now I understand that the battles for nuclear disarmament and gender equality are inextricably linked.'

The alternative lifestyle presented by many in the peace movement tended to make the rest of the country think that the idea of nuclear disarmament must be rather eccentric as well, and the issue undoubtedly damaged Labour as it approached the general election. With three million unemployed, with prices and interest rates rising, most voters were more preoccupied with paying the rent or mortgage. And for a million families in council houses, it was about to switch from one to the other.

New front door lays down challenge to Joneses

In former times the Conservative supporters with whom the leader felt most comfortable owned their own estates. Under Mrs Thatcher they sort of shared it with the council. The policy of permitting council tenants to purchase their properties at a discounted rate was a huge vote-winner for Mrs Thatcher, and was central to her ambition of creating a 'property-owning democracy', even if some of the properties did have a skinhead upstairs who kept a Rottweiler on his balcony. A new front door was the public declaration of independence for former council tenants; the message to the outside world was that they had bettered themselves and didn't have to wait five years for the council workman to come round and say he couldn't fix the window.

Part of the treacherous journey to the heavily fortified border between the upper-working and lower-middle class involved off-loading some other unnecessary baggage, such as the tradition of voting Labour. With false but believable rumours put about that Labour authorities would compulsorily repurchase all former council houses, over 60 per cent of those Labour voters who bought their council house voted Conservative at the 1983 election. The idea of allowing council tenants ownership of their homes was, in principle, a fair and progressive policy and the Labour Party was too slow to endorse it. Except the scheme's Machiavellian secondary purpose was exposed by the fact that councils were forbidden by law from spending the receipts of council-house sales on building more public housing. Millions of people may have been waiting for council houses, but Margaret Thatcher was determined to diminish the public housing stock (and the Labour voters who lived in them).

Westminster Council was caught keeping council houses empty in marginal Tory wards, while another of Thatcher's favourite authorities actually emptied an entire estate under the pretence of asbestos removal and then sold all the blocks off to private developers for luxury flats. You didn't have to be a Wandsworth Council tenant to buy a massively discounted slice of the public housing stock; you just had to live in the borough or get a job in the borough to take a cheap house off their hands. Just getting stuck in the Wandsworth one-way system probably entitled you to a small flat. It's a miracle that lifers in Wandsworth Prison weren't offered the chance to buy their own cell.

Mrs Thatcher wanted to go further in 'rolling back the frontiers of the state', and in the hubristic afterglow of the Falklands victory a document was prepared that would radically cut public spending and, she believed, force people to become more self-reliant. Produced by the government's own think tank, it proposed a complete replacement of the National Health Service with an American-style insurance system, ending all state funding for higher education, the abolition of student grants* and the freezing of benefits. The so-called 'wets' in the cabinet were horrified, and despite Mrs Thatcher and her Chancellor wanting

* This policy was of course eventually brought in by a Labour government, ostensibly to pay for a widening of the numbers attending university.

to pursue this radical agenda further, they managed to kill off the paper by leaking it to *The Economist*. In the outcry that followed, Mrs Thatcher had to pretend to know nothing about it and claimed that it had appeared on the cabinet agenda by mistake.

The wets were not just opposed to such extreme policies in practice, they were also anxious about the forthcoming general election. Surprising though it may seem now, given the resounding victory that was to follow, Tory ministers were nervous as they headed into 1983, unsure how the political pendulum would swing now that the SDP/Liberal alliance had added a third dimension. In fact, the Tory vote did drop slightly in June 1983. But it was the Labour vote that utterly collapsed, almost knocked into third place by the SDP. Mrs Thatcher is usually credited with ending post-war consensus politics in the United Kingdom, but by re-electing her, British voters rejected a far greater wrench with the past. Labour's 1983 manifesto proposed withdrawal from the EEC, withdrawal from NATO and unilateral disarmament. It was famously dubbed 'the longest suicide note in history' and was almost universally derided. It even proposed a National Investment Bank, for goodness' sake, with a threat to take the major clearing banks into public ownership – as if that was ever going to happen.

A split opposition utterly lacking in any credibility with the public meant that Mrs Thatcher was re-elected with a landslide victory and a majority of 144 seats. Some governments lose momentum as they enter their second term. Mrs Thatcher was only just getting into her stride.

Chips with everything

The beginning of 1984 brought a nightmare scenario more horrific than anything George Orwell had envisaged. 'What is the most terrifying thing in the world, Winston? It is endless semi-topical parodies of *1984* written by lazy hacks padding out their newspaper columns. "No! Please! I will talk . . . Just don't subject me to any more *Daily Mail* articles asking if that over-zealous traffic warden proves that Orwell was right."'

Other post-war writers had foreseen that the arrival of computers would bring a different sort of tyranny, but frankly, when computer technology did come along, The Rise of the Machines was rather less terrifying than the science-fiction doom-merchants had predicted. Sometimes the video recorder taped the bloody *Horse of the Year Show* because you had set the timer incorrectly. Sometimes the man behind you at the cinema would have a digital watch that went 'beep' on the hour. But it didn't quite add up to a tyranny of computers that had gained consciousness and enslaved mankind.

This was the decade when the mass production of silicon chips unleashed the commercial possibilities of digital technology. Primitive mobile phones appeared, though they were about the weight and dimensions of a breeze block, and if you used a 'cell phone' in public in the 1980s, you were basically saying, 'I'm a bit of a prat!' Compact Discs went on sale, although the first albums in the shops were all the cheesy middle-of-the-road LPs. 'It is impossible to scratch or snap this copy of *Hotel California* by The Eagles,' said the technology correspondent on the evening news. It was a challenge many young music fans were determined to rise to, with the assistance of their parents' power tools.

The huge craze for Space Invaders had already passed; the Space Invaders sacked their agent and were stuck doing corporate work and short turns on cruise liners as the public attention moved on to Asteroids. Various primitive and cumbersome home computers went on sale, such as the Sinclair ZX or the BBC Micro, and everyone agreed that this was definitely the future, except the BBC, who got out of computers and invested in local radio instead.

Then Alan Michael Sugar Trading, shortened to 'Amstrad', produced a home computer so cheap and easy to use that soon millions of people were loading up 'Locoscript', the word-processing software, and taking a week to learn that you didn't have to press the return key to make the sentence go on to the next line. The tiny blinking cursor against the glow of the green screen provided a more advanced type of headache than the one you'd got from the BBC Model B, and the Amstrad's dot-matrix printer brought the possibility of a choice of fonts and letter sizes printed on cheap perforated printer paper. It was the breakout moment for computers in Britain and it made Alan Sugar a very rich man. Then a lot of far superior computers came along at much better prices and the British public declared, 'Amstrad – you're fired!'

'The enemy within'

Despite the fact that computers were now fundamentally trans-forming the crucial area of pub games, the world of work was still dominated by the traditional 'heavy' industries: steel, car-making, the railways and the coal mines. All of these were state-owned and heavily unionized, with the unions generally led by people who made no attempt to disguise their northern accents. Mrs Thatcher had been part of a Conservative government that had twice been defeated by the National Union of Mineworkers, and fairly early on in her premiership it was clear that she was preparing for a confrontation with the Elite Republican Guard of the British labour movement. During her first term her government had quickly settled with the miners to avoid a strike; the battleground had not been adequately prepared. But now huge stockpiles of coal were built up at the power stations and a picture of Arthur Scargill was pinned to the dartboard. New laws against secondary picketing were passed, the police were equipped with riot shields and helmets* and a tough anti-union head of the National Coal Board was appointed. In the spring of 1984, Ian MacGregor announced the closure of Cortonwood Colliery, right in the heart of the Yorkshire coalfield and a pit that the miners believed to be economically viable. Just in case the NUM had not got the message, he then listed another twenty pits that were to be closed. The miners had been lured into a strike at the worst possible time. Not only was it nine months until the winter and eight months after the government had won a landslide victory, it was also the worst possible time because Arthur Scargill had become NUM President.

No one can question the commitment of the leader who saw his union's membership shrink from 200,000 to just him. He had previously been ridiculed for his paranoid warnings about the number of closures the government were planning. In fact, even his dire predictions turned out to be conservative. He had toured the country telling union meetings that workers would eventually have to make a stand to defend their industry (a great night out for all the family), but was not the sort of individual to build alliances across the industry that might have avoided the miners splitting. In his office was a huge painting of himself posing in the style of a Soviet revolutionary leading the workers forward to victory. But his support for trades unions did not extend to supporting Solidarity in Poland, whom he considered to be anti-Soviet counter-revolutionaries, and he became increasingly vocal in his support for Stalin. That invitation to come along to the SDP's cheese and wine soirée was looking less likely by the day.

Scargill knew he might not win a national strike ballot of miners, and so the miners' greatest ever national strike was in fact

---

* These were ostensibly introduced as a response to the riots in Brixton and Toxteth, but forces which had not experienced any serious rioting were also equipped. Mind you, things can get pretty hairy in the Isle of Wight when Shanklin play Ventnor at carpet bowls.

just a collection of local disputes, all ratified by the union executive invoking Rule 26, Paragraph c (as you will remember from when you chose the NUM Constitution for the book club). 'King Arthur', as the tabloids dubbed him, declared that no man had a right to vote another out of a job, and that not a single miner should be laid off on the grounds of a pit being uneconomic or exhausted. This allowed Mrs Thatcher to point out that he was therefore in favour of keeping miners in work to dig for mud. And digging mud was the preserve of the government's various job-creation schemes.

Coal not dole (if there's like, you know, a choice)

Within a month, over 80 per cent of miners were on strike. Not, it should be pointed out, for higher wages or shorter hours, but in defence of their fellow miners' jobs; which was to make the enormous sacrifices of the coming year all the more heroic. But in the traditionally less militant areas such as Nottinghamshire and Leicestershire that did hold a ballot, a significant majority voted against strike action, with the result that around 50,000 miners kept working. Flying pickets were sent to try and close these coalfields down and thousands of police were about to discover that 1984 would be the year of unlimited overtime and paying off the mortgage.*

By the summer the miners' families were enduring real hardship, as food parcels arrived from fellow trade unionists across Europe, and the Labour Party grassroots organized cash collections and food convoys. Constituency parties were twinned with collieries and friendships were formed across regional and

---

* There were just under 10,000 arrests during the year-long strike, with an average of 3,000 extra officers being deployed each day.

class barriers. Even gay support groups taught the miners a thing or two (about tolerance and uniting to fight oppression, I mean; they didn't teach the burly miners anything beyond that). The miners' wives formed support groups and became empowered and politicized in a way that meant their lives would never be the same again, whatever the outcome. And Arthur Scargill may have sounded like a paranoid Marxist, but then a Marxist analysis of the behaviour of the establishment and the agents of the 'ruling class' would not have looked that outlandish as the strike progressed. Volunteers shaking buckets for the miners in provincial high streets were randomly arrested by police officers. Phones were tapped, judges invariably sided with the government, and the media (including the BBC) distorted the stories to such an extent that it strayed into the realm of deception. The narrative of the picket-line violence was too unpalatable to be served up as it actually happened, and so when the television news broadcast the shocking scenes from Orgreave and other flashpoints, the order of events was helpfully reversed. Miners throwing punches or chucking rocks was shown as justifying the shocking police violence, when in fact the anger of the strikers had been in response to unprovoked police charges.

In another England Torvill and Dean may have skated to a dramatic Olympic gold in 1984, but that was not the most powerful image of Britain that was beamed around the world that year. The ice-skating triumph was overshadowed by Britain's gold medal in the Freestyle Picket-line Violence event, in which the British team scored a perfect 6.0 from every single judge. To the gentle opening strains of Ravel's 'Bolero', massed ranks of police in riot gear lined the entrance to the Orgreave coke works in preparation for the elaborate dance-off against the flying pickets, who stepped forward in perfect formation towards the truncheons that were now beating on the riot shields in time to the music. Tum-ta-ta-ta-tum-tum, tum-ta-ta-ta-tum-tum, went the pulsating beat of 'Bolero', as the rumbling approach of the lorry convoy cranked up the tension. Mounted policemen take up position, a thousand strikers push against the police lines and then the lorries rumble past, wire mesh on their windscreens, a striker breaks through but is wrestled to the ground, a helmet on the floor, a kick to a head, tum-ta-ta-ta-tum-tum. 'Bolero' reaches its dramatic climax and now millions of TV viewers gasp as the truncheons rain down on strikers in T-shirts and jeans, blood pouring from heads, bodies dragged into waiting vans, half bricks flying through the air, a policeman bleeding from his forehead, tum-ta-ta-ta-tum-tum, and the mounted police gallop across the field raining truncheon blows onto the heads of fleeing miners, but the lorries are through, the missiles fall short as teeth are knocked from the mouth of a striker in the back of a police van, boots, fists, truncheons; the choreography is impeccable and in the dramatic finale the miner lies prostrate on the floor as if unconscious – the music stops and it's over. 'Oh that is magnificent!' exclaims the commentator, 'that is magnificent!' to the orgasmic applause of the crowd.

The drift back to work

The intellectual argument was that the government could not justify keeping open 'uneconomic' pits. But overall it cost Great Britain plc more to pay ex-miners unemployment benefit and then import coal from the oppressive regimes of Poland and South Africa. The arguments went back and forth, but the lights stayed on even as winter set in. News crews drove up to the pit villages to ponder what sort of Christmas the miners' little children would have. 'Do you wish your daddy would go back to work?' said one particularly impartial TV reporter. In January 1985 the Energy Secretary Peter Walker announced that there would be no power cuts that winter, and the miners' demoralization sank to a new low. Many of them had sold pretty well everything they owned to keep going, getting into serious debt and irrevocably falling out with family members who had broken the strike. Lives were lost on both sides, including three children of striking miners crushed by a collapsing slag heap as they scavenged for tiny lumps of coal.

But after a whole year on strike, more miners were now working than not, and a divided NUM executive reluctantly voted for a return to work. Miners across the country marched back with as much dignity as they could muster behind banners and brass bands as if to emphasize a way of life and sense of community that was about to disappear for ever. In 1985 there were 170 pits across the country. A decade later there were fewer than fifty, and even the miners of the East Midlands who had worked through the strike and formed a breakaway union were to discover that the promises of job security made to them were meaningless. Cortonwood, the colliery that triggered the strike, is today the 'Cortonwood retail and leisure park' complete with McDonald's, Argos, Matalan and Asda. Whether the closure of Cortonwood Pizza Hut would precipitate a heroic national strike to protect the jobs of pizza delivery drivers remains to be seen.

Apart from that, Mrs Thatcher, how was your stay?

For Mrs Thatcher the experiences of 1984 seemed to raise her to an even greater level of indestructibility. On 12 October at 2.45 a.m. she had just been putting the finishing touches to her party conference speech when an IRA bomb ripped through the Grand Hotel in Brighton. The bathroom she had been in two minutes earlier was completely wrecked. It was the closest anyone had come to assassinating a Prime Minister in modern times, and a major embarrassment for the security services. Who knows what will be revealed when the official papers are released thirty years after the Brighton bomb. One bit of correspondence from the Grand Hotel has already been removed: *Dear Mrs Thatcher, Thank you for your letter and under the circumstances we accept that your request for a refund is a reasonable one. However, after the search of your bomb-damaged room we were still unable to locate two towels and a hotel ashtray and wonder if by chance you might have accidentally packed . . .*

Despite the rude interruption, an unscathed Mrs Thatcher saw the importance of starting the conference bang on time, and she strode up to the platform at 9.30 the next morning with not one hair out of place as if nothing whatsoever had happened. Most of her cabinet were there, kitted out in new suits that had been provided by the local Marks & Spencer. But a Tory MP had been killed, as had the wife of the chief whip John Wakeham. The television news had shown images of her Industry Secretary Norman Tebbit in his pyjamas being carried out on a stretcher. His wife was permanently disabled and he was never quite so combative again.

An IRA statement declared, 'Today we were unlucky, but remember we only have to be lucky once.' In fact, Mrs Thatcher was extremely lucky all through her premiership. Lucky to have survived the Brighton bomb. Lucky in the Falklands that so many Argentine missiles failed to detonate. Lucky that Ronald Reagan was in power and prepared to allow Britain to pursue a war in the Americas, lucky that Arthur Scargill was such a disastrous leader of the miners, lucky that her period of office saw the opposition collapse, lucky that North Sea oil began to flow ashore in vast amounts just as the government received a huge social security bill for the three million unemployed.

Napoleon always said he wanted lucky generals, that he could teach them everything else. On this basis Maggie Thatcher would have replaced him as French Emperor and invaded Russia during the first ever January heatwave.

The newly elected Labour leader Neil Kinnock may have been the son of a miner, but for him the miners' strike had been a whole year lost. His huge task of setting Labour back on the road to becoming a creditable alternative government had been put on hold for a month while he worked out the facial expression he would adopt when he finally stood on a miners' picket line. Labour had not only suffered a catastrophic election result in 1983, virtually wiping it out in the south of England, but also the rump of two hundred MPs that remained were divided and in thrall to their constituency parties, some of whom had been taken over by far-left entryists. After a landmark conference speech in 1985, Neil Kinnock began the process of expelling members who were believed to be Trotskyist, although putting an ice-pick in their head was judged to be outside party rules.

It wasn't always so easy to tell which Labour members were also members of Militant. Just because they were standing outside the meeting beforehand trying to sell a newspaper called *Militant*, you can't necessarily infer anything from that. There had been a strong body of opinion within the Labour Party that Militant should be defeated not by expulsion and party rule books, but by debate and persuasion. The trouble was that the prospect of an evening at a Labour Party ward meeting arguing politics with half a dozen Militants, who denounced you as a *fascist-Tory-fascist* if you even questioned the logistics of reinstating all sacked miners at non-existent pits, did not sound very enticing when *Back to the Future* was on at the Odeon and the curry house was doing all-you-could-eat for a fiver. And so nearly a decade later than it should have done, Labour began to deal with the entryists on a constitutional basis. Those on the far left called it a 'witch-hunt', just because the National Executive Committee threw the Militants into a pond to see if they would float, and then put them in a ducking stool before burning them in front of a mob of angry villagers. David Owen later admitted that the day Neil Kinnock took on Militant was the day he realized that his new centre party had no future.

Don't tell Sid . . .

Labour was perceived as old-fashioned and northern, the party of flat-capped pigeon fanciers who drank brown ale and read the *Daily Mirror* on the outside toilet. And so when British Gas shares were advertised with the strapline 'Don't tell Sid', it was almost as if there was one section of stubborn old working-class blokes who were deliberately being excluded from this modern-day gold rush.

The sell-off of British Gas raised a record £5.4 billion and was massively oversubscribed, adding credence to accusations that the huge advertising campaign was politically rather than commercially motivated. During the 1980s the proportion of the population owning shares increased from 7 per cent to 29 per cent, and more significantly almost a million former public-sector workers now found themselves employed in the private sector. It didn't just raise billions of pounds; it was a central part of the government's ideological mission of 'popular capitalism'.* Privatizations during the Conservatives' first term had been minimal. Investors might have been nervous of buying a company when Labour activists talked of 'the next Labour government renationalizing without compensation'. But now that 'next Labour government' looked like it might be a couple of millennia away, the coast was suddenly clear. As the date for British Gas share applications came closer, the slogan was updated: 'If you see

* The original phrase 'people's capitalism' had been rejected by Margaret Thatcher because it sounded like something from an East German collective.

Sid, tell him.' Now everyone was invited to be part of the big cash give-away that had already proved so lucrative for all the people who had bought (and quickly sold) shares in British Telecom and BP. Everything from British Airways to the Central Electricity Generating Board was sold off below its real value, so that the scheme remained visibly popular and the grateful voters could pocket a quick few hundred quid when they sold the shares on to some foreign bank that would now be in control of the UK's infrastructure. The Chancellor asserted that anything that was owned or funded by the state would be sold off unless an unanswerable case could be made for it remaining in the public sector, which must have made the royal family and the Church of England a bit nervous.

Privatization was a brilliant scam; it's amazing that the shady gang involved were never featured on the BBC's popular new detective show, *Crimewatch UK*. 'Police are keen to talk to anybody who may have witnessed an elaborate fraud which they believe has been perpetrated right across the country. Many of its victims may still be unaware that their property has been taken away right from under their nose. Some may have even been persuaded to buy their own property back!' And then they showed a photo-fit photo of Nigel Lawson and had the audacity to say, 'Don't have nightmares . . .'

Give us your fookin' money

Although millions succumbed to this offer of free money from the government, or voted to have their building society convert to a bank so they'd get a large unearned cheque in the post, it didn't mean that everyone had somehow performed a reverse Ebenezer Scrooge, turning from selfless do-gooders into miserly money-grabbers overnight. In 1984 a famine in Ethiopia prompted former Boomtown Rats frontman Bob Geldof to organize a charity record featuring most of the best-known singers of the day, which became the best-selling British single to date. 'Do They Know It's Christmas?', with its less well-known B–side, 'No, Because Ethiopia Is A Muslim Country', tapped into an enormous well of charitable sentiment and the desire to do something, even if it was just buying a popular single. It was followed up with Live Aid, a huge concert at Wembley Stadium, on the same day as a similar event in Philadelphia. All the great French rock stars offered to play at an equivalent event in Paris, so no event was organized there. It was an incredible achievement for Bob Geldof (whose first single had been called 'Looking After Number 1'). He cajoled previously apathetic rock stars and even pressurized the government into donating the VAT raised on the original record to famine relief. The synchronized concerts across two continents in response to a tragedy in a third prompted commentators to judge that we now lived in a 'global village' and David Bowie wondered if world famine could be ended by doing events like this every year. And the answer was no. But Band Aid was a remarkable achievement, all the more so for the supposedly mean times from which it emerged, even if it did set a pattern for increasingly contrived fundraising singles down the years that ultimately caused more pain than the tragedy they were raising money for.

Here comes the chopper . . .

As she approached the middle of her second term, Mrs Thatcher seemed unassailable. She had defeated Galtieri and Scargill, she had a massive parliamentary majority and her eye operation had been a complete success; she was now completely unable to see other people's points of view. Then from nowhere came a crisis that for a moment looked like it might see her toppled from power.

A British helicopter manufacturer was in financial trouble and in need of a rescue bid. There were two options on the table. Mrs Thatcher (and to be fair, the board of Westland) favoured an American company; the Defence Secretary, Michael Heseltine, thought the government should back a European consortium. On a grand geo-political level, the Westland crisis was about the fundamental direction of Great Britain's strategic alliances: were we to become an American client state or an integral part of an ever closer European Union? But in fact the Westland crisis wasn't about that at all: it was about the more traditional matter of two politicians who hated each other's guts. Thatcher feared the popular and ambitious Michael Heseltine, and he could no longer abide being bullied by the increasingly presidential Prime Minister. She encouraged her Trade Secretary Leon Brittan to brief against Heseltine. When she declared in cabinet that all his department's press statements on Westland would have to go through the cabinet office, Heseltine stood up, gathered his papers and declared, 'In which case I can no longer be part of this cabinet,' and walked out to give an impromptu resignation announcement to a rather surprised journalist who'd been hanging around outside Downing Street.

Heseltine had always had the air of a man who intended to succeed Mrs Thatcher. Julian Critchley MP, a university contemporary, recalled how they had once written down their lifetime's ambitions on the back of a menu, and that Heseltine's carefully worked-out plan culminated in him becoming Prime Minister in the 1990s. It was said of Heseltine's barnstorming conference speeches that he could always 'find the clitoris of the Conservative Party'. Thatcher had been determined to rein in her most serious rival whatever the means. Both the Defence Minister and the Prime Minister had authorized leaks against one another – which of course they both denied. But Downing Street's account of who leaked what and when did not stand up to detailed examination. The Westland crisis wasn't the first time Mrs Thatcher had been caught lying. But on previous occasions the intricate details had been drowned out by the noise of battles in the South Atlantic or the coalfields. For a day in January 1986 it looked like she might be forced out. 'I'm afraid this is a resignation issue . . .' she said to her closest advisors and ministers, and they were all shocked at what this meant. 'So off you go, Brittan. No, on the bus, you don't have a car any more . . .' In the end the media gods were appeased with the sacrifice of her Trade and Industry Secretary. But the whole episode had exposed the ugly face of politics. Well, Leon Brittan's face to be precise.

Win it three times and it's yours to keep

'The next move forward' was the Conservatives' election slogan for 1987, which the lefty cartoonists all changed to 'The Next Moves For War'. Despite the growing concerns about Mrs Thatcher's leadership style, the government were in confident mood as they approached polling day. There had been some elections the Conservatives had persisted in losing, such as those for the Greater London Council and other metropolitan boroughs, but Mrs Thatcher solved that problem by simply abolishing the authorities. County Hall, the home of London local government since 1888, was sold off and turned into a luxury hotel, while its basement was converted into an aquarium and filled with sharks in order to assist satirical commentators trying to write a searing piece about property speculators and the death of local democracy.

After the results were in everyone was agreed that Labour had run an excellent campaign. A stirring film with Neil Kinnock on the clifftops had been directed by *Chariots of Fire* director Hugh Hudson. Labour's new red rose symbol adorned professional-looking leaflets and posters. Left-leaning musicians such as Billy Bragg and Paul Weller had toured marginal constituencies under the banner 'Red Wedge', encouraging young people to vote Labour. All in all, the Labour Party could feel pretty pleased with the way the whole campaign had been organized. Admittedly there had been the minor matter of being completely trounced at the polls for the third time in succession, but some people will always find something negative to say.

Mrs Thatcher had returned with another huge majority, and became the first Prime Minister to win three elections in a row since Lord Liverpool in the 1820s. Despite a net loss of around twenty MPs, the Tories actually gained a handful of seats in London and the South, as the country became increasingly polarized politically and philosophically. It had once been believed that no government could win an election while there were three million unemployed. But Mrs Thatcher won two majorities of over a hundred by appealing to the self-interest of enough people in the south of England to make the fate of those who felt the consequences of her policies completely irrelevant. To be fair, she seemed to have noticed that there were some areas that didn't seem to be enjoying the benefits of the fastest-growing economy in Europe, and declared that something had to be done about Britain's inner cities. She dashed to Teesside and met just one unemployed man, who showed her a thousand job rejection letters. She told him he should retrain, which was helpful. She was photographed standing in the middle of an expanse of flattened industrial waste ground. The next day one cartoonist redrew the image under the caption 'If you seek a monument, gaze around.'*

---

* This is the inscription on the memorial to Sir Christopher Wren inside St Paul's Cathedral, although the original was in Latin so that most of us read it, nodded meaningfully, and hoped that onlookers couldn't tell that we didn't have the faintest idea what it meant.

Greed is good*

If the millions of people who found themselves significantly worse off during the 1980s were wondering where all the money had gone, they could have done worse than toured the sprouting towers of Docklands and the City of London. The importance of the City as a global financial trading centre had developed well out of proportion to Britain's economic status, and huge fortunes were now being made by braying yuppies, which didn't prompt any resentment at all.

The government had abolished exchange controls almost immediately on taking office, and in 1986 the so-called 'Big Bang' further deregulated the City, widening the choice of loud ties, gaudy jackets and big red braces for all the podgy rugger buggers ambitious to have their first heart attack before they were forty. Screaming into several phones at once was now positively encouraged and the traditional stockbrokers from Surrey were shocked that a new breed of trader had arrived in the City. For one group in society, the ostentatious display of wealth became culturally acceptable in a way that would have been seen as incredibly vulgar in previous decades (and, in fact, still was incredibly vulgar to nearly everyone else). Harry Enfield struck a chord with an avaricious working-class character initially called the Plasterer but immediately rechristened by his catchphrase 'Loadsamoney!' Nigel Lawson's 1988 budget was pretty much in the spirit of this satirical take on the age of greed. 'What are we going to give the rich? Loadsamoney! Bish, bash, bosh, giveaway budget; tax rebate, cut top rate, flash the cash, loadsamoney!'

Flaunting your wealth became acceptable in the 1980s. The lavish lifestyles of the super-rich were chronicled in soap operas

* 'Greed is good' was the essence of a speech given by the 1980s icon Gordon Gecko in the film *Wall Street*, although rather disappointingly he never actually says those exact three words.

such as *Dallas* and *Dynasty*. There were stories in the City of London of young traders playing a game in which whoever came to the wine bar with the least cash in their pockets had to foot the bill for the entire evening, with the result that fat wallets containing tens of thousands of pounds were being waved about by drunken yuppies in the watering holes of EC1. For this, the firemen of the Blitz had saved the City of London.

Although British traders made money as individuals, the main beneficiaries of the booming City of London were foreign banks, particularly American ones. An analogy was made between the City and the Wimbledon lawn tennis championship. Both British institutions were world leaders, but neither saw much success for British participants. But at least Sue Barker wasn't deregulated, asset-stripped and sold off to Japanese bond traders.

Mrs Thatcher's Methodist father would surely not have approved of the way his daughter ushered in the money-lenders bashing on the doors of the temple. The British population was suddenly bombarded with invitations to get into debt. Once upon a time, the bank or building society might have offered grudging terms for a modest loan, but now mailshots by everyone from Marks & Spencer to the Automobile Association were fighting to lend you money; you were lucky if you got a birthday card from Grandma and it didn't include a glossy leaflet offering you the chance to get the exclusive 'Grandma Credit Card'.

And then in one rather confusing week it all came tumbling down. A stock-market crash happened at exactly the same time as the worst hurricane in hundreds of years, and old people struggled to understand how a collapse in the financial markets had resulted in all the trees falling over in Kew Gardens. Share prices went crash, the trees went crash; the Porsche had to be sold but it had just been crushed by a falling plane tree anyway. Would Bob Geldof do another charity appeal for all the yuppies who had nothing left but a fat Filofax and unpayable mortgage on an executive flat in Docklands? Frankly, no.

Who would have possibly thought it? A huge consumer boom built on borrowing and people selling each other money turned out to be unsustainable. 'Well, we've definitely learnt our lesson,' said all the financiers. 'We won't be letting greed get the better of our financial judgement again.'

Look, no safety net!

The government had a vague formula for how they saw British society working, but for the first time there was a whole group of people completely left out of the equation. The destruction of Britain's manufacturing industry had left millions of people un-employed and fearing that they might never work again. Convinced that many of the long-term unemployed must be work-shy, the government made it increasingly difficult for the jobless to claim unemployment benefit. In the mid-1980s, charities placed frank and undramatic advertisements on bus shelters and tube stations explaining that if the government's latest benefit changes were put in place, then some people would be forced to sleep on the streets. And sure enough, soon there were people lying in subways or huddled in doorways, failing to keep warm under bits of cardboard that had originally packaged some luxury gadget purchased in the contrived consumer boom. It happened almost overnight, something that British people had only witnessed on holidays to the third world; suddenly people were begging in the streets of England for cash. Well-meaning liberals were so appalled that their fellow citizens had been reduced to this that they gave generously, a pound coin maybe, sometimes two. And then a couple of years later the homeless were still there and they pretended not to see or hear them as they walked straight past.

Apart from the danger of falling trees or stock markets, there was a whole series of disasters in the late 1980s which collectively gave the impression that Britain's infrastructure was suffering from under-investment and that corners had been cut with safety. Preventable tragedies such as the Piper Alpha oil disaster, the King's Cross fire, the Zeebrugge ferry sinking and the Clapham rail crash took hundreds of lives and were generally followed up with footage of the Prime Minister visiting survivors in hospital. As if they hadn't suffered enough. Satirical opponents of the government distributed the 'Thatchcard', which looked much like the kidney donor card but said that, in the event of an accident, 'I do not wish to be visited in hospital by the Prime Minister'.

Another subtler disaster was befalling homosexual men, as the disease known as AIDS was finally identified as posing a serious public-health threat. In 1987 the government launched a publicity campaign declaring 'Don't die of ignorance', urging the use of condoms and informing intravenous drug users of the dangers of sharing needles. There were many in the government who would have preferred a more moralizing campaign advocating sexual abstinence or monogamy, but they were advised that this would simply fail. Although heterosexual partners were also at risk of contracting this lethal new virus, the most vulnerable groups were those on the outside of traditional family units, causing one police chief constable to comment that AIDS victims were 'swirling in a cesspit of their own making', which was helpful of him. Homosexuality had been legal for barely two decades when gay men had this calamity befall them. There was a discernible homophobic backlash and in this atmosphere the government rushed through an amendment to the Local Government Act of 1988 declaring that homosexuality could not be 'promoted' as anything other than abnormal in schools. The infamous 'Clause 28' effectively instructed teachers that if they were to mention homosexuality in schools they had to say it was abnormal. The suggestion seemed to be that children might be exposed to the concept of homosexuality and decide to convert. Just one reading from the works of Oscar Wilde and the morning assembly would spontaneously abandon hymns as the kids burst into 'YMCA' by Village People.

'Another brick in the wall'

Mrs Thatcher had previously served as an Education Minister when she was famously dubbed the 'milk snatcher' after she cut the funding of free school milk. But under her government it actually became illegal for schools to choose to spend their own money on a mid-morning drink of milk, and so some inner-city head teachers went out and bought fruit or bread just so the most deprived kids had something in their stomachs before lessons. In 1988 her government finally got round to addressing what was perceived as the problem of the nation's schools and universities, introducing the Great Education Reform Bill, known as GERBIL for short. Ministers who hadn't been listening at the beginning sat there for hours wondering why the idea of the school getting a gerbil had gone all the way up to cabinet level.

The 1988 bill was arguably the most significant education act since Rab Butler's landmark 1944 bill. It introduced school league tables, which helpfully pointed out that pupils at schools in Surrey were achieving at a much higher level than those in Hackney, so the Surrey teachers must clearly be doing a much better job. The theory was that parents would then all choose the high-performing primary school full of middle-class kids learning the French for 'I'd like to buy a villa in Provence, please'. Meanwhile the bad school where the kids' reading was well below standard just because the kids didn't speak English would have to buck its ideas up or close. Making the comparison was enabled by the introduction of a national curriculum that would standardize what children learnt across the whole country. Mrs Thatcher took a keen interest in what should be taught, particularly in history, where she favoured listing the Kings and Queens of England, even if she was surprised not to see herself included at the end. 'Key stages' were introduced and soon afterwards 'SATS' exams would measure how good children were at being crammed for their SATS exams.

None of these reforms would apply to private schools, where pretty well the entire cabinet had been educated and where they all sent their own children. In fact, their understanding of how ordinary schools functioned seemed to be based mainly on reading *The Bash Street Kids* in the *Beano*. As far as ministers could ascertain, 'Teacher' failed to keep discipline in the classroom, and there was no evidence of lesson plans or differentiated learning with the result that pupils such as Plug and Smiffy were held down a year for three decades in a row. Bash Street School was later put into special measures after failing its Ofsted and reopened as a City Technology College specializing in business studies and maths.

'The NHS is safe in our hands' (especially this one with the fingers crossed)

The central idea of the Education Act was that 'money would follow the customer'; the customers in this case being the pupils, although few of them tried taking their teachers back to the staff room to exchange them for a different model. The attempt was also made to apply the same market principle to the National Health Service, which had looked increasingly vulnerable throughout the Thatcher years. 'The NHS is safe in our hands,' she had declared a few years into her premiership, which made everyone think, 'Oh no, she's going to abolish the NHS.' Like schools, hospitals had suffered from serious under-funding and staff were demoralized and overworked. Government ministers said that you couldn't just throw money at these problems. Problems like shortage of money. Then in January 1988 Mrs Thatcher used an appearance on *Panorama* to announce a 'fundamental review' of the Health Service. The NHS was a black hole, said Mrs Thatcher, constantly sucking in money and resources. There seemed to be no limit to what it could absorb, it had suffered a stellar gravitational collapse and its escape velocity exceeded the speed of light; frankly, the 'black hole' metaphor got rather out of hand.

The ensuing review seriously considered the abolition of a free health service but kept coming up against the political un-popularity of such a move. The government was determined to introduce the rigours of the free market into this state-run monopoly, even though it was transparent that the idea of customer choice and competition didn't really apply to a man in the back of an ambulance who had just suffered a major heart attack. 'Thank you for travelling with Virgin Ambulances today; please help yourself to a complimentary newspaper, fresh coffee and croissants. We'll be along later to ask which Accident and Emergency Department you have chosen from the brochures.'

Instead the idea of an internal market was introduced, which attempted to split purchaser from provider, making hospitals compete for patients on the basis of efficiency and cost. The BBC's gritty new hospital drama *Casualty* suddenly took on a whole new feel. Now when the ambulance pulled into Holby City hospital, the patient was greeted by a crack team of highly qualified accountants: 'Quick, get him into the finance depart-ment, fast. We need a double-entry cash accounting flexible interest buy-back. Fetch my calculator and invoice pads, we're going to need Geoff from auditing and fast!'

Like the grant-maintained schools that were being allowed to opt out of local authority control, hospitals could choose to become self-governing. These would be quasi-independent units operating under the NHS franchise; a sort of 'medical McDonald's'. Instead of getting burgers and fries to go, you could have a health service to go. 'Hmmm,' contemplated Mrs Thatcher, '"Health Service to go." Yes, I like that; it has a certain ring to it . . .'

Rolling back the frontiers of the state

The fundamental dichotomy of the Thatcher government is that her personal philosophy centred around 'rolling back the frontiers of the state', and yet every time she allowed people a measure of independence or political freedom, they didn't do what Mrs Thatcher wanted them to. Because of this, power became dramatically more centralized during the decade, as executive control passed from elected authorities to quangos packed with retired Tory members and compliant government appointees. An astonishing average of ten Acts of Parliament a year were passed during this period to curb the powers of local government. 'Rate-capping' limited what councils could raise; 'competitive tendering' forced them to put council services out to private contractors, irrespective of whether the local electorate had voted for it. If Thatcher had stayed in power any longer, local councillors would have been banned from being left-handed or having beards.*

Although voters could not bring themselves to elect a Labour government, they felt so full of self-loathing for choosing Margaret Thatcher that they regularly assuaged their guilt by

---

* Mrs Thatcher once said she would never have a bearded man in her cabinet, which seems fair.

supporting Labour at a local level in between times. The authorities that she hadn't got round to abolishing then proceeded to annoy her immensely as she learned in the *Daily Mail* about them funding lesbian direct-action training workshops and fact-finding jollies to Cuba.

But only property owners were paying directly for local government (even if most of a council's budget came directly from the Treasury). What if the cost of local government was shared equally among all local residents? That might stop them voting for expensive socialist policies like putting rubber matting under the swings. Thus was conceived a radical replacement for the rates. Various names were toyed with, such as the 'residents' charge' and the 'services charge', before they settled on the 'community charge'. 'It doesn't matter anyway, because every-one's going to call it the poll tax.'

'It's a funny old world'

The rope that hanged Mrs Thatcher had many interweaving strands. She had often willingly put the noose over her own head. Perversely, she had been turned on by the danger and the sensation of intense pressure; the risk she subjected her own political life to was a form of auto-erotic asphyxiation. But now the thickening threads of Europe, the poll tax, economic policy, her own personal style and hubris tightened around her, putting her in far greater danger than she could possibly realize.

After a record third successive election victory, there seemed no reason why, as she had once said, she would not go 'on and on and on' (at which point the switchboard at the Samaritans had begun emitting smoke and then exploded). But to those on the inside the tensions were already apparent. Before his famous tax-cutting budget of 1988 she had seriously fallen out with the man she had called 'my brilliant chancellor', who was that most dangerous of senior ministers: a man who no longer minded if he left politics. The issue had been Britain's membership of the European exchange rate mechanism (ERM), which both Lawson at the Treasury and Howe at the Foreign Office were adamant was vital to Britain's national interest. For a woman whose mind was locked in a time when nations around the world had based their economies on the value of sterling, the idea of Britain following Germany (of all countries) had her scrambling the bombers and flying across the channel to the theme from the Dam Busters. But little did she know it was already happening. Lawson had secretly pursued a policy of having the pound track the deutschmark, which he had absentmindedly forgotten to mention to her, the five hundred times they had met over the past few years. Every time an interest rate was raised or lowered, every time the currency was bought or sold, it was all designed to keep the pound at D2.90, but the First Lord of the Treasury had no idea about this policy what-soever, even when it was perfectly clear to every financial journalist and City analyst what was going on. He would have gone round to tell her but 10 Downing Street was a bit of a schlep from Number 11. And then there was that other consideration that she would have gone mental. Lawson rather proudly recalls that she finally learned of it when she read it in the paper.

Relationships with her long-suffering Foreign Secretary were also about to get a lot worse. Some bright spark at the Foreign Office wondered if it was time for Mrs Thatcher to make a land-mark speech signalling Britain's passionate commitment to be at the heart of Europe. 'You've not met Mrs Thatcher then?' said the bloke on the desk opposite. But to everyone's surprise, Downing Street accepted the invitation to speak at Bruges. Even better, Downing Street said they would like to write the speech themselves, so keen, it seemed, was the Prime Minister to express her enthusiasm in her own words. Her landmark address to the Europeans was scheduled for September 1988.

The Belgians had had their fill of English football hooligans over the previous decade, but this one looked strangely familiar. Wrapped in a union flag, and in a bulldog T-shirt captioned 'Brits on the Piss!', the British Prime Minister chanted 'Two world wars and one world cup!' as she threw empty lager bottles in the direction of the riot police. 'Ing-ger-land! Ing-ger-land!' she continued, while the officials from the Foreign Office feverishly scanned the pre-agreed text. 'Oh, you'd all be speaking German but for us! Yes, you'd all be speaking German but for us!' and then she threw a café chair in the direction of the water cannon and exposed the bulldog tattoo on her chest, which quickly had the Belgian police running in the opposite direction.

The Bruges speech was met with horrified disbelief across Europe and utter despair by her Foreign Secretary. She had made enemies of her two most senior cabinet colleagues, and now they resolved to force her hand over the ERM. Unless a date was set for Britain to join, they would resign. Mrs Thatcher was not used to being bullied, but had no choice but to agree.

As she passed the tenth anniversary of her accession to power, another ten years looked increasingly unlikely. The following month Labour won its first national election for fifteen years, as millions of people decided that the key issue when electing a member of the European Parliament was to express their extreme dislike of Mrs Thatcher. Those close to her increasingly found her impossible to deal with; Chris Patten privately wondered if she had actually gone mad. She defended the use of the royal 'we' by claiming that she used the plural to denote the whole cabinet, an argument that rather fell apart when she emerged from Downing Street and announced to journalists, 'We are a grandmother.'

In July 1989 she took her revenge on Sir Geoffrey Howe, demoting him from the Foreign Office. He successfully haggled for the title 'Deputy Prime Minister', an honour that was rather spoiled the following day by Downing Street saying it was a meaningless post. 'It's just a courtesy title,' went the briefing, skilfully using the concept of courtesy to be as insulting as possible. Nigel Lawson resigned in acrimonious circumstances in October, exasperated at Mrs Thatcher's interference in monetary policy, and her employment of a personal financial advisor whose policies were at odds with the Chancellor's. He was replaced at the Treasury by John Major, who had risen apparently without trace, replacing in turn each of the two key figures of her government. Polls continued to show Mrs Thatcher as the most unpopular leader since King Herod, and in December an unknown Tory backbencher challenged her for the leadership in the hope of tempting bigger guns to emerge in a second round. Sixty Tory MPs voted for the challenger, abstained or spoilt their ballot papers – revealing that Thatcher did not have the support of one-sixth of the parliamentary party.

Can pay, won't pay! (Until I get a second reminder)

But more than anything else, the fall of Thatcher was about the highest principle of all: money. The community charge was supposed to relieve homeowners of the burden of paying the rates, and yet the government had somehow contrived to create a system in which it seemed everyone faced the prospect of higher bills. In Middle England Mrs Thatcher's natural supporters had to completely rethink their finances; there would have to be less money spent on porcelain figurines, the net curtains would only be washed once a fortnight. The 'community charge' (as nobody called it) was vilified as a fundamentally unjust tax in which a 'duke pays as much as a dustman' and half-remembered comparisons were made to the peasants' revolt under Richard II. 'He brought in a poll tax, and then Wat Tyler made him sign the Magna Carta and, erm, that's how he got his hump before he killed the Princes in The Tower.' The system had already been piloted in Scotland, with millions of people refusing to pay. On April Fool's Day 1990 it was introduced in the rest of the country. Thousands marched through London in protest, and television histories of this period always focus on the drama of the ensuing riot, because the footage of flames in Trafalgar Square and police horses charging protestors wielding scaffolding poles makes such good TV. In fact, it was the little protests around the country that were terrifying Tory backbenchers. Middle England was furious. People were looking skywards and tutting.

Watching all this in the wings was Michael Heseltine, who had spent the previous four years on the 'rubber chicken circuit' speaking to Conservative Associations around the country to remind them what a good Prime Minister he might make. In order to appear loyal he had always maintained that there were 'no foreseeable circumstances' in which he would challenge Margaret Thatcher for the Conservative Party leadership. And then the most unforeseeable event imaginable came to pass: Geoffrey Howe made an exciting speech. After eleven and a half years of being undermined, bullied, humiliated and ignored by his leader he finally snapped and resigned in protest at . . . something, something, she never really got to the end of the letter.

All the big hitters of the previous decade were now against her. Indeed Sir Geoffrey likened her to a cricket captain sending her players to the crease 'only for them to find the moment the first balls are bowled that their bats had been broken before the game by the team captain'. Frankly, it was a rubbish metaphor. You'd have to be pretty useless at cricket not to notice your bat was broken until the first ball was bowled. In any case, you couldn't just break a cricket bat, you'd need power tools and a Black and Decker Workmate. But they faked hysterical laughter anyway; his barely suppressed fury was clear, as a packed House of Commons continued to listen and gasp or wince as Nigel Lawson nodded sagely on his right-hand side. Television cameras had only recently been admitted into the Palace of Westminster, so the dramatic speech was seen by millions in the modern-day public gallery. He ended with a challenge: 'The time has come for others to consider their own response to the tragic conflict of loyalties with which I have myself wrestled for perhaps too long.'

Back in his dressing room after the speech it was high-fives all round: 'Geoff-baby, you was well sick out dere, blud!' 'Slap me some skin, man!' 'She is well dead, blud; she's gone buried, innit?' Michael Heseltine announced his candidacy for the party leadership the following day. In a double turn of the knife he promised a review of the poll tax. By a curious twist of timing Heseltine was untainted by any collective responsibility for the government's most unpopular policy. On the very day he had walked out of cabinet in January 1986, the approval of the community charge had been the next item on the agenda.

'Treachery with a smile on its face'

The self-certainty that had seen her rise to such heights would now be a deciding factor in her catastrophic fall. Overconfidence led her to take little personal involvement in her own campaign, and she refused to make a single call to any potential waverers. Her campaign managers were lacklustre and complacent; Peter Morrison was found asleep in a leather chair in the middle of the afternoon. When he was asked why a certain MP had not been approached he cryptically replied, 'Oh yes he has! But he doesn't know it.' It had been Downing Street that had set the deadline for nominations for the leadership at 20 November, without checking whether Mrs Thatcher would be available that day. In fact, she was booked to go to Paris for a conference, and so while Heseltine was working overtime to maximize his support, she appeared remote and above it all.

She awaited the result dressed for a night at the Paris ballet. When the figures came through, she was just four votes short of avoiding a second ballot.* She confirmed that she would fight on, and then joined the waiting Prime Ministers and Presidents who, unlike her, would still be leading their country in a week's time. Back in London she decided to talk to her cabinet ministers one by one. One or two cried. Others said they wouldn't be voting for her. But none thought she could win the second ballot and defeat her nemesis. 'It was treachery,' she later recalled; 'treachery with a smile on its face.' She decided to sleep on it, but whether she slept at all is not recorded. The next day she announced she would be resigning as Prime Minister. Shame.

'A middle-class hero is something to be'

Among modern commentators it has become fashionable to view the Thatcher years in the same light as the bombing of Libya† and Ronald Reagan's bowel surgery: an unpleasant business but it

---

* There had been a subtle change to Conservative Party rules in 1975. Previously the winner of a leadership election had to get an outright majority plus a margin over the nearest challenger of 15 per cent of all Conservative MPs. In the year she became leader, this was adjusted to 15 per cent of *those who had voted*. Under the old rule she would have won the first ballot outright, and no doubt carried on as Prime Minister, most probably leading the Conservative Party to defeat in the 1992 general election. Without that minor arithmetical adjustment in 1975 there probably would have been no John Major as Prime Minister and no New Labour under Tony Blair.

† In 1986 Mrs Thatcher had permitted Britain to be used as a base for American planes bombing Libya in response to Colonel Gaddafi's alleged sponsorship of terrorists. They were denied permission to fly through French airspace, and then managed to hit the French embassy in Tripoli.

had to be done. That a large dose of a very bitter medicine was the only thing that could possibly cure the sick man of Europe. Oh, and then to throw the sick man down the stairs and kick him in the head a few times for good measure. He'd thank her for it later. But that analysis presumes that it worked. That Britain is a better place for having endured the cathartic experience of mass un-employment; a happier society for having cut adrift an underclass left to fend for itself. It is certainly true that she brought an end to the strikes that had crippled British industry for so long. But as the Roman historian Tacitus would have put it, 'There they make a desert and they call it peace.'

In former centuries history was 'written by the winners'. Now, whether they win or lose, history is written by the middle classes. So just as the late 1940s were deceptively portrayed as a time of austerity, the 1980s have been chronicled as the shake-up that made today's prosperity possible. But of course that is the prosperity of the triumphant middleclasses, for the 1980s was the decade when the class war was finally won. Not everyone in Britain today is sitting around in Starbucks doing spreadsheets on their laptops. Whole swathes of industrial Britain have never recovered from being totally flattened with no plan for what else those places might be for. (Or if there was a plan, one that didn't decide that the first small businesses to move into the derelict mill towns should be the heroin dealers and car-stereo thieves.) Of course the heavy industries would have declined anyway, but that transition could have been managed and considered. The industrial heritage museum was only going to employ so many former steel workers, especially once the booking office was manned by call-centre workers in Bangalore. Today, in the places ravaged by Thatcherism, there are still millions of people reliant on state handouts, areas where a third generation is now entering a culture of dependency.

The 1980s was the first time in modern history when the poor actually got poorer, in absolute as well as in relative terms. The average weekly income of a family at the bottom end of the pay scale fell from £69 to £61. But perhaps more significantly, now it was somehow their fault. The destruction of the trades unions was just part of a wider and quite open hostility to Britain's working class that has continued to this day. Jokes about chavs and men in white vans are the modern descendants of a message that has come down from on high ever since 3 May 1979: 'It is not all right to be working class.' And as millions of ordinary people lost their sense of purpose and cultural identity, Britain became a more fearful, meaner and more divided society after Downing Street itself became a gated community. In hundreds of little ways the difference in British society was perceptible. In 1979 every motorway junction was lined with expectant hitch-hikers confident that they could rely on the kindness of strangers. Ten years later the lay-bys were deserted now that drivers were too frightened to stop. Data from the Institute for Fiscal Studies revealed a steady decline in charitable giving over this period, suicides rose significantly in the 1980s (they eventually started to fall after 1998) while overall recorded crime rose by 78 per cent between 1981 and 1991, eventually falling back in the late 1990s.

Fear for the safety of children was a recurring theme throughout the 1980s; by the end of the decade, it was no longer common practice to let your children go out and play on their own. For centuries parents had got on with their lives while children played together unsupervised in the open air, but in the course of one generation, this was deemed to be too dangerous to contemplate. Venturing outside the security zone of the family home was now only acceptable if a parental chaperone was in attendance, with the result that children exercised and socialized with their peers far less. If it hadn't been for *Emmerdale Farm*, they wouldn't have got any fresh air at all. The generation currently running the country is the very last one to have grown up exploring, discovering and making decisions on their own; so look out for the next cohort of national leaders who'll get into government and then start looking around for their parents to tell them what they're supposed to do.

Not all of these social trends can be laid directly at the door of Mrs Thatcher's government, but more than any other European government she took the spirit of the times, and pushed it further and faster without worrying about the consequences. So Thatcherism worked if the problem was that the already comfortable were being denied the chance to improve their standard of living yet further. But if the purpose of a government and the ambition of a society is to bring greater cohesion, peace and happiness for the greatest number possible – Thatcherism was an utter disaster which would surely take generations to put right.

Some in Westminster have talked about her receiving a state funeral when she dies, which seems a bizarre sort of tribute to someone who believed the state should do as little as possible. It would be far more appropriate to allow competitive bids from private companies to run the funeral arrangements. 'And we now go over live to Westminster, where state leaders are lining up for Lady Thatcher's funeral sponsored by McDonald's. And there we see the coffin respectfully borne on the shoulders of six part-time burger-flippers dressed in the official Ronald McDonald costume, before the private cremation when the body will be flame-grilled with gherkins and a slice of cheese.'

It's what she would have wanted.

6

1990–1997

*How Eastern Europe fell apart, Western Europe came together and
John Major rose to the historic times with a traffic cone hotline*

In 1989, the Berlin Wall was set upon by demonstrators with pick-
axes and coal chisels as Western journalists gushed at the historic
symbolism of it all. 'And as I speak, one young demonstrator has
a sledgehammer, and he is attacking the top of the wall; this is incredible! And, well, he doesn't actually seem to be making much
of a dent in it yet; it is a very solidly built wall, but now he's been
joined by a fellow freedom seeker, and goodness, that one's bent
the end of his pickaxe. I think they may need to come back with
some power tools or something, because this is going to take for
ever. These Western tools are a bit rubbish, quite frankly . . .'

The end of the Cold War should have ushered in a period of
world harmony and economic prosperity as Britain cashed in its
peace dividend, welcomed exchange students from Moscow and
saw its US nuclear bases converted into children's playgrounds or
the Greenham Common Peace Camp Heritage Centre.
Unfortunately things never work out quite as you hope they
might. The Soviet Union may have been a big scary power bloc
with nuclear missiles pointing at the Isle of Wight, but at least you

245

knew where you stood. Eastern Europe was now in flux; its anxious people didn't know where their next two hundred cigarettes were coming from. Would the future see them living on a diet of root vegetables and travelling by horse and cart? These luxuries at last seemed possible.

Regimes fell from Prague to Moscow, and the politics of the whole continent were altered. And although in the United Kingdom the governing party would win one more election victory, there is a direct causal link from the fall of the Berlin Wall to the collapse of the British Conservative Party's economic policy on 16 September 1992, and the subsequent loss of confidence that would keep them out of power for a generation. The protestors might not have made much of a dent in the Berlin Wall, but events in Europe, East and West, would ultimately bring the Conservative house crashing down.

Ground control to Major John

Mrs Thatcher had left Downing Street with great dignity and poise, if you discount the scraped fingernail marks where she'd been dragged down the corridor, and the missing chunks in the doorframe where she had tried to cling on with her teeth. For five days the country was in a strange state of limbo as the tiny electorate of Conservative MPs decided who was to become the next Prime Minister. Once they'd had her heartlessly evicted from Number 10, the Conservative Party experienced a collective pang of guilt and felt compelled to opt for whichever candidate received her backing. Little had changed since Macmillan had advised the Queen to send for his chosen man. Now the outgoing Prime Minister just announced who she wanted to succeed her and that tiny electorate duly voted for him.

Heseltine had been well aware that 'he that bears the dagger rarely wears the crown', and in any case had made too many enemies to be the right leader to heal the wounds of a traumatized Tory Party. His vote dropped back significantly from the number he had received when he had possessed that special 'anyone but Mrs Thatcher' quality. The rank outsider was Douglas Hurd, who in the inverse snobbery that had overtaken the Conservative Party, was apparently disadvantaged by being an old Etonian whose father had been a baron and whose grandfather had been called 'Sir Percy'. He managed a paltry fifty-four votes. By contrast, John Major had lived in a run-down block in Brixton, left school at sixteen with three O levels and then failed to qualify for a job as a bus conductor, which apparently made him the perfect man to inherit the mantle of Churchill, Eden and Macmillan.

When the result of the first ballot came in, Major was significantly ahead (although not enough to win it outright) and the other two candidates withdrew. John Major became Prime Minister without even winning an internal Conservative Party ballot as the rules demanded, gaining the Tory leadership with fewer votes than Margaret Thatcher had received when she lost it. Though of course she would never have been unsporting enough to point this out. No, that must have been someone who just looked like her. With her favoured successor in Downing Street, she now helpfully commented that she was 'a very good backseat driver'.

Glad to be grey

'Well, who'd have thought it?' quipped John Major at the beginning of his first cabinet meeting. And there was a good-natured chuckle around the table, although one or two of the laughs went on slightly too long to be convincing, and Heseltine's turned into a sort of forlorn sobbing. The man who had been nothing more than Chief Secretary to the Treasury in

July 1989 was as surprised as anyone else to find himself Prime Minister less than eighteen months later.

Rather bizarrely, John Major had been excused public appearances during the Thatcher leadership crisis as he was 'having his wisdom teeth out', according to the note from his mum. To cynics everywhere it sounded like a sneaky excuse to get out of having to comment on whether he was after the top job himself. No doubt when secret government papers are released in 2020, we will finally learn that whilst he claimed he was having his wisdom teeth out, he was in fact, well, just having his wisdom teeth out. But Major was certainly a deft political operator, building political friendships across all sections of the party, and earning a reputation for reliability, integrity and hard work, for those who could remember which one he was (which was not very many of them).*

His apparent dullness contrasted with a comically exotic family background; his twice-married father had been a circus performer and music hall artiste who had fallen on hard times. It was joked that John Major was the only man to have run away from the circus to become an accountant. He became a Lambeth councillor in the Conservative landslide of 1968 and after a thrilling, roller-coaster career in banking, was elected to Parliament in 1979. As Mrs Thatcher waved on the steps of Downing Street, the Westminster new boy could have never imagined that he would be next.

---

* Major's preferred form of exercise was walking, but with the Downing Street garden so small, a special arrangement was made so that he could go for private walks in the gardens of Buckingham Palace. Obviously he couldn't go walking in the public parks; people would have recognized him. Eventually.

'Let's deal with Saddam Hussein once and for all'

The new Prime Minister had an immediate international crisis to
deal with involving some tough choices about whether to go along
with what the Americans wanted or go along with what the
Americans wanted. In the summer of 1989, just as the world was
focusing on the dramatic events unfolding in Eastern Europe,
the former British protectorate of Kuwait was coming
under intense pressure from its large neighbour Iraq and its
charming dictator Saddam Hussein. Despite having an
appalling human rights record, Hussein had been supplied with
weapons and support by Western governments who would
take any ally they could get against the even more feared
Iranians.

Oil-rich Kuwait had heavily underwritten Iraq's disastrous war
against Iran, but now was unwilling to go along with Saddam
Hussein's inspired idea that they wrote off his $65 billion debt.
'But it's like, *oh I didn't eat any garlic bread* – why don't we forget
about all the petty who–owes–what-to-who and just call it quits?'
'Because we don't owe you anything, and you owe us $65 billion.
And it's *whom*.' That was the last straw, and on 2 August 1990
Iraq invaded and declared Kuwait the nineteenth province
of Iraq.

The Western powers could not sit back and have this dictator
redraw the borders of the Middle East. The historic nation of
Kuwait dated back many decades, ever since its boundaries had
been set by some Foreign Office chappie with an atlas and a ruler
in the 1920s. President George Bush Snr gathered a coalition that
crucially included many Arab countries and the United Nations
force finally attacked on 16 January 1991. The American forces
gave the liberation of Kuwait the name 'Operation Desert Storm',
while the British forces used the rather less dramatic name of
'Operation Granby', which somehow seems less likely to inspire a

PlayStation game. A few conspiracy theorists had some interesting ideas of their own about why the West was really going to war: 'You know what this war's really about, don't you? It's about *oil*.'

'Oil, that's right, yes it is,' confirmed the American conservative. 'Petro-chemicals are fundamental to our whole way of life; industry, transport and trade depend on the availability of oil – nearly all wars in history have been about trade, this oil war is no different.'

'Er, yeah, but, I reckon it's really all about *oil*!'*

Of the thirty-four countries involved, the United States played by far the biggest role, followed by Saudi Arabia and Britain. An SAS patrol was dropped behind enemy lines to find scud missile launchers or, failing that, maybe a literary agent for the bestselling books they were all planning to write about the operation. Although 40,000 British service personnel were deployed in the Gulf, British casualties were low. Almost as many British soldiers were killed by American friendly fire as they were by the Iraqis.

There was much fate-tempting talk of 'smart bombs' that were supposed to be able to locate their intended targets, but unsurprisingly they often destroyed civilian centres by mistake. But given the original Iraqi aggression, it was a less controversial war than its sequel a decade later. This was the United Nations doing what it was founded to do, legally forcing an invading army back to its own borders. In that sense it was the high point of the new, post-Cold-War world order. With such a broad coalition, America had to stick to the basic war aims of liberating occupied Kuwait, much as they might have wanted to continue to Baghdad and topple Saddam Hussein. Given the human and political cost of going in a second time, George Bush Jnr might have wished his

---

* The Kuwaiti Petroleum Corporation sold fuel at British service stations with the logo 'Q8' (not to be confused with the Spike Milligan sketch show of the same name). The Q8 brand disappeared from British streets in 2004 following a corporate takeover, which fortunately was not by Saddam Hussein.

dad had bypassed the United Nations, involved fewer Arab states and then pressed on for regime change in Iraq. When the Bush dynasty returned to the region over a decade later, Britain would be one of the very few countries still prepared to go along with the Americans when the case for war was so much murkier. Thus it was that the First Gulf War made John Major more popular, while the Second Gulf War would severely damage Tony Blair.

John Major's personal rating soared as the television news featured footage of the new Prime Minister looking relaxed and unassuming as he chatted to British soldiers in the Gulf. Not even his appalling taste in casual wear could prevent him achieving an approval rating higher than Mrs Thatcher had ever managed even in the afterglow of the Falklands. Concerned about the attacks upon Kurds in the north of Iraq, he is credited with persuading his European counterparts of the idea of a no-fly zone in northern Iraq, which was then successfully sold to the Americans. Occasionally, it seemed, Britain could be a bridge *from* Europe *to* America. Aid for the Kurds hiding out in the mountains was dropped by parachute, although one of the crates landed on a refugee and killed him, which has to go down as one of the most unfortunate deaths of the decade.

Taking some of the credit for a swift military victory fighting alongside the Americans would be the easiest part of John Major's premiership. It was international affairs closer to home that would dominate his six and a half years in power and split the Conservative Party down the middle. From here on, the 'friendly fire' would be no accident.

Tunnel vision

Britain had always been psychologically separate from continental Europe, perhaps as a consequence of its geographical isolation.

But in December 1990, England's historic moat was finally breached. The French and British engineers working on the channel tunnel finally met under the seabed, to the astonishment of everyone else who had fully expected the two tunnels to miss each other. Four years later the tunnel was officially opened. The Queen and the President of France were whisked by high-speed rail link across the French countryside and under the English Channel to Ashford International. Then due to essential engineering works they were put on the replacement bus service, which took them as far as the Swanley Hoppa, where Her Majesty was told they were only accepting off-peak tickets purchased with a railcard.

International borders were not just counting for less in terms of new tunnels, breached walls and cheap package flights to Ibiza; capital now flowed effortlessly around the world and multi-nationals rivalled nation states in terms of their gross domestic product. Britain's economic leverage was not just below that of Japan or Germany, corporations such as Procter and Gamble or Unilever were looking alarmingly powerful as well. The day that McDonald's decided to acquire its own army would be the point at which even the SAS might decide that the enemy territory was simply too dangerous. 'Right, men, we're going in; some of us might come out with heart disease and diabetes, but whatever you do don't order a shake or we'll be bogged down there for months.'

The era when Britain or France could hope to independently micro-manage the economic conditions within their own borders was long gone. British sovereignty wasn't surrendered by the politicians; it was chipped away by global capitalism. The European Community was an attempt to have more control over our destiny, not less. In any case, the petty nationalism and local rivalries of Europe were surely a thing of the past. You just had to look at the voting patterns of the Eurovision Song Contest to see that. The problem for the government was that the great posh marquee that was the British Conservative Party had always been held up by the two big tent poles of patriotism and business – and now the two poles were being pulled in opposite directions.

The world turned upside down

Towards the end of the traditional historical drama genre comes the compulsory section where the natural order of things seems to have been turned on its head. 'Good is become bad and godly men wouldst worship the devil,' laments the baron in the unconvincing medieval costume. 'Beggars have become dukes, and dukes beggars!' he continues in an accent that suggests everyone in the olden days spoke with a West Country twang.

So it was as the twentieth century came to a close that the traditional positions of the two main parties seemed to be reversed. It wasn't just the petty matters of class and background: an unqualified nobody from Brixton winning the leadership of the Conservative Party by promising a classless society, while Labour elected a public schoolboy and former barrister. The internecine warfare of Labour was also forgotten as the people's party stole the Tories' secret weapons of loyalty and unity. Now divisions tore apart the Conservatives as, most significantly of all, the two main parties swapped positions on the grand issue of the times: Europe.

Hugh Gaitskell had been firmly against British membership of the Common Market in the 1950s and Labour had gone into the 1983 election with a commitment to withdraw from the EEC. But the European Union became less about simply promoting trade and business and more about a whole range of issues from human rights to safeguards for workers. A Labour Party that had failed to get any form of socialism through the House of Commons began to see another route by which its agenda might be realized.

The President of the European Commission was Jacques Delors, who horrified the Conservatives by turning out to be not just a socialist but French as well. Many Conservatives who had been alarmed about the prospective loss of British sovereignty were now apoplectic about the left-wing ideas that seemed to be gripping Brussels. The prospect was described as 'socialism by the back Delors', which is such a weak pun that it makes you take Delors' side before you've heard the remainder of the arguments. When Delors spoke to the British TUC, he described a vision of improved workers' rights as part of a progressive package far bolder than anything the British trades unions would have dared suggest. Ron Todd, the leader of the Transport and General Workers Union and once a fervent opponent of the Common Market, was so enthusiastic he urged his members to learn a European language!

So it was that many of those on the right were dismayed when John Major announced soon after becoming Prime Minister that he wanted Britain 'to be at the heart of Europe'. Enoch Powell suggested that John Major should have another look at the map. 'Britain is not at the heart of Europe, Germany is.' Many Conservatives were instinctively hostile to the idea of surrendering the symbols of British independence: the dark blue British passport, the pound, the right to shout at foreigners in over-simplistic English. Known as the 'Euro-sceptics', many were in favour of complete withdrawal from the Common Market. Their patriotism took a narrow form; it was hard not to conclude that they would rather see their constituents poorly paid in pounds than well paid in euros.* John Major had seen his predecessor destroyed by the issue of Europe, and now had to navigate with

---

* At this point discussion about a single currency centred around what was called the 'ECU' – the European Currency Unit. There was also talk of the 'EMU', but this acronym was used less as it tended to conjure up images of it attacking Michael Parkinson with Rod Hull's hand up its bottom.

care as he found himself swimming against the tide of greater European integration.

But for some reason, the monumental issue of Britain's future as a nation state failed to grab the attention of the average British voter. The fate of Europe was only a fascinating subject if it involved Spitfires and Nazis, with clearly definable goodies, baddies and a guaranteed satisfactory outcome sorted out nearly half a century earlier. But though modern history was now being made under their noses, the British people seemed to greet the issue of Europe with a collective yawn before switching over to the snooker. People knew that the Maastricht Treaty was probably quite important, but it failed the crucial test of being interesting as well. All that people gleaned from what happened at Maastricht was that John Major seemed to have stood up to the Europeans and managed to get his own way, which surely made him a strong leader. What Major had in fact succeeded in doing was negotiating an opt-out of the so-called Social Chapter so that British workers would not enjoy the same rights as their counterparts on the continent; there would be no minimum wage or guaranteed right to join a union. How the patriots' hearts swelled that Britain had made such a principled stand.

It turned out that John Major did not really want Britain to be at the heart of Europe; he wanted it to be at the appendix of Europe, the toenail of Europe, at most the left testicle of Europe; it's just that that wouldn't have sounded so good in his speeches. But the outcome of the Maastricht negotiations were well spun by the Conservative Party, described as 'game, set and match to Britain'.*

Major was greeted like a returning hero by the Conservative backbenchers and, buoyed up by the positive media coverage in

* A fax with this line was sent to the home of every Conservative Minister before they had even woken up. This was the first time that such a concerted media line had been organized this way.

March 1992, the Prime Minister announced the expected general election.

But for the first time in a generation, the Conservatives approached polling day with real trepidation. The country was deep in recession with over a thousand businesses closing every week; millions were stuck in so-called 'negative equity', in which they found their mortgages were now greater than the value of their homes; the hated poll tax had not yet been replaced, and the Conservative Party's leader seemed to have gone from being an unknown nobody to just a nobody.

Conservatives hold Basildon

The other day upon the stair, I met a man who wasn't there. He wasn't there again today; I think he may be the Prime Minister. John Major chose to capitalize on his ordinariness, standing on a 'soapbox'* in provincial town centres to address everyday passers-by, most of whom seemed to be waving Socialist Workers banners in the background. Obviously he wasn't hoping to reach thirty million voters by standing in market squares; he had judged that this would look better on television than visibly attempting to look good on television in the slick and professional manner employed by the Labour Party. Getting hit by a couple of eggs also added to the air of a Prime Minister who was actually the beleaguered underdog.

A week before the election, three separate polls gave Labour a significant lead over the Conservatives and Labour's euphoria was clearly evident at a rally in Sheffield. Neil Kinnock let his natural exuberance get the better of him, shouting, 'Well all right!' several times like a karaoke Bruce Springsteen, and millions of TV

* The famous 'soapbox' was actually an upturned milk crate. After they had the idea of the soapbox, the Tory election machine discovered that you just can't buy soap in large wooden boxes these days.

viewers cringed all at once. Many serious commentators have since discounted the significance of this episode, insisting that one outburst could not possibly turn a whole election. However, there is no doubt that for many it was a defining moment, crystallizing something they had never liked about Neil Kinnock, and it was the Labour leader, as much as his party, who was targeted by the Conservatives and their supporters. On polling day the *Sun*'s front page declared, 'If Kinnock wins today will the last person to leave the country please turn out the lights?' The *Sun* also helpfully featured a very overweight bare-chested lady on page three, warning that this is what their topless model would look like every day if Labour won the election (which, to be fair, was a central plank of Labour's economic policies).

Polls had narrowed as the election approached but the Conservatives were still expected to lose on 9 April. A BBC exit poll, conducted in the style of a secret ballot, predicted a hung parliament. In fact, the pollsters were to join Labour as the big losers of the election. The difference between the opinion polls and the actual result revealed a deeply conflicted electorate, many of whom felt that they ought to say they were voting Labour, but could not actually bring themselves to do so. Not only did a significant proportion lie to pollsters, many even compensated for voting Conservative in the polling booths by voting Labour in the BBC's secret ballot immediately after – as if that somehow made it fair! The actual result was a tiny 2 per cent swing to Labour, and, against all expectations, a twenty-one-seat majority for the Conservatives. It was a personal triumph for John Major; on a high turnout he had gained more votes than any party leader in history.*

* The population had grown, giving him more actual votes even though he got a smaller share of the poll than Labour and the Conservatives had got in the 1950s. Neil Kinnock got more votes losing the 1992 election than Tony Blair got winning his third victory in 2005.

There was a widespread sense that if Labour could not win in the middle of a recession, it might never win an election again and that Britain had already become a one-party democracy like Japan or the London Borough of Kensington and Chelsea.

A sufficient number of the British it seemed were more interested in their wallets than their society. In 1992, everything, it seemed, was about money. Even the beautiful game was about to be kidnapped by the money men, as the greed and mean-spiritedness of the times took over the national sport.

Football's coming home (if you live in a bank)

The 1980s had been a particularly grim time for English football. English clubs had been banned from Europe following the Heysel disaster in 1985 when Liverpool fans had attacked the supporters of Juventus FC, with the resultant stampede and collapsing wall claiming thirty-five lives. At the 1989 FA Cup semi-final, ninety-six Liverpool fans were killed by the crush at Hillsborough Stadium and the inquiry that followed saw all-seater stadia made compulsory for top-flight clubs, although Justice Taylor killed off Mrs Thatcher's pet scheme of a national identity card scheme for football supporters.

To be interested in football was almost vulgar in some circles; the sport certainly didn't have the widespread popularity and social acceptability it enjoys at nearly all levels today. England's performance at the 1990 World Cup is usually credited with kick-starting football's renaissance, although the change could actually be felt before that. Gates started to rise, and the sport began to attract a certain degree of intellectual and cultural attention.

However, the fans were growing restless. They looked at the FTSE index and felt their teams should be further up the table. On the terraces they began chanting the names of their favourite accountants and corporate strategists. In the pubs after the match, fans would endlessly argue about restructuring the club's loans to offset capital costs against projected revenue streams. 'If that's what the fans want, maybe we *should* try and make more money out of the game . . .' pondered the reluctant chairmen.

With rising TV revenues coming into the game, the bigger clubs realized that by breaking away from the century-old Football League, they'd be able to keep far more cash for themselves and give more money to their top players to spend on gaudily furnished mansions in Essex. In 1992 the twenty-two clubs of what was then the first division resigned en masse from the Football League. The old second division became the first division, and so on; so the clubs that were about to lose out financially could at least pretend to themselves that they'd been promoted.

England were hosts for the 1996 European Championships, but for the second time in the decade went out at the semi-final stage following a penalty shoot-out against the Germans. England's St George's flag was rediscovered and football was now firmly established as a major feature in British life. In his final conference speech as leader of the opposition, Tony Blair paraphrased the lyrics of the England Euro 96 song and told the country, 'Labour's coming home.' In the run-up to the election he was filmed playing 'keepy-uppy' with Kevin Keegan, heading the ball back and forth many more times than Mrs Thatcher had ever managed.

The Premier League has since become the richest league in the world, followed by billions of fans around the world, who each have their favourite English team called Manchester United. In the era of globalization, football was one British invention where, at club level at least, Britain was back to being a world leader. However, the disingenuous claim of the breakaway league's founders that part of their motivation was to assist the England national team has not been borne out by a horde of international honours. And with so many of the world's best players now coming to England, there are fewer opportunities for British players to make their living from the sport. Of the original twenty-two clubs that resigned from the Football League to avoid sharing the money with clubs from the lower leagues, thirteen of them are now in the lower leagues.*

Interest rates suddenly interesting

In the 1992 European football championship, England failed to get past the group stage, not even winning a game. On the financial front, too, a humiliated Britain was about to be knocked out of Europe. England manager Graham Taylor was on the touchline angrily shouting at the linesmen, 'You realize that we joined the exchange rate mechanism at too high a rate, don't you?' The UEFA fourth official was trying to restrain him, but he wouldn't stop. 'Currency convergence is right off the agenda now. Do I not like that!'

The exchange rate mechanism (or ERM, as it was called because *erm?* was roughly the noise made when anyone was asked if they understood it) was the agreed system by which European currencies remained in relative proximity in advance of monetary union. It was the economic policy pursued by the British government because shadowing the strong German deutschmark was perceived to be a good way of preventing inflation – it didn't mean the British Conservatives were yet ready to commit to a single European currency. But it was central to the government's economic policy that this particular squad of marathon runners continued to jog along in a pack, that the pacesetting Germans did

* At the time of writing, being the end of the 2008/9 season. To date, forty-three clubs have competed in the Premiership, but only four have won the title.

not get too far ahead, and that the wheezy Brits and Italians managed to keep up, despite having forgotten to bring their shoes and claiming to have a cold. On 16 September 1992, the UK didn't just fail to keep up the pace, the podgy British Chancellor was bent double by the side of the running track, dripping in sweat and throwing up into the long-jump sandpit. On the day that became known as Black Wednesday (a name quickly coined by the new shadow Chancellor Gordon Brown), the Treasury spent billions trying to prop up the pound but its value continued to plummet. During the tumultuous day the base rate was raised to 10 per cent and then to 15 per cent in the hope of attracting investors, but it was so obviously an unsustainable bluff that investors continued to sell pounds. Keeping the base rate of 15 per cent would have made millions of mortgages unpayable and as many small businesses collapse. At the end of the day, the British currency was helped into the St John's Ambulance as the other runners disappeared over the horizon. Britain's membership of the ERM was suspended, base rates brought down to 12 per cent* and a shell-shocked Norman Lamont appeared in front of the television cameras announcing that Britain was leaving the ERM, as a fresh-faced public schoolboy who worked as his special advisor hovered behind him looking excited about being on telly. For as long as anyone could remember, opinion polls had shown that the Conservatives were the party most trusted to run the economy, but they lost that trust in one single day in 1992. They would not regain it until that 26-year-old special advisor David Cameron (who'd obviously given really special advice) became leader of the Conservative Party.

The government's poll rating fell drastically after Black

---

* Then down to 10 per cent the following day. This was of course at a time when the Chancellor had the power to set interest rates – it was partly because this lever had been used as a political rather than economic device that Labour surrendered this power to the Bank of England on coming to office in 1997.

Wednesday, never to recover. Not only had Britain suffered a national humiliation, but more importantly an incredible £27 billion of Britain's reserves had been lost pursuing a doomed economic policy. If the government had faced up to the inevitable, they could have actually made a profit out of devaluation, but now their economic and political policies were completely in pieces. On the night of Black Wednesday, John Major rang up the editor of the *Sun* to see how they were going to cover the story. 'Well, John, let me put it this way. I've got a large bucket of shit on my desk. And tomorrow I'm going to pour it over your head.' To which the Prime Minister summoned up all his intellect, his negotiating skill and tactical nous and managed the rejoinder, 'Oh, Kelvin, you are a one.'

Had Germany not been so crippled by the expense of reunification, then it would have probably listened to John Major's desperate pleas to lower their interest rates and avoid the British humiliation. But the knock-on effect of the collapse of the socialist regimes of Eastern Europe was the collapse of one of the weaker capitalist governments of Western Europe. The British government was only five months into its term and already it was effectively over. The following five years were little more than a desperate attempt to hold things together as the Conservatives split in all manner of directions. A press pack smelling blood tore the government apart over a series of scandals that would have been given less prominence in a different political climate. The Black Wednesday debacle strengthened the resolve of the Euro-sceptics who would now continue to undermine John Major for the rest of his blighted premiership. The anti-Europeans had drawn a line in the sand – they said they were determined that Britain should not be ruled by the Germans. To which the royal family replied that they didn't actually have that much constitutional power any more.

Annus horribilis

In the 1980s the royal family had enjoyed a surge in popularity as the addition of Diana Spencer and Sarah Ferguson brought some intellectual rigour and scholarly depth to the Palace with their sober reflections upon the works of Voltaire, Rousseau and Wham! Was Jean-Paul Sartre's landmark *L'existentialisme est un humanisme* a paradigm shift in Western philosophical thought, or merely a continuation of the neo–orthodoxist work of Heidegger and Kierkegaard? And just how dishy was Simon Le Bon from Duran Duran?

The stuffy old-fashioned royal family had always kept the media at a certain distance, but these fun-loving newcomers brought a breath of fresh air for the royal correspondents and were clearly enjoying the media spotlight: dressing up as policewomen to gatecrash Andrew's stag party or openly discussing a pregnancy with the eager press corps. They were young, rich and famous; and it was great the way the tabloids were building them up. 'Golly, I wonder what comes next?' they pondered optimistically.

The grandeur of the House of Windsor came crashing down in one terrible year during which all of the Queen's married children separated from their partners in less than dignified circumstances. Although parents always try to put a positive spin on things, the round robin that went inside the Queen's Christmas card telling all her old friends what the family had been up to in 1992 did not make for very happy reading. 'Well, it's been another wonderful year for all of one's children. Andrew was so busy with his royal duties to one's subjects that he was unable to accompany dear Sarah and the girls on holiday, so the Duchess went without him and, well, was photographed with her tits out having her toe sucked by some Texan bastard.' The Duchess of York's boyfriend was described as her 'financial advisor'. Given that she was millions of pounds in debt, it was almost as if he must have spent his time with her doing something else. 'Toe-sucking' briefly enjoyed some status as bizarre upper-class kinky foreplay as portrayed in sex manuals such as *The Joy of Financial Advice*. Princess Anne announced that she was to separate from her husband Mark Phillips; it transpired that they'd only stayed together this long for the sake of the horses. Anne also became the first royal with a criminal record after she was found guilty under the new Dangerous Dogs Act. Her bull terrier Dotty had attacked two children, and she was fined £500, which must have been a blow. She agreed to a court order to give her dog more training, after which the same dog fatally savaged the Queen's favourite corgi.

But the biggest storyline of all in the new high-class soap opera *Pallas* was the collapse of the marriage of Diana Princess of Wales to the future king. *Diana, Her True Story* hit the bookshelves in a blaze of publicity, and publishers thought, 'OK, there's been a Diana book now; so there's no point in doing another one.' Claiming to be based on the testimony of insiders,* the exposé alleged that Diana was deeply unhappy in her marriage and had attempted suicide on several occasions, and that the British royal family was utterly dysfunctional, manipulative and dishonest. So there was a bit of an atmosphere when one of the ladies-in-waiting suggested it for the Queen's book club that month.

Just when it looked as if nothing else could go wrong, a major fire at Windsor Castle caused extensive damage to the state apartments and to many priceless oil paintings of important fat people from the olden days. The blaze would have been put out earlier, but as over two hundred firemen rushed into the royal residence, the Queen and Prince Philip kept saying, 'Hello, and what do you do?' The Queen finally acknowledged her disastrous year, in

---

* After her death Andrew Morton claimed that his chief source had been the Princess of Wales herself. Oh no, I've just given it away that Diana dies.

which the royal family had been accused of being remote and out of touch, by referring to her 'annus horribilis'. To most people this sounded like a posh phrase for haemorrhoids. Further PR disasters were to follow and the public image of the royal family never fully recovered.

The sudden death of Old Labour

When the result of the 1992 election came in, Neil Kinnock said, 'Well, that's it – I've just wasted the last nine years of my life.' What everyone else said to attempt to cheer him up is not recorded, but it was probably along the lines of: 'Yeah, loser, what were you doing?!' Kinnock resigned the Labour leadership and made a guest appearance on *Have I Got News For You*, but unfortunately lost that as well. With so many Conservatives convinced that Brussels was a hotbed of socialism, it was decided that the best way to wind them up was to give the former Labour leader a job as a European commissioner. There was little doubt as to who would succeed Neil Kinnock as Labour leader: John Smith had come across as a solid and dependable shadow Chancellor. There were even tales that he had served as a minister in 'the last Labour government', which by now sounded like some fabled Arthurian legend, lost in the mists of time.

John Smith had a reliable solidity to him, possessing a certain gravitas that made it possible to imagine him prudently managing the country's finances. Pictures of him in the red tops usually featured his beautiful grown-up daughters beside him; in fact, the photographers generally tried their best to get the boring bald bloke to move out of the way altogether. During Kinnock's time as leader, he had been seen as a potential rival. One *Spitting Image* sketch had shown John Smith tucked up in bed recovering from the heart attack he suffered in 1988, with Neil Kinnock visiting him and recommending he eat lots of lard and take up smoking.

But having experienced such a major scare, Smith had apparently confronted his health problems, adjusting his diet and setting himself gruelling challenges walking in the Scottish mountains. And it's not as if trying to hold the Labour Party together was a particularly stressful job. The new leader of the opposition believed that with cautious reform and considered criticism of the government's incompetence, the next election would be Labour's. This 'one more heave' approach deeply frustrated two of the party's rising stars, Gordon Brown and Tony Blair, who wanted Labour to reinvent itself completely, to appeal directly to people who had aspirations or who had done quite well under the Tories. Tony Blair fell out with his party leader and even considered leaving politics altogether. A few changes were made, most significantly the abolition of Labour's infamous 'block vote', which had given so much influence to individual union leaders at the Labour Party conference. Instead the leadership of the Labour Party would be decided on a principle of 'one member one vote' – an issue on which Smith threatened to resign if he did not get his way. But the principles enshrined in Clause IV were fiercely reaffirmed at the same conference, and Labour Party members reasserted their right to nitpick about obscure points of order at general management committees.

Fortunately for John Smith, the government were making the job of leader of the opposition a lot easier than it had been for his predecessor. The Conservatives' poll rating sank to below 30 per cent after Black Wednesday, where it remained marooned for the rest of their disastrous term. With the Tories bitterly divided over Europe, with scandals and botched ministerial sackings, Major's government continued to look like it was 'in office, but not in power', in the damning words of the embittered ex-Chancellor Norman Lamont. At the May local elections in 1994, Labour enjoyed a staggering 24 per cent lead, winning in the south of

England as well as the north, and it looked like John Smith was well on the way to Downing Street; the movement he had worked all his life for would finally be returned to power with him as Prime Minister. But it was never to be – for just one week later he was dead. After suffering a massive heart attack at his London flat on 11 May, Smith was rushed to hospital.* He never regained consciousness and was pronounced dead at 10.35 a.m.

A shocked House of Commons was informed that afternoon by the new Speaker, Betty Boothroyd. Such was the unity of the House of Commons that afternoon, and so respectful were the tributes from all sides, that there was speculation that the old 'ya-boo' confrontationalism might be gone for ever. Obviously a week later they were cat-calling and jeering as usual, but it was a nice thought while it lasted. The following morning on breakfast TV, party veteran Denis Healey was asked who he thought should be the next leader. His answer was Tony Blair. Whether taking their cue from the great leader that Labour never had, or reaching the same conclusion independently, newspaper commentators and political pundits were suddenly all declaring Blair the next leader before his friend Gordon Brown (and the former favourite) had finished writing obituaries of his friend and fellow Scot.

Brown had always had respect for his protégé Tony Blair; he had even predicted that Blair might be leader of the Labour Party after him. But he hadn't noticed Blair coming up on the outside, showing decisiveness and ruthless ambition at the moment of tragedy. With the polls already showing Blair as the most popular choice, Brown travelled to Blair's home turf in Islington, to a restaurant so fancy that it didn't have its name on the front, and then had to travel up and down Upper Street trying to locate it.

* St Bartholomew's Hospital was threatened with closure by the Conservatives; a month earlier, Smith had toured Barts in support of their campaign to save it. The doctor who showed John Smith round was the same man who tried in vain to save his life.

The 'deal' struck at table 13 in Granita restaurant has become the stuff of political legend, the famous dinner when there was only one pasta special left, and Tony said, 'OK, well, *you* have the last special and then *I'll* be Prime Minister for ten years. That makes it fair.'* So many people have written about the meeting with such confidence and certainty that you might have thought it was a table for two politicians and twenty-seven political journalists with tape recorders. In fact, the only other notable person reported to have been in the restaurant that night was the *EastEnders* actress Susan Tully. She probably thought all the arguing and shouting coming from the table in the corner was a bit over the top: 'Leave it, Gordon, it's not worth it!' What does seem likely is that Gordon Brown, already knowing that he would not win a leadership contest, managed to extract a guarantee that he would control social policy from the Treasury and perhaps an undertaking that Tony would stand aside for him after a set number of years. Both of these things did come to pass, but both sides seem to think that the other broke the terms of what was agreed, while Cherie Blair's memoir says that the deal wasn't done in Granita at all. What is historically significant is that the unassailable power of the Treasury was cemented in May 1994. The Chancellor, it seemed, wouldn't just raise the money, and allocate the money; he would tell all the other ministers how they should spend it as well.

Granita closed shortly before Gordon Brown became Prime Minister and reopened as Desperados.

Major minor

An early test of the supposedly closer European Union came with a crisis in its own backyard, as Yugoslavia disintegrated in an ugly

---

* In fact, Brown didn't eat at all.

and complex war. Germany had been quick to recognize the Balkan states declaring their independence from the increasingly nationalist Serbia, but as war followed, European neighbours were reluctant to get involved. Britain sent troops to protect food convoys, but full-scale military intervention was judged to be an impossibly difficult and open-ended prospect.

It was an incomprehensible but brutal conflict played out nightly on television screens across Europe. But the United Kingdom was never going to show much of a lead on a genuine European crisis when John Major had his own European civil war within the Conservative Party. The painful passage of the Maastricht Bill through the House of Commons saw Conservative rebels siding with Labour on the Social Chapter (even though they opposed its provisions) as Euro-sceptics lost the Conservative whip or resigned from the party. Bosnian Serbs and ethnic Kosovans must have looked at the factions and historic enemies and wondered how peace could ever come to the war-torn Conservative Party.

John Major looked at the shifting tectonic plates of global power, at the new world order in which the Soviet Union had disintegrated, with America now the only superpower but with an emerging rival in the European Union – and he saw clearly that what was needed was for people who served you in the Post Office to wear clearly legible name badges. Major's Citizens' Charter was his first big idea in government, a collection of guarantees about service standards and accountability that would make you slightly less cross when you tried to get through to someone at the local council.

'And in the bathroom, the bottles should say "Shampoo" or "Conditioner" in bigger writing, because you never have your glasses on in the shower . . .'

'Sir, the communists have retaken power in Moscow . . . Gorbachev has been toppled . . .'

'. . . and when you go to the cashpoint machine, there should be a little canopy because you can never read it when the sun's shining . . .'

'Hang on, Boris Yeltsin is defying the coup, he has climbed onto a tank . . .'

'. . . and if the buttons on pelican crossings were a little bit higher, then toddlers wouldn't be able to press them when their mother has no intention of crossing the road . . .'

League tables for schools were introduced, league tables for council efficiency, league tables for hospitals, even league tables for football clubs were suggested, but that was going too far. Most visionary of all was the celebrated Traffic Cones Hotline, a telephone number advertised on the motorways for people to call up and report that traffic cones seemed to be deployed on a motorway for no apparent reason. At that point the call usually went dead, as the caller crashed after using their mobile phone while speeding down the M1. In fact, a regular message to the cones hotline was, 'Can I have a vanilla 99 with raspberry sauce on top, please?' The scheme was abandoned after three years, entering the political lexicography as a symbol of a petty government initiative akin to rearranging the deckchairs on the *Titanic*. They also abandoned Major's idea for the 'Someone-Has-Taken-a-Chocolate-From-The-Lower-Tray-When-There-Are-Still-Some-On-The-Top' Hotline.

And it was by this time that the British public finally worked out what they did not like about John Major. He was supremely naff. When he had addressed the nation on television before the First Gulf War, he had ended with the homely message 'God bless' (despite the desperate pleas of an advisor to cut that from his script). A typical 'joke' when he was resisting calls to resign was, 'Give up? Give over!' With Tony Blair steaming ahead in the opinion polls, the best putdown he could manage for the man who sought to be the next Prime Minister was: 'Sorry, Tony; job's taken!' His audience dutifully laughed and clapped, but inside must have been thinking, 'Yes, but Blair is the leader of the opposition. It is sort of his job to seek yours.' In one particularly bizarre speech he shared his sentimental impression of a nation that few would have ever recognized: 'Fifty years from now, Britain will still be the country of long shadows on cricket grounds, warm beer, invincible green suburbs, dog lovers and – as George Orwell said – old maids bicycling to Holy Communion through the morning mist.' After this speech Major was given the disappointing news by his advisors that there were in fact no such people as the Famous Five, so they wouldn't be able to help him solve the riddle of the missing treasure. But behind the cricket-loving Middle England persona, there was another side to John Major. He could be petulant and resentful, bearing grudges and sometimes being pointlessly stubborn. A live microphone caught him referring to 'the bastards' in his cabinet who opposed him on Europe; fortunately the microphone failed to pick up any more of the language that the South London boy had learned on the streets of Brixton: 'I is gonna put a cap in their ass, innit?'

Fat Controller to get fatter

Aside from the charters and the hotlines, the government's more ambitious pieces of domestic legislation did not impress much either. With all the profit-making industries having been sold off by Margaret Thatcher, the late afternoon of this particular car boot sale saw John Major left just flogging the loss-making bits that nobody much wanted, like British Rail and the Post Office. The sale of the Post Office was eventually abandoned, probably because no one could be bothered to queue for the special form, but Britain's ramshackle rail network was another matter. Mrs Thatcher had always backed off from railway privatization, saying that it would be her 'Waterloo', and all the train buffs wondered why it would be her south London terminus serving the south-west and Surrey suburbs. But now John Major harked back to the days when the railways had been romantic private companies, such as Great Western and LNER. The Majoresque obsession with tinkering and pointless rebranding had already spread to the railways before privatization. Passengers waiting for delayed trains were wound up even more by being addressed as 'customers', although this new status did not go down particularly well at the busy ticket office. 'Yes, can I see the ticket for the 5.15 to Manchester Piccadilly, please? Hmmm, that's quite nice, have you got one in blue?'

The government seemed determined to try and sell off a central part of the country's infrastructure, despite no one quite knowing how the railways might be converted into a profit-making business without closing all the railway lines and just concentrating on selling overpriced croissants and cappuccinos at the stations. The Conservative chairman of the House of Commons Transport Committee famously described rail privatization as 'the poll tax on wheels'. Various permutations of a private railway system were examined and none of the models seemed quite stupid enough. Until they hit on the idea of one company owning the track, and another company owning the trains, and another company owning the stations, and another company owning all the bit of sloping land covered in brambles and bindweed growing through old shopping trolleys. A ludicrously complex system of subsidies, infrastructure maintenance units, cross-ticketing, rolling stock leasing, rail regulators and twenty-five train-operating companies was created. The madness of it all was summed up in one memorable piece of news footage. A company needing to get a train from one part of the country to another found that it was cheaper to put it on the back of a huge lorry and have it driven down the motorway. The privatized (but still heavily subsidized) railway network ended up costing the taxpayer more than it did when it was plain old British Rail.

Privatization-for-the-sake-of-it also loomed for the diminished coal industry, and in preparation for the sell-off, it was announced that another thirty-one pits were to be shut down. These further closures got a remarkably negative reaction from the general public; the government now seemed vindictive as well as incompetent. For a while it looked like Mrs Heseltine and Mrs Major might have to launch a ministers' wives support group, Women in Favour of Pit Closures, giving out badges saying 'Dole not Coal' and organizing food parcels of Harrods hampers. Back in 1984 the Nottinghamshire miners who'd worked throughout the year-long strike had racked their brains for the precise wording of that famous political slogan. 'How does it go? *Divided we stand! United we fall!* – is that it?' They had made the government victory possible and were now rewarded with the sack. 'Oh, no, it's *Divided we fall!*, isn't it? That actually makes more sense now I think about it . . .'

Mad cows and Englishmen

Not content with completely alienating most of urban Britain, the government set about angering the rural community as well. During the 1980s there had been some concern among dairy farmers about the way some of their cows started to bark at the moon or think they were Napoleon. Some of the nuttier ones even developed paranoid conspiracy theories that the humans were only feeding them so they could eat them later. It was declared that these creatures had some sort of bizarre brain-eating disease, and the best thing to do would be to slaughter them and feed their offal to all the healthy cows. For as anyone who watches the Discovery Channel will remember, wild cattle are of course voracious cannibals. When wildebeest migrate across the African savannah, the greatest danger are carnivorous gnus lying in wait by the watering hole, where they pick out the weakest member and tear him to shreds. The lions and crocodiles avert their eyes at the brutality of it all.

Nobody had dared say the words 'mad cow' to Mrs Thatcher because they couldn't trust themselves to keep a straight face. While concern was mounting that a major health crisis was on the way, the Ministry of Agriculture was desperate to play it all down. Farmers could wait for some sort of guidance until the cows came home, which considering that they were now all staggering sideways and then falling over might be some time.

In the summer of 1990 the Agriculture Minister John Gummer famously offered his four-year-old daughter a hamburger in front of the cameras and young Cordelia recoiled as it was shoved in her face.* Instead the minister eagerly ate it himself to demonstrate that he was in no danger of going mad. Six months later he broke down in tears because Mrs Thatcher was resigning.

Eventually the scientists told the government: 'We believe that bovine spongiform encephalopathy leads to variant Creutzfeldt-Jakob disease.' 'Well, that's easy for you to say.' But by the mid-1990s the government's assertion that mad cow disease could not be passed on to humans had fallen apart. When they finally admitted the link, beef sales fell by 90 per cent in one day (even though by now steps had been taken to make the beef safe). It became clear that the Ministry of Agriculture had been too slow to react and had been selective with which scientific information it had shared. Now thousands of cattle had to be destroyed as the European Union banned the export of traditional British Big Macs. 'Cattle

---

* The footage shows that she actually thought it was too hot, but eyewitnesses say that the half-eaten burger in Cordelia's hand in the staged photo featured a burger that had been bitten into by a loyal civil servant.

derivatives' were also outlawed, such as gelatin, tallow and semen. No one was quite sure just how much bulls' semen Britain had previously exported ('Is that what's in those huge tankers sailing out of Milford Haven?') but mad cow disease helped turn the traditionally Conservative countryside against the government. Somehow it seemed symbolic of the times that under this government even the roast beef of old England was off the menu.

Ambitious Major decides to stand for Tory Party leadership

By the summer of 1995, the constant chatter of plots and intrigues against John Major made a leadership challenge in the autumn seem inevitable. In an attempt to take control of events, John Major decided to stand for the leadership of the Conservative Party himself.

'But, Prime Minister, you're already leader of the Tories!'

'No, someone has to make a stand. It will send a clear message to the Prime Minister.'

'But, sir, you are the Prime Minister. It's you.'

'Thank you for your optimism. But let's see how I do in the ballot first, shall we?'

The news of John Major's surprise resignation sent shockwaves through the country, which was quickly followed by a disappointed 'Oh' when it was explained that he wasn't resigning for ever, just to try and get elected again to stop everyone being so mean to him. The bombshell was announced in the garden of 10 Downing Street. 'It is time to put up or shut up!' said Major, sounding about as macho as a slice of quiche. He had forewarned his key cabinet allies, most importantly Michael Heseltine, and as soon as the news broke, the cabinet were seen on the evening news emphasizing their full support for the Prime Minister and all citing 'the-Prime-Minister's-political-courage-his-bold-leadership-and-decisiveness-please-read-this-out-on-the-telly'. But after a day or two, somebody did a head count and noticed that one minister had been ominously quiet. 'John Redwood hasn't said anything yet.' 'Who?' 'He's Secretary of State for Wales apparently.' It transpired that John Redwood was refusing to answer the phone to journalists or indeed Number 10. He had not been in the inner circle who had been prewarned, and was clearly so cross that the Prime Minister had resigned that he decided to resign. When finally he was tracked down in his cricket whites, it was clear that a proper contest was on the cards and the public were about to be subjected to yet another string of laboured cricketing metaphors.

The Secretary of State for Wales continued to avoid the TV cameras, with the result that the BBC kept playing an old clip of him looking like a rabbit in headlights, pretending to sing along to the Welsh national anthem. His little wiggle of the head seemed to say 'Oh yes, I love this bit', while his terrified eyes revealed that the actual words of 'Hen Wlad fy Nhadau' had escaped him for a moment. Just in case this didn't make him look ridiculous enough, at his first press conference, the man dubbed 'the Vulcan' allowed himself to be surrounded by the even weirder-looking misfits of the anti-European lunatic fringe: Tony Marlowe in a stripy public-school blazer, Teresa Gorman in a gaudy lime-green creation, Edward Leigh gurning like an upper-class twit from a Monty Python sketch. From that opening photo-inopportunity Redwood's campaign was strangled at birth. Other right-wingers watched with interest at whether events would allow them to enter the contest at the next stage. The embittered ex-Chancellor Norman Lamont had been considering his own challenge in the autumn, and was indignant that Redwood was suddenly the standard-bearer for the right. Michael Portillo was not-very-secretly preparing a campaign headquarters in Lord North Street, where extra telephone lines were being installed in front of watching journalists. When Major was asked his views on this at Prime Minister's Questions, he quipped that it demonstrated the efficiency of a privatized British Telecom.*

Redwood may not have been a particularly credible alternative, but Major had still taken a considerable gamble. And when the figures came in, the reality was a bad result for the Prime Minister. Over a third of the parliamentary party had failed to support him and, as he admits in his surprisingly readable memoirs, his total votes were only three above the minimum target he had set himself to carry on as PM. But now a remarkable bit of spin was successfully sold to the waiting press hounds. Over forty senior Conservatives appeared at key points around College Green, all peddling the same story of a famous victory. Bold claims were made about the greatest ever win in a Tory leadership contest (even though a contest like this was unprecedented) and the unprepared press bought the lie that it was a good result. By the time they had fully digested the figures and realized that Major had actually done badly, the public's attention had moved on to other things, like the first pub quiz night in *EastEnders*. John Major had hoped that he had lanced the boil of dissent in the Conservative Party. In reality, he had clumsily squeezed it with grubby fingers, and it would swell and seep poison for the next two years.

'Hello? I'm on a train!'

The reporters who had arrived in the Downing Street garden to be told the surprising news of John Major's resignation had all

---

* This joke was given to Major by the Scottish Secretary Ian Lang, who had once been a writer for *That Was The Week That Was*.

had their mobile phones confiscated to prevent the story leaking out before the Prime Minister's official statement. By 1995 everyone, it seemed, could talk to anyone at any time. As they approached the final decade of the century, the scientists had looked at all the predictions from the 1950s about what life would be like in the year 2000 and realized they had left it a bit late. And so there was a mad dash to get everyone holding portable computers and talking on personal communicators before the year 2000 so the millennium wasn't too much of a damp squib.

Mobile phones went from being an ostentatious status symbol to a virtual necessity in a period of a couple of years. By the mid-1990s the streets seemed to be full of people talking into handsets to ascertain whether or not their friends were on a train. A whole new etiquette would need to be developed regarding when exactly it might be acceptable to answer your cell phone in company, where and when your handset should be switched off, and the degree of courtesy that should be accorded to strangers who might not want to overhear your conversation. And that new etiquette should be along any decade now.

One unexpectedly popular new form of communication was texting. This facility had been added on to mobile phones almost as an afterthought and amounted to a tiny proportion of mobile phone use to begin with. But very quickly the operators discovered texting offered a quick and efficient way of dumping a boyfriend without having to talk to him. A whole new language was devised to irritate linguistic purists, and now the Prime Minister didn't need a formal weekly audience with the Queen, they could just text each other when they were stuck in boring meetings. *Hi Lz, omg – gr8 bg wr in Bznia. wl snd bmbrs 2moz : – (*

The other major transformation of the decade was of course the world wide web. Although the development of the internet had been a complex and protracted evolution, involving the

American military, university computer departments and rather bizarrely the British Post Office, the actual invention of the world wide web is directly attributable to British computer scientist Tim Berners-Lee. So advanced is his knowledge of computers that he actually understands the difference between 'the internet' and the 'world wide web'. Berners-Lee explained his plan to take the hypertext and connect it to the transmission control and domain name system, and rather than admit they didn't have the faintest idea what he was talking about, the government decided they'd better give him a knighthood to acknowledge his achievement. Crucially he resolved that access should be freely available to everyone. 'That's wonderful, darling,' said Mrs Berners-Lee. 'I mean, you could have copyrighted it for yourself and we would have been multibillionaires; richer than Bill Gates and the Sultan of Brunei put together. But much better that everyone gets their pornography and stolen dissertations for free . . .' and she walked briskly through to the kitchen where the sound of crockery being smashed could be heard soon after.

Throughout the 1990s the idea of the internet promised an exciting future in which you would be able to get your domestic gas supply via the internet into your mobile phone, or something, nobody quite understood any of it, but the technology was clearly epoch-making. The internet promised to be the solution to everything – anyone needing a cure for cancer or a peace plan for the Middle East would simply be able to look it up on the internet. At the Labour Party conference in 1995, Tony Blair made what seemed at the time an incredibly exciting promise: revealing that he had already negotiated a deal with British Telecom whereby every school in the country would be connected to the internet! Like Harold Wilson's white hot heat of the technological revolution, Blair's technological promise made him look modern and relevant, without having to deal with any of that difficult business about tax rises or the distribution of wealth.

Nice and sleazy does it

Once a government is as discredited as John Major's was after the humiliating collapse of its economic policy in 1992, then every little scandal and embarrassment will be seized upon to underline just how rotten is the regime clinging to power. A story that might have merited a few columns on the inside pages will be splashed across the front page day after day, and the next related story to come along will somehow warrant even more coverage. That said, the Conservatives didn't have to give the newspapers quite so much entertaining ammunition. The word 'sleaze' was skilfully landed upon to bring together all the financial and sexual improprieties that plagued John Major's government in its dying years. It was particularly unfortunate for the Prime Minister that he had attempted to establish a theme of 'Back to Basics' at the 1993 Conservative Party conference, which although not primarily about public morality certainly provided something of a hostage to fortune when so many of his MPs were caught with their fingers in the till while their trousers were down around their ankles.

David Mellor, 'the Minister for Fun', set the ball rolling by having a bit too much fun with an unknown actress. Extra humiliating details were made up about sex in a Chelsea kit and toe-sucking, knowing that the minister was hardly in a position to say, 'No, hang on, OK, we did have sexual intercourse, but I wasn't wearing a Chelsea kit, I was in black socks and a vest from Marks & Spencer.' Mellor did a rather cringeworthy photo-call with his wife and children, but was so damaged that a second ministerial indiscretion (accepting an inappropriate free holiday) was enough to finish him off soon afterwards.* There were trivial scandals involving a married MP sharing a holiday bed with

---

* The *Sun*'s gleeful headline was *From Toe-Job to No Job*.

another man, another on holiday with a young man below the legal age of homosexual consent. And then there were shady business deals, Jonathan Aitken procuring prostitutes for Arab business-men or Michael Mates taking cash and gifts from the disgraced businessman Asil Nadir.

The string of sleaze scandals came at a time when Conservatives were attempting to make a principled stand on the sovereignty of the British Parliament. 'We must defend the supremacy and great traditions of this House of Commons and its honourable members . . . whoops, Tim Yeo has fathered a child by another woman and kept it secret . . . er, only in this historic chamber can the interests of the British people be served by honourable members acting on behalf of their constituents . . . oh dear, Graham Riddick and David Tredinnick have been caught asking parliamentary questions for cash payments . . . and oh dear, Alan Duncan's had to resign after getting his elderly neighbour to buy a discounted council house so he could get it off her at a huge profit, and a minister has admitted lying about arms sales to Iraq . . . well, anyway, all that aside, the British people have entrusted us with power and we must honour that . . .'

One Tory MP was found dead in his London flat, hanging from a noose of electrical flex, dressed in nothing but stockings and suspenders with an orange in his mouth and a plastic bin liner over his head. It was hard for John Major to say, 'Well, we've all done it, haven't we? I mean, who can honestly say that at some time or another they haven't masturbated while hanging by a homemade noose, sucking on amyl nitrate and wearing ladies' lingerie? I know I have!' The bizarre auto-erotic asphyxiation death did not exactly fit in with his agenda of Back to Basics or the image of old maids cycling to communion.

There were even rumours that the Prime Minister himself had had an affair, which Major was swift to crush with legal action. Few people believed it anyway, he just didn't seem the womanizing type. And so in 2002 when it was finally revealed that John Major had in fact conducted a four-year liaison with Edwina Currie before he became a minister, it caused astonishment and amusement in equal measure. The bombshell was leaked in order to promote Edwina Currie's political diaries. People briefly pictured the two of them having sex and then put it out of their heads as quickly as possible, with the result that Currie's book was a publishing disaster.

With the string of so-called sleaze scandals, a government already perceived as incompetent, divided, petty and occasionally nasty was now judged to be utterly sordid as well. Looking back it's hard to work out how they managed to get any MPs elected in 1997 at all. In fact, when a general election in Canada returned just two Conservative MPs across the whole country, pundits began to wonder if such a total wipeout was possible in the UK. Especially now that the Labour Party was working so hard to make itself presentable to the widest possible constituency.

'One cod with chips, with some of that avocado dip, please'*

Tony Blair had moved fast on becoming leader of the Labour Party in 1994. On 4 October he gave his first conference speech, declaring, 'Let us say what we mean and mean what we say.' The delegates applauded this noble sentiment, completely unaware that what he was in fact proposing was the abolition of Clause IV. He never mentioned the socialist fourth commandment by name; instead, the real meaning of his coded speech was conveyed by

---

* There is an apocryphal story (spread as an after-dinner joke by Neil Kinnock amongst others) that during a by-election campaign in the north of England, Peter Mandelson saw some mushy peas and thought it was guacamole.

party managers to political journalists around the hall immediately the speech ended. So on the evening news the diehard party activists saw themselves applauding wildly as the caption announced that Labour was abandoning its historic commitment to public ownership. Had the posh new leader just stood up and said that the old lefty Clause IV had to go, there would have been booing and walkouts, but managing appearances was to become central to the revitalized Labour Party under Tony Blair. Putting the best possible spin on any story was part of this management of the news agenda, and the word 'spin' entered the English language as if it was some sinister new development, even though propaganda was as old as politics itself. In order to make it completely clear that Labour had changed, the party was rebranded as '*New* Labour'. Delegates at conference remained determined to keep singing 'The Red Flag', hoping the lyrics hadn't been changed to incorporate five pledges to encourage private enterprise.

The New Labour project was the work of a small team of modernizers close to Tony Blair and Gordon Brown. Peter Mandelson was a key media manager and political fixer, who in his youth had been a member of the Young Communist League. Alastair Campbell was hired to manage Blair's press relations. A former political correspondent at the *Daily Mirror*, he had once punched his counterpart on the *Guardian* for making a joke about the death of Robert Maxwell. Campbell's recently published political diaries recount every detail of the Blair–Brown axis, recalling how the two most powerful men in Britain skipped through ten happy years of government holding hands and laughing at one another's jokes. The team were disciplined and occasionally ruthless, but were undoubtedly effective. In the dying days of the Major government, it felt as if power had already been transferred to New Labour, such was the media interest in Labour's policies and personalities. The Conservative majority had been chipped away by by-election defeats and defections until by the beginning of 1997 the Prime Minister found himself leading a minority government. Finally in mid-March John Major announced the date of his own execution. Polling day was to be the first of May. The cartoonists portrayed him as the pilot of a plane engulfed in flames and spinning out of control, screaming, 'Mayday! Mayday!' I don't know why they had to write 'Conservative Party fortunes' on the side of the aircraft; we all got the joke.

Taxi for Mr Major!

There was a point about three and half hours into the coverage of the 1997 election results when the words 'Con hold' finally flashed up on the television screen. After hours of 'Lab holds' and 'Lab gains', a Tory MP had finally been elected. In the studio Cecil Parkinson joked that this was wonderful news as now John Major could actually have a leadership contest with someone.* By that point it was clear that Labour were about to win a landslide election, greater than any since the advent of universal suffrage. It made no difference whether Conservative MPs were pro- or anti-European, whether they had bravely rebelled against Major's government on points of principle or had employed a rent boy as their private researcher to trick old ladies out of their savings and spent the money on cocaine and bribes to fugitive Iraqi business-men. The public just wanted the Conservatives out and were canny enough to use tactical voting to make absolutely sure it happened. In previous elections the anti-Conservative vote had been divided; now it was strategically deployed by voters in a

* Earlier in the evening Jeremy Paxman had said to Cecil Parkinson, 'You're the chairman of a fertilizer firm – how deep is the mess you are in?'

calculated two-pronged attack in which voters supported whichever party had the best chance of ousting a sitting Tory. Thus it was that the greatest majority in modern politics was achieved with a voter share of just over 43 per cent – less than Labour had managed throughout the 1950s when it had lost three elections in a row.

At the beginning of the campaign the *Sun* backed Labour with the sort of courage that saw Argentina declaring war on Germany at the end of March 1945. John Major had called the election six weeks before polling day hoping that a longer campaign might see Labour trip up, but it just allowed more time for further financial and sex scandals to surface and embarrass the Conservatives. Neil Hamilton and his feisty wife Christine guaranteed maximum coverage for the sort of Conservative that John Major would have preferred to keep off the TV screens. Hamilton had been caught accepting cash in brown envelopes from Harrods boss Mohamed Al Fayed to ask questions in Parliament, but refused to resign his rock-solid Tory seat. Instead, both Labour and the Liberals stood aside and the BBC correspondent Martin Bell became the first independent MP for forty-seven years to be elected to the House of Commons.

John Major's final years in office had seen a discernible shift in public opinion; people who were not normally interested in politics seemed to develop a passionate sense that drastic action had to be taken. And as with mad cow disease before the election, it seemed that the only cure for the psychosis that had gripped the Conservative Party was an extensive cull. So on 1 May 1997, veterinary surgeons were called to constituencies across the country, where a swift bolt through the forehead saw 178 Tory MPs dispatched as humanely as possible. Famous Conservatives to go included Michael Portillo, Malcolm Rifkind, Ian Lang, William Waldegrave, David Mellor and Davros, leader of the Daleks, who decided to concentrate on show-business. The Tories didn't win a single seat in Scotland or Wales, and would have to find shadow secretaries for Scotland and Wales from English Tories who'd been there once on their holidays. Despite a slight dip in their vote, the Liberals had their best result since 1929, winning a total of forty-six seats. But of course the real story of the result was a sensational victory for Tony Blair and his rebranded Labour Party.

Labour won seats in leafy suburbs and historic market towns where Labour activists would have been pariahs a dozen years earlier. There were Labour MPs for coastal towns in the south of England, and for places where they had come third in 1992. Over a hundred women were elected to the House of Commons; 'And we will not be patronized or defined by our relationship to a man,' said one of 'Blair's Babes'. New Labour gained a majority over all other parties of 179 seats; with 418 MPs they couldn't all fit on the government benches in the House of Commons.

In the unseasonably warm weather of May 1997, there was an optimism and a sense of a new beginning across the country as a young family posed on the steps of Downing Street. On their first day in office, the government granted independence to the Bank of England, surrendering the power to set interest rates to ensure that henceforth such decisions would be taken for economic rather than political reasons. It was hailed as a political master-stroke by the handful of people who were still listening when its fiscal significance was fully explained. The weekend after Labour's victory, Britain won the Eurovision Song Contest. It seemed like anything was possible.

John Major had known there was little he could do to prevent a defeat that had been coming for nearly five years and on 2 May he resigned as leader of the Conservative Party and went off to the Oval to watch the cricket. No one can pretend that he was a lucky Prime Minister; he led an unleadable party, and pretty well everything that could go wrong, duly did.

It is a widely held belief that elections are decided on the state of the economy, but in 1997 the country's finances were in better shape than they had been for years; certainly far better than in 1992 when Britain's economic woes should have seen John Major thrown out of office. In fact, the surprise 1992 victory turned out to be a poisoned chalice; whoever was in power when the over-valued pound came under attack from the international speculators would have been irrecoverably tainted. It is possible that a Kinnock government would have devalued the pound on taking office and remained in control of the economic situation, but most politicians would put off such an unpopular decision. The other great 'what-if' of the Major years is what would have happened if John Smith had not died so suddenly? It seems fairly safe to presume that he would have won in 1997, although there is a school of thought that governments only implode when faced with dynamic opposition – the media only turn on the incumbents when the alternative looks totally credible and much more exciting, as happened with Wilson in 1963/4. A John Smith premiership would probably have seen a more conventional European social democratic government; his social conservatism would have meant that there would not have been the rapid equality achieved in areas such as gay rights, but neither would there have been hobnobbing with the rich and famous that many found distasteful in a Labour Prime Minister. It seems unlikely that a Smith victory would have been quite so spectacular as Tony Blair's, leaving the Conservatives with less of a mountain to climb before they could once again become a credible alternative government.

For that was the other legacy of the Conservatives' rout in 1997. Such was the wipe-out of their worst result since the Great Reform Act of 1832 that the Tories were clearly out of power for some time to come. Tony Blair had at least two terms in office ahead of him; he had a huge majority, a healthy economy, the goodwill of the public and a talented team of ministers around him. If only there had been a song that could have expressed the likelihood of things generally getting better.

7

1997–2008

How New Labour gave the poor a bit more cash, the rich a lot more cash and then watched the banks lose the whole lot anyway

Tony Blair's big tactical mistake was not getting himself killed soon after he'd been elected. Such was the optimism and the impossible expectation on 1 May 1997 that only a tragic, pointless death in the first few months could have preserved his saintly status as one of the country's greatest ever leaders. Great Britain's own JFK, cut down before his best work could be done: 'He was, in every sense, the *People's Prime Minister.*' In fact, if he'd sat in the back seat between Princess Diana and Dodi we could have got it all over with at once.

Because by its very nature, political euphoria can never last for very long. It's like the overwhelming joy a parent feels on the birth of a child – a few years later you are shaking your head in despair at their terrible behaviour and appalling choice of friends. 'I can't believe young Tony's bombing Baghdad and going to stay with Cliff Richard. We had such hopes for him . . .'* In truth, the fierce antipathy that developed towards Tony Blair was just as out

---

* Tony and Cherie went to stay at Cliff's Portuguese holiday retreat early in 2000. They say the drinking went on till nine o'clock at night.

of proportion as the adoration that had greeted his arrival. Perhaps some of the anger came out of a feeling of humiliation: the love-struck political adolescents ended up feeling jilted and betrayed as if somehow Tony had let them down personally.

But the media commentators had only needed political change to inject some fresh characters and storylines into their eternal national soap opera. The people who really needed a new government were far from the gaze of the opinion-formers and agenda-setters. In the great Venn diagram of British society, there is no overlap between those who write the newspapers or edit the TV news and the invisible millions who directly benefited from the minimum income guarantee or the working family tax credit. Most of the columnists of the broadsheets probably thought Sure Start was a ladies' deodorant. The lives of Britain's poorest were significantly improved during the Blair/Brown decade and that *is* sort of the point of a Labour government. Blair won an unprecedented three elections in a row for Labour, pumped billions of pounds into schools and hospitals (not to mention Derry Irvine's* wallpaper) and yet the left remained deeply ambivalent about him. Many were frustrated at New Labour's failure to narrow the gap between the rich and poor and by a growing sense that the opportunity for radical change was only half seized. But most of all Blair's premiership was blighted by a war of questionable legality, the subsequent damage done to the Western alliance and the shifting, sometimes duplicitous case that was made for military action. Without Osama Bin Laden and Saddam Hussein, the story of the New Labour government might have been very different. If Tony Blair had known that in May 1997, he'd have had them both round

* Lord Irvine was Tony Blair's first Lord Chancellor and a man ahead of his time. Years before the MPs' expenses scandal, he was widely castigated for spending thousands of pounds of taxpayers' money on rather fancy wallpaper for his official apartments.

to Chequers for a game of tennis and then a no-nonsense chat about sorting out the Middle East . . .

'Call me Tony'

Tony Blair was not born into the Labour tribe in the impoverished manner of the party's greatest heroes. He couldn't hark back to a working-class boyhood spent delivering Labour leaflets down cobbled streets, going down the pit at fifteen and then having to dig coal with his fingernails and teeth after the mine owner took away his pickaxe for being a union activist. 'When I were a lad . . .' Tony would say at Labour Party meetings, 'we was sent off to t'top private school with nowt to look forwar' to 'cept eking out livin' in t'law courts. Some days we didn't know where t'next food hamper were coming from.' His father had been a Conservative activist and likely Parliamentary candidate until a stroke ended his political aspirations. However, after leaving Oxford University, young Tony joined the Labour Party and was made ward secretary at his first meeting. He met and married a fellow trainee barrister and with a certain amount of good fortune just managed to get himself a safe Labour seat in time for Labour's disastrous 1983 election result.

Fourteen years later the youngest Prime Minister for over a hundred and fifty years stood on the steps of Number 10; Downing Street was a family home for the first time in living memory. Next door, the Chancellor would be trying to work on his budget, but all he could hear was the swing-ball in the back garden, the tutor-tapes for the French conversation classes and the electric guitar pulsating through the wall. When the kids got home it was even worse. For Blair's three children it would take some getting used to; on one occasion Euan Blair arrived home to find a large group of foreign diplomats lining up to be formally welcomed. Not wishing to push in, he joined the back of the line, before finally getting to the door to be told, 'No, Euan, you don't have to queue to be greeted by the Prime Minister. He's your dad. You live here.'

Tony Blair adopted an almost studiedly casual manner, chatting to the press with a mug of tea in his hand and telling his ministers, 'Call me Tony.' There were no big surprises in his cabinet; a radical plan to include Paddy Ashdown had been rebuffed by the Liberal leader before polling day, and by the time Labour had won such a huge majority, any idea of giving out jobs to Liberals risked alienating Labour MPs. Already wondering how long he would have to wait for the top job, Gordon Brown was promptly told that 10 Downing Street was his. However, it turned out that this was only the accommodation upstairs; the Blair family took the larger flat above Number 11.* The new Foreign Secretary was Robin Cook, who declared that Labour would pursue an 'ethical foreign policy', a line he had failed to clear with his boss who was not wild about such a high-profile hostage to fortune. The new Prime Minister was keen to damp down the euphoria of May 1997, understanding that the bigger the hype now, the greater the disappointment later.

Blair's cabinet meetings were short, and some felt that Tony was more interested in listening to the results of the famous focus groups than finding out what his ministers thought. 'So this focus group represents a genuine cross-section of the electorate, does it?'

'No, Prime Minister, these are your ministers, this "group" is a cabinet meeting . . .'

'Hmmm . . . that blind man is saying he's Minister for Education – do a lot of voters feel that way?'

---

* So it was Gordon Brown who had to endure the Number 10 flat as it had been furnished according to the taste of Norma Major. The Majors left behind various personal items, including his and hers knitted boiled-egg warmers.

'No, PM; that *is* the Secretary of State for Education and Employment. David Blunkett is one of your most important ministers.'

'And are all these voters planning to support Labour at the next election?'

'Well, yes, they are the New Labour government, Prime Minister; you should sort of expect them to all vote Labour.'

'Well, that's an excellent sample – 100 per cent backing New Labour! That's much better than that one-to-one session this morning with that definite non-voter wearing the crown.'

Tony Blair did not spend a great deal of time in the House of Commons, and almost immediately reduced the knock-about showcase of Prime Minister's Question Time to just once a week. He was accused of being Presidential, though fortunately not because he was locked in a stationery cupboard with an intern.* In fact, Britain's Head of State would soon have cause to thank him, when in the first major news event of his premiership, he accurately judged the national mood when the royal family clearly did not. The first day of summer had been one of euphoria; the last day of summer was to be overwhelmed with shock and grief.

The People's Ex-Princess

And finally on the news tonight, Diana, the former wife of Prince Charles, has died in a car crash in Paris. She was a popular Princess of Wales, but latterly became estranged from her husband and the royal family, and announced in December 1993 that she would be

---

* After the Monica Lewinsky scandal engulfed President Clinton, Gordon Brown came up with a joke for his conference speech that he was only dissuaded from using at the last minute. 'In Downing Street, there will be no right turns, no left turns, no u-turns and definitely no interns.'

*retiring from public life. A private family funeral will follow. That's
all from the news team here tonight, and now the weather in your
local area, sponsored by Legal and General.*

Perhaps somewhere in a parallel universe, there is another 1990s
Britain where the death of the Princess of Wales was mentioned
in passing as an insignificant news event, like the death of a
former sitcom star or the closing of a famous London boutique.
The news was unimportant in the general scheme of things,
clearly having no bearing on the people's standard of living, the
economy, party politics, the state of schools, hospitals or housing
– but was probably worth just mentioning as it might be of trivial
nostalgic interest for its own sake.

But the point had now been reached where the news did not
simply report things that affected people's lives; the media
consciously dictated public anger or cynicism by the stories it
selected and the moods it created. The tail now wagged the dog to
such an extent that the Head of State was commanded by the
Fourth Estate to come to London, to mourn in public and to break
royal protocol and fly her royal standard at half mast. And the
Sovereign duly obeyed the ultimate power in the land.

Of course, the sudden death of Diana was a massive news
event, but only because of the way she had been built up over the
previous years as one of the lead characters in the national soap
opera which had fused 'news' with the meaningless adventures of
celebrities. And so when the nation woke up on the last day of the
summer to the shock news that Diana was dead, suddenly an individual whose highs and lows had been shared with them for a
decade and a half had been brutally snatched away at the point
when she had perhaps found true love at last . . .

The bare facts of her death were these. Finally divorced from
Prince Charles the previous year, and increasingly public in her
criticism of her former husband and the royal family, Diana had

begun a romance with Dodi Al Fayed, playboy son of the dodgy multimillionaire who owned Harrods. On the night of 30 August, the couple had dinner at the Ritz in Paris, and were then driven away at speed by a driver employed by Al Fayed. Henri Paul was drunk, and in attempting to lose the photographers that followed the car on motorbikes, he crashed into a concrete pillar in a tunnel at the Pont de l'Alma. The car had been travelling at more than double the legal speed limit, neither Di nor Dodi were wearing seat belts and unsurprisingly both were killed.

Or the bare facts of her death were these. The Duke of Edinburgh, in collusion with MI6, the *Daily Mail* and the French security services, conspired to have Diana killed by the cunning method of getting her driver to drive very fast into a concrete pillar. They did this to prevent her marrying a Muslim, because she might have been pregnant with Dodi's baby, and because Prince Philip had just bought shares in that florist's next door to Kensington Palace.

What certainly did not happen next was a national outpouring of sensibleness about the importance of wearing seat belts. Elton John did not record a special health and safety ballad entitled, 'You See? You Should Always Wear Your Seat Belt'. Diana's brother Viscount Althorp did not give a moving eulogy which included incontrovertible data about road deaths and seat belts. Instead the nation embarked upon an utterly surreal week of very public mourning, which mutated itself into self-righteous outrage about the paparazzi who provided the photographs over which they had pored so eagerly. Tabloid-inspired fury was directed at the royal family for not being seen to tie any petrol station carnations to the gates of Kensington Palace complete with little soft toy and poem from Hallmark cards. It was a nationwide Nuremberg rally of contrived sentiment and displacement grief; people were genuinely weeping, but crucially doing it in public, whipped up by other mourners all around them re-enacting the sobbing they had seen on the news the night before. In the four weeks after the funeral, the national suicide rate rose by 17 per cent (45 per cent among women aged between twenty-five and forty), while cases of self-harm (an alleged symptom of Diana's own unhappiness) went up by 44 per cent. Fortunately none of this identification trauma went as far as anybody taking off their seat belt and speeding into the thirteenth pillar of the Pont de l'Alma.

It was simply not permissible to question the sanity of this. WHSmith refused to display copies of *Private Eye*, which drew attention to the hypocrisy of the media whose photographers had been chasing Diana. In separate incidents a couple of tourists who had picked up soft toys left outside Kensington Palace as souvenirs were given jail sentences.* The flowers piled outside Kensington Palace were five feet deep; around a million bouquets were purchased and left in tribute, creating a stunning image in colour and scale and producing an overpowering fragrance of fresh petals. And then they began to decompose and turn brown, and the putrid compost of rotting cheap flowers still in their polythene stank as a symbol every bit as potent as the intended one.

At her funeral Elton John sang a hastily reworded version of 'Candle In The Wind', which became the highest-selling single of all time, and thankfully the Queen was not slammed in the tabloids for failing to wave her arms in the air in time with the music.† Millions of people lined the route of the funeral

---

* Both jail sentences were subsequently reduced to fines when the country had returned to its senses, although two days in prison were served in the first case, and in the other the Sardinian tourist who had his sentence reduced to a £100 fine was punched in the face as he left the court.

† On the night of the funeral, the BBC was hyper-conscious of making sure that nothing in the schedules could be possibly seen to be in any way insensitive or disrespectful. So they selected the family film *Free Willy*. One caller is recorded on the duty log to have rung in to complain that on the day that the nation buried the Princess of *Wales*, the BBC had been so insensitive to broadcast a film about a *whale*.

(those taking photographs were shouted at in anger after the manner in which she had died). Thousands of them cast flowers onto the hearse as it passed slowly by; frankly by the time they were on the A428 the driver was getting pretty fed up with having to turn on his windscreen wipers to clear all the gladioli. It was many, many months before the first newspaper appeared that did not mention Diana, Princess of Wales.

But what was a great comfort to all of us in this dark hour was the exceedingly high quality of the souvenirs produced as a tribute to the life of the so-called 'Queen of Hearts'. Diana porcelain dolls that featured some of her most memorable dresses, hand-painted and individually numbered by the traditional royal potters of Taiwan. Commemorative mugs, featuring that un-mistakable coy smile. A children's Diana doll, which allowed you, simply by pulling a string on her back, to relive those favourite catchphrases: 'There were three of us in this marriage, so it was a bit crowded.' 'I'd like to be a queen in people's hearts.' The Princess of Wales memorial plate for that tiny half piece of lettuce that could be puked up later. Let it never be said that due reverence and dignity was not maintained.

Into the vacuum left by the silence of the royal family had stepped the new Prime Minister, a young and refreshing national leader who understood the power of the media like few before him. Appearing shocked and slightly emotional, Tony Blair described Diana as 'the People's Princess' (in a phrase concocted by Alastair Campbell) and his approval rating shot up to over 90 per cent. It was reportedly his intervention that persuaded the royal family to come to London to be seen to be responding to the intense national tragedy, and nobody would have been much surprised if the Prime Minister had got up in Westminster Abbey and improvised an extended guitar solo in the middle of 'Candle In The Wind'.

The long honeymoon

The voters' honeymoon with the new government continued for three years, despite the cautious and pragmatic approach of the Prime Minister to the nation's problems. It is said that in any general election, each political party is psychologically fighting the previous one. By this logic, in July 1945 the Liberals should have campaigned against appeasing Hitler while promising to defend Abyssinia against Mussolini. But in 1997, despite its huge poll lead, Labour had still been haunted by the shock of the 1992 defeat and the party leadership was not prepared to take anything for granted. To the disappointment of many Labour supporters, the desire to appear sensible and cautious had expressed itself in a promise to stick to the Conservatives' spending plans for the first two years of a Labour government.

So in one sense John Major remained in power for another two years after the Conservatives' most crushing election defeat. By rights Tony Blair should have been tucking his shirt in his underpants, calling his cabinet 'bastards' and secretly shagging Edwina Currie. The outgoing Chancellor Kenneth Clarke later said that if the Tories had won the election, even they wouldn't have stuck to the Conservative Party spending plans, so for Labour to voluntarily put themselves into such a straitjacket was incredibly frustrating for the Labour ministers itching to begin the task of reversing years of underinvestment. The chance for symbolic gestures such as abolishing museum charges or introducing free eye tests for all was lost, and the 'prudence' of the Chancellor even involved some miserly adjustments such as cutting lone-parent premium on income support.* It was not until two years into their first term that the government's attack on poverty

---

* This particular cut was later made up with an increase in child benefit, but not before one or two Labour MPs had rebelled against the measure, thereby ending their chance of a ministerial career before they'd even got started.

began in earnest. Thus it was that Gordon Brown repeatedly told the 1999 party conference, 'We've only just begun.' Some politicians quoted Churchill, Voltaire or Nelson Mandela. Brown preferred the words of Karen Carpenter.

Tony Blair had made much of a new philosophical credo which he called 'the third way'. Previously right-wing economists had argued that courageous entrepreneurs (i.e. slimy tax-dodging sweatshop owners) should be allowed to keep more of their money. With such incentives more overall wealth would be created, much of which would then trickle down to those beneath (i.e. estate agents in Tuscany). Conversely, socialist commentators would argue that governments had a moral duty to redistribute wealth. Only by taxing the richest in society could it help the poorest to help themselves (i.e. by buying a lottery ticket). Like an embarrassed son-in-law during a bitter family row at Christmas, advocates of the third way would say, 'Well, you're both right . . . Erm, I mean, there are valid points on both sides.' Blair wanted to pay Peter without robbing Paul. Indeed Paul would probably get a knighthood and an invitation to Downing Street in the hope that he might make a donation to the Labour Party.

Politicians of the 'radical centre' (which included many of Blair's contemporaries such as Clinton, Schroeder and Jospin) believed that if the conditions were created in which businesses could thrive, the increased tax yield would be worth more to reforming governments than punitive tax regimes that stifled enterprise or drove businesses abroad. What Tony Blair patently did not understand is that the membership of the Labour Party wanted to clobber the rich *for the sake of it*. They didn't want economic arguments on attracting investment and public-private partnerships; they wanted special levies on BMW convertibles and 4x4s with a 'Countryside Alliance' sticker in the back. They wanted a one-off windfall tax on the name 'Rupert'.

'A hand up, not a handout'

But having your cake and eating it was actually possible during the Blair decade because his premiership coincided with a remarkable period of sustained economic growth for which the Chancellor was more than happy to take the credit. The global economic collapse when he became Prime Minister was obviously a different matter entirely. With a top rate of tax that was lower than it was for most of Margaret Thatcher's premiership, the New Labour government made massive investments in schools and hospitals while raising the living standards of millions at the bottom of the social scale. New Labour did not redistribute wealth; indeed the gap between rich and poor got wider. But it did spend a much greater proportion of the growth on helping the poorest while nobody was really looking.

A range of initiatives was branded together as the 'New Deal' by the Chancellor in a deliberate echo of Roosevelt's social policies of the 1930s, although thankfully it didn't culminate in all-out war with Japan and Germany. The minimum wage was introduced against a howl of opposition from the Conservatives and the CBI, who said it would create unemployment and damage business. It was set at £3.60 an hour, which today doesn't sound very much, and back then didn't sound very much either. What was shocking for many was that £3.60 an hour would actually constitute a pay rise for around a million and a half people. At the 2001 general election, the government promised to raise it to £4.20 an hour, and by the time Blair had left office it was over £5, so if his 'Middle East Peace Envoy' thing didn't work out he could always earn twenty quid on Saturday mornings stacking the shelves at Lidl.

'Sure Start' was a progressive initiative that targeted the families in the poorest areas of Britain, providing early education, health and family support. In community halls on some of

Britain's most deprived estates, young mothers were soon bringing their toddlers to educational playgroups where the parents
themselves got access to advice about everything from quitting
smoking to learning English. (As it happened all their cigarettes
were now illegally imported, so many of them could already read
the health warnings in Spanish or Portuguese.) Child benefit was
now paid to a mother several months before she gave birth; it
was recognized that buying baby clothes and a buggy might be
something you'd want to do before you actually had the baby. An
impoverished single mother hoping to return to part-time work
after years of childcare might not have a suitable outfit for a job
interview; now a one-off grant allowed her to buy clothes at
selected stores. Suddenly there was a government *that got it*. A
hundred new women MPs and influential female advisors in 10
and 11 Downing Street helped create an atmosphere in which the
practical problems facing single mothers or unemployed families
living in poverty were considered without moralizing disapproval.

During his weekly audience with the Queen, Blair would try to
explain the social problems caused by Britain's dependency
culture. 'We have to do something about these single-parent
families who expect to live off the state all their lives . . .'

'Well, I'm sorry, but at least Edward's getting married and
working.'

However embarrassing the kids could sometimes be, families
with children got increasingly generous tax breaks throughout the
decade. Benefits were increased and help was given to get parents
with children of school age back to work. Over a million children
were lifted above the poverty line, and Blair even made the
ambitious pledge that the government would lift all children out
of poverty* within twenty years. Even the government optimists

---

* Across the European Union 'poverty' is defined as living below half the average
income (although the British average shot up quite a bit when Roman Abramovich
moved over here).

thought, 'That's OK, he'll definitely be out of power and in the clear when that fails to happen.'

The elderly were another group singled out for special help. They got a winter fuel allowance, a free TV licence and a national bus pass scheme, which the government hoped they might not take up if they were now staying in by the fire watching telly. These benefits were given to Britain's pensioners without any pre-conditions: they were not required to desist from standing chatting in the fast lane at the swimming pool or complaining that there was a black man reading the news.

When New Labour first came to power it had been announced that the benefits system was to be radically reformed, and Tony Blair called in the maverick Labour MP Frank Field who was told to 'think the unthinkable'. Field's conclusion was ignored because it turned out to be unthinkable. But half a century after Attlee's Labour government brought in the welfare state, the system had developed a fundamental flaw. In 1945, a man who lived to the age of seventy paid taxes for fifty years and lived on a state pension for five. In 2000 a man who lived till he was ninety paid taxes for fifty years and drew a state pension for twenty-five years. Simple economics meant that the state could no longer support the millions who were being so selfish as to stay alive. Clearly the solution was for old people to stay in work longer – preferably in really lethal jobs like motorcycle stunt driver or gangland drug dealer. Fortunately, there is a solution to this seemingly impossible pensions time-bomb; and that is to tell our children that we intend to be an enormous burden to them.

In September 2000 the Chancellor raised the minimum income guarantee so sharply that in one stroke it pulled all pensioners above the poverty line. Perhaps the idea was to shock a few of them into having heart attacks. The Chancellor's generosity more than made up for the miserly 75p pensions increase that did the government so much damage the previous year when they had stuck rigidly to a formula linking increases to inflation. Such is the way of politics that more people remember the cock-up of the 75p increase than acknowledge how much life for Britain's poorest was significantly improved by such a sustained assault on poverty and 'social exclusion'.

But people judge a man by his friends as much as by what he does. Tony Blair liked to mix with the rich and famous. Perhaps if he had wanted people to acknowledge him as the friend of the most needy, he should have chosen to holiday with impoverished pensioners, instead of with rock stars and millionaires. 'Tony Blair left today for his annual holiday. He will be taking a day trip on a coach to Eastbourne, during which he will listen to Ethel Johnson talking about her grandson who is something to do with computers. He will return from holiday this evening, with a packet of Werther's Originals and a porcelain figurine of a shepherd.'

Ulster says yes!

The politics of Northern Ireland are not like the rest of the United Kingdom. You don't get Surrey Conservatives painting the sides of their houses with great big murals celebrating the day the residents' committee heroically stopped local school children using the tennis courts. The historic divisions of Ireland had defeated many politicians before Tony Blair, but his government inherited a stumbling peace process that with skill and careful diplomacy might possibly see an end to the decades of bombs and puzzled sports shop-owners wondering why they were selling so many baseball bats.

The reasons for peace finally becoming a possibility in the 1990s are complex and diverse, but at the centre of it all was a growing realization within the IRA leadership that blowing people up wasn't really getting them anywhere. If anything, it seemed to make them *less* popular. Following overtures from SDLP leader John Hume, secret talks began which culminated with the IRA announcing a ceasefire in 1994. It was almost as if the New Labour craze for moderation had crossed the Irish Sea. 'New IRA: working for a United Ireland, but only if that's what everyone else wants.' John Major's weakened government, dependent on the support of the Ulster Unionists, failed to capitalize on this historic opportunity, and the ceasefire ended in February 1996 with the explosion of a huge bomb in London's Docklands.

But with a new Prime Minister came another chance. Like the troubled province itself, Tony Blair was half-Irish, his late mother having come from Donegal, though he had never particularly emphasized his Irish roots or expressed any sort of Irish national-ism. Mind you, once the IRA don those black berets and dark glasses, you never know who's behind the disguise.* Blair worked hard on the renewed peace process, his ministers were prepared to talk to terrorists if that's what it took, and the Republic was per-suaded to abandon its historic claim to the six counties of the north, which had given some sort of legitimacy to terrorists down the years. In 1998 the momentous Good Friday Agreement saw a deal hammered out that would establish a north–south ministerial council, a range of cross-border initiatives, a timeframe for the decommissioning of terrorist weapons, IRA prisoners released if their ceasefire was observed, a new, less sectarian Ulster police force, and Celtic were allowed to have a turn at being Scottish champions. Tony Blair said, 'A day like today is not a day for soundbites, really. But I feel the hand of history upon our shoulders.'

---

* In fact, Tony Blair's mother was from a Loyalist family, though they lived in the Republic, in the Catholic bit of Ulster, though they were Protestants, though Tony later became a Roman Catholic. Nobody said Northern Ireland was simple.

Inevitably there were die-hards opposed to the compromise and a massive bomb in Omagh in August 1998 killed more people than any since the troubles had begun. But in the decade since the Good Friday Agreement, terrorist incidents have been dramatically reduced, the IRA has been seen to destroy its weapons and Martin McGuinness and Ian Paisley* now enjoy nothing more than sitting down over a pint of the black stuff and listening to the fiddler play a medley of Republican and Loyalist anthems. Under the terms of the Belfast Agreement (to give the deal its proper name), there will be no change in the constitution of Northern Ireland against the wishes of the majority of its people. So now the Protestants' best chance of remaining in the United Kingdom is to try and persuade the Pope to change his position on contraception before the Catholics are in the majority. 'Another cache of condoms was found in Nationalist West Belfast this morning,' the news will soon be reporting. 'The IUD, a shady loyalist group, has admitted responsibility for the so-called switch from Semtex to Durex.'

In a hundred years' time it seems unlikely that they will be singing Irish folk songs to Tony Blair, but if it does transpire that peace has come to Ireland, it will be in no small part down to his skills as a patient negotiator and determined pragmatist. Perhaps it was his success in Ulster that convinced him it was worth trying to find a peaceful solution to the Middle East. Last time anyone looked, that challenge seemed to be taking a little bit longer.

---

* Ian Paisley had refused to take part in the negotiations that led to the Good Friday Agreement, although regularly turned up to claim he was being excluded. Sky's Adam Boulton recalls that during one cross-examination by reporters he told a female journalist, completely without irony, 'Woman, know your place! Why aren't you at home tending your family?'

Scotland says Yes! Wales says 'S'pose so'

When John Smith died, his successor jettisoned much of the former leader's cautious reforming agenda, but one commitment was too far advanced and high profile to be abandoned. For some time now, Scotland and Wales had been perplexing the mandarins of Whitehall by claiming that they weren't in fact large counties on the edge of England, but were actually nations in their own right, with their own languages, traditions and amusing accents useful for minor characters in BBC sitcoms. Such fanciful notions were generally dismissed out of hand by whoever was Secretary of State for Scotlandshire, but since the nationalist cause had gained political momentum in the 1970s, the case for regional assemblies had refused to go away.

Sticking by Labour's manifesto promise (that had seen the Tories left without a single seat in either country), the government organized referendums in Scotland and Wales on whether they wanted their own parliaments. Scotland responded with an overwhelming Yes vote, but the response in Wales was decidedly lukewarm.*

The New Labour machine did not have the best of luck with either of the candidates to lead these assemblies. The only significant Westminster politician to be persuaded to move to Edinburgh was Donald Dewar, who became the first First Minister of Scotland and then promptly died. In Wales Ron Davies was the preferred candidate and was selected at the Welsh Labour Party conference in September 1998. Two days later he resigned. Davies admitted to what he called 'a moment of madness', having been walking around on Clapham Common at night and then going off to Brixton with a man he had met there. The

---

* One Downing Street witness claimed that Blair declared 'Fucking Welsh!' when the results came in, which amazingly prompted a police inquiry on the grounds of anti-Welsh racism.

man then mugged Davies at knifepoint, which Davies kept insisting was the point of this whole story, but everyone kept going back to the beginning and saying, 'Sorry, I'm a bit confused: why did you go to this well-known gay haunt at night and go off with a stranger that you had met there?' When he was later spotted at another gay haunt off a motorway slip road, Davies claimed that he was 'watching badgers', which as euphemisms go is up there with the best of them.

It was unfortunate that such an incident should have so damaged Ron Davies, since 'badger watching' was an area in which the Blair government could be seen at its most progressive. The age of consent for watching badgers was reduced to sixteen, badger watchers were permitted in the armed forces, and if two badger watchers wanted to join together in a civil partnership to watch nocturnal mammals then they were at liberty to do so. Today, when our TV screens are packed with sexually explicit gay jokes from Graham Norton or *Little Britain*, it is difficult to imagine just how different the atmosphere was for homosexuals in previous decades. Tony Blair proved to be consistently on the side of tolerance and equality, and for a politician often accused of playing to conservative Middle England, he had little to gain politically from such a stand. In fact, so consistent and principled was his policy on gays that the *Daily Mail* were rather disappointed that his major personal announcement after retiring was his conversion to Catholicism, and not an admission that he had left Cherie for an air steward called Rodney.

New Labour press release: 'Labour have stopped spinning – official'

Prime Ministers are either judged to be weak and dithering like John Major or autocratic and domineering like Margaret

Thatcher. Fairly quickly Tony Blair was pigeon-holed in the 'control freak' category by the media, intervening in every department and obsessed with trying to dictate what the newspapers wrote. Alastair Campbell became the chief bogeyman for those feeling unable to criticize the hallowed St Tony just yet, with Peter Mandelson apparently hovering shadily behind as some sort of cynical Machiavellian spin doctor whom everyone decided they didn't like, without knowing very much about what he did or why he aroused such strong feelings.

New Labour's alleged 'control freakery' was born out of a determination not to let the party slip back into the divisions and political posturing of the 1980s. Although the government was willing to devolve power from the centre, creating regional assemblies and elected local mayors, the New Labour leadership would then tie itself into all sorts of knots as it struggled to put its favoured candidates into the new posts. Ken Livingstone had been a popular London leader, and had kept a high media profile since Mrs Thatcher had attempted to abolish him in 1986. But for Tony Blair, Gordon Brown and others, 'Red Ken' was in the same Axis of Evil as the hugely damaging Tony Benn and Arthur Scargill. Elaborate procedures were considered for selecting Labour's mayoral candidate by whatever means would keep out Livingstone and put in the favoured Frank Dobson. 'How about we limit the selection panel to just Mrs Dobson?' they wondered. 'Why not split the job in two,' joked the Tory Leader William Hague, 'with Frank Dobson as your day-mayor and Ken Livingstone as your night-mayor?' Denied the chance to be Labour's choice, Livingstone ended up standing as an independent, winning the election and pushing Labour into third place. He had been leader of the GLC and returned as London's figurehead fourteen years later. His first words at the podium were, 'As I was saying before I was so rudely interrupted . . .'

The voting public had seen Livingstone as a victim of the control freakery of the government. Before long the spin doctors had ceased to be the medium and became the message. Stories of Labour MPs forced to carry pagers and accounts of aggressive spin doctors shouting their rebuttals down the phone at those poor journalists all helped the country fall out of love with New Labour.

World finally learns how to spell 'millennium'

As the year 2000 approached there was a rash of nostalgia shows looking back over the past 1,000 years. 'What was your favourite showbiz moment? Was it Nasty Nick's eviction in *Big Brother*, or Falstaff's faked death in *Henry IV Part 1*? Top politician: Tony Blair or Cardinal Wolsey?' In the year 999 they had feared that God would bring chaos and disaster. A thousand years later the same powers were attributed to computers. The so-called 'millennium bug' threatened to bring modern civilization to collapse with doom-mongers predicting that all the world's mainframes would simultaneously shut down when confronted by a date that came after 1999. Planes would fall out of the sky, life-support machines in hospitals would pack up, Amazon.co.uk might even send you inappropriate book recommendations. Around the world over $300 billion was spent preparing for the terrifying Y2K moment, but even in the territories that did very little, no great disasters were ultimately reported. In Australia, a couple of states reported that bus-ticket-validation machines had failed to operate, but mankind managed to bounce back.

More predictable perhaps was the disaster taking shape in Greenwich. The Millennium Dome project had originally been developed by the previous Conservative government, but Labour had more than enough time to look again at the plans and realize they were unworkable. Saddled with too many bosses and competing agendas, and crucially based on unrealizable visitor numbers, the Millennium Dome soon became the first point of call for anyone wishing to bash the government. Every spending shortfall was contrasted with the waste of money that was the Dome, which was in fact doing a fairly good job of providing an outlet for the great British passions of queuing and moaning. Those who despised Blair before he had even started worked themselves up into such a lather about the Millennium Dome that they had no higher level of fury available during Blair's second term when he went to war against Iraq.

On New Year's Eve 1999, the memorable image was of the uncomfortable-looking Queen linking arms with Tony Blair singing 'Auld Lang Syne', but the guests who had got into the Dome on the night had experienced many hours of queues and security checks and were all in a filthy mood by the time it was midnight. 'A River of Fire' was promised on the Thames, which, like the Dome, never quite lived up to the hype. Politically speaking it might have been wiser to promise something that could realistically be delivered. Like 'A River of Water'.

'Purer than pure'

Tony Blair ended up apologizing for the Dome, but it wasn't the only embarrassment of his first term. From the outset, Tony Blair demonstrated that his government was just as accident-prone as any other. It was just that there was such a reservoir of goodwill for him that to begin with the popularity of 'Teflon Tony' seemed unaffected. An early scandal involved party donations. Labour had pledged to end tobacco advertising in sport, but had exempted Formula One racing, because they had lots of tobacco advertising. And anyway, Formula One isn't a sport; it's just driving inconsiderately. Questions about the exemption were raised when it turned out that Formula One boss Bernie Ecclestone had donated a million pounds to the Labour Party before the election. The suggestion was that government policy was being decided on the basis of party political donations. Tony Blair was too intelligent a politician to have consciously allowed such a thing to happen. But Ecclestone had had access to the PM to argue that Formula One would be forced overseas if the ban stood. The less glamorous sports of snooker and darts did not have a spokesman who had purchased a ticket for the top table. The Labour Party quickly gave the money back, but the first damage had already been done to the reputation of a Prime Minister the papers were sure had promised to be 'purer than pure'.

Other embarrassments included the extra-marital affair of Robin Cook, the business affairs of Geoffrey Robinson, and Peter Mandelson resigning from the government not once, but twice, which is pretty good going in a four-year term. Blair was certainly not loved everywhere; he was slow-handclapped during a speech to the Women's Institute, and the pro-hunting lobby was furious about Labour's plans to abolish hunting with dogs. The so-called Countryside Alliance organized marches through London purporting to be about a range of issues affecting rural communities, but the banners all seemed to be about the right to kill foxes for fun, with not a single mention of the way the supermarkets were virtually squeezing farmers out of existence. The marches were well attended, although those estimating the numbers may have made the mistake of counting the farmers' wives and the farmers' sisters as two different people. But it was not until opponents of the government began taking direct action that the government's poll rating briefly slipped behind the Conservatives for the first time in eight years.

With Labour having promised not to increase income tax, revenue was raised with so-called 'stealth taxes' that saw higher duty levied on items such as fuel. By 2000, tax accounted for over 80 per cent of the cost of a litre of diesel. Petrol prices in Britain were higher than most of the rest of Europe, particularly Russia, where they were now drinking it with tonic and a slice of lemon. Road hauliers and farmers had held various lacklustre protests demanding a price reduction, but in September 2000 a group calling itself Farmers for Action blockaded an oil refinery in Cheshire, and other copycat blockades soon prevented petrol tankers getting out of the depots.

The government urged people not to panic-buy petrol, which obviously was the cue for everyone to jump into their cars and drive down and join the fractious queue outside the Shell garage. While everyone agreed that car usage would soon have to be reduced if Planet Earth was not to shrivel up and die, people understood that this reduction would be in general terms, and obviously didn't apply to the trips they were planning later that week. Suddenly motorists had to enjoy their cars without the bonus of petrol, children had to walk the half mile to school, BMW drivers had to get on a bus: it was truly a painful time for millions.

But the unforeseen shortage of fuel was also threatening essential services; some schools closed, the Health Service was put on red alert and then supermarkets warned they might run out of supplies (which caused panic-buying of food as well). The government had been taken by surprise by the effectiveness of the campaign, and accused the petrol companies of doing little to try and get their tankers out of the depots (the oil companies obviously would have preferred lower fuel tax as well). The surreal week exposed modern society's total dependence on oil, and for all the lip service paid to green issues, the token wind farms and recycled newspapers, it was clear that our love affair with the car was just as strong as ever. The fuel crisis had been a painful double whammy: not enough petrol to drive to the garden centre at the weekend, but not so little that they had to cancel *Top Gear*.

Just William

The episode had been the only glimmer of hope in a dismal four years for the leader of the opposition. William Hague had first come to national attention at the 1977 Tory Party conference when as a teenage boy he had spoken of his fears for the future. Luckily he concentrated on politics and not his worries about O levels or eventually having sex. Two decades on, he was leader of the party as the Conservatives opted for someone even younger than Tony Blair.

When the Conservatives' candidates had been vying for position before the leadership contest, Hague had agreed to run as Michael Howard's deputy. It seems as if William must have got home to be roundly told off by his mum or something: 'You said *what*? You go right back out there and tell him that you want the top job yourself!' Whatever happened, the next morning the deal was off, and Hague ended up topping the poll. He struggled to be taken seriously by the media, but was not helped by his decision to pose in a baseball cap at Alton Towers or a claim that he used to drink fourteen pints of beer a day. Meanwhile the Tories continued to be associated with 'sleaze' with Jonathan Aitken sent to prison for perjury and Jeffrey Archer looking like he'd soon be joining him. Compared to Hague's impossible job of leading the Tory Party into the general election, they looked like they were getting off lightly.

'Whoever you vote for, the government always gets in'

Poor Peter Snow. There he was with his great big swingometer and computer-generated election battleground, all ready to leap around the studio of *Election Special* projecting the exit polls onto the key marginals, predicting famous scalps and estimating majorities. And nothing changed in the slightest. The result of the 2001 election saw a tiny dip in Labour's massive majority, and the Conservatives increase their total number of MPs by one.

The election campaign was so expertly organized that Labour had timetabled all its gaffes for the same day. On 17 May, the day of Labour's manifesto launch, Tony Blair was harangued by a woman on live television about her husband's inability to get hospital treatment, while the Home Secretary Jack Straw was slow-handclapped by the Police Federation. None of this particularly damaged Labour because everyone was eagerly watching the seventeenth slow-motion replay of the Deputy Prime Minister punching a voter in the face. The pro-hunting protestor had shoved an egg into the side of John Prescott's head at almost point-blank range; Prescott had thought he was being struck and turned round to return the compliment with more force than British boxers normally seem to manage. The couple grappled against a wall for a moment with rather less dignity than had been hoped for when Prescott was told to go and meet some ordinary voters, until rather disappointingly the fighters were separated by Labour Party minders whose job of getting some publicity for this ministerial visit now seemed to be accomplished. Frankly the whole election would have been a lot more entertaining if the pair had been allowed to compete in a full-blown American-style wrestling bout, complete with spangly pants, character masks and climatic victory for the Deputy PM as he landed his wobbly naked belly onto the face of the mullet-haired young farmer. Far from damaging the government, perversely the news footage of the event seemed to help the Labour Party campaign – probably by waking everyone up to the fact that there was supposed to be an election going on.

In the reshuffle after Labour's expected victory, John Prescott was made 'cabinet enforcer' – basically, if ministers didn't deliver, then he would come round and thump them. Robin Cook was demoted to Leader of the House, Jack Straw was moved to the Foreign Office, while David Blunkett became Home Secretary. Gordon Brown was very open to the idea of being moved from the Treasury in the reshuffle: 'I could have a bash at being Prime Minister, I suppose . . .' he suggested helpfully. It was politically impossible for Blair to move his Chancellor without alienating him further and precipitating a prolonged Heseltine-like leadership campaign. Thus it was that Gordon Brown became the longest-serving Chancellor in modern history. On Sky TV's *Neighbours From Hell* a familiar-sounding man filmed in semi-darkness would complain about this Scottish bully who lived next door, who kept tutting at everything he did and tried to get him evicted at every possible opportunity.

Quiet Man asked to be quieter

With barely even a minor dent in Labour's massive majority, it looked like the next election was probably already decided as well, and William Hague resigned the Tory leadership to make a lucrative living on the after-dinner speaking circuit. The Conservative Party became even more divided and demonstrated that it had learnt nothing about appealing to a wider electorate by choosing quite the most uninspiring leader available, and to date Iain Duncan Smith remains the only leader of a major political party never to become a celebrity. At the time they hoped his elevation to the position of leader of the opposition would get him all over the papers and the TV screens. 'OK, the date's in the diary: 12 September 2001.'

The former Scots Guards officer had been a thorn in the side of John Major as a leader of the rebels opposing the Maastricht Treaty, and it was this hard-line anti-Europeanism that made him attractive to the dwindling Conservative Party membership. As a public speaker, Duncan Smith's main concern seemed to be not waking up the pensioners in the front row of the Tory Party conference. He attempted to cast himself as 'the Quiet Man', as if that made up for projecting with less range and passion than Stephen Hawking. The *Newsnight* journalist Michael Crick uncovered some embarrassing untruths in his curriculum vitae, in which he claimed to have attended the University of Perugia (he had done a short language course nearby), and when Duncan Smith gave a second appalling conference speech, Tory insiders secretly approached Crick with further revelations that Duncan Smith's wife was claiming a salary as his assistant without seeming to do very much work. The story was enough to finish him off; just two years after becoming leader he lost a vote of no confidence of the Parliamentary Party and was replaced by the Member for Transylvania South, Michael Howard.* Howard had come fifth out of five last time he had stood for the Tory leadership, so this time they didn't bother with a vote.

Shoulder to shoulder

Three months after the 2001 general election, Tony Blair prepared his speech for the Trades Union Congress, expecting a certain amount of booing, heckling and perhaps even a WI-style slow handclap. As it turned out he received a warm and dignified ovation, although this was for going up on the stage and saying he would not be giving a speech at all. It was the afternoon of 11 September and news had come through that America was being subjected to unprecedented terrorist attacks.

---

* Michael Howard had never quite recovered from the damning words of his former Home Office colleague Ann Widdecombe, who had said there was 'something of the night about him'.

Some news events are so momentous that you know immediately things will never be the same again. So it was when the smile of the Manhattan skyline had its two front teeth knocked out. Great Britain too felt the force of that blow, and not just because many Britons were feared to be among the thousands killed. For all the shared institutions of Brussels and Strasbourg, the British people felt a deeper affinity with the English-speakers across the Atlantic Ocean, and most observers agreed that Tony Blair's immediate response to the 9/11 attacks was perfectly judged. A short public statement, a strategic assessment of what the events would mean in the short and long term, followed by immediate efforts to build a European consensus. Some American commentators contrasted all of this with George W. Bush's response, which was basically to hide under the kitchen table for a day and a half.

Most British people were utterly in agreement with Tony Blair when he said that the United Kingdom would stand shoulder to shoulder with the United States in the fight against global terror. However, if they had thought about it a little more deeply, they might have preferred him to add the caveat: 'For as long as we are feeling as strongly about this as we do at the moment.' At the time senior civil servants in the Home Office feared that the events of 9/11* would prompt dissident Irish terrorists to raise their game; the prospect of Islamic suicide bombers operating within the UK was not at the front of their minds. But the British government produced a document outlining what was known about Osama Bin Laden and the support he had received from the Afghan government. The following month Blair travelled 5,000 miles in two days as he tried to build a consensus for action against Afghanistan, while Cherie checked he was registering his air miles.

* In Britain, of course, we arrange our dates the other way round, but this didn't seem quite the moment to interrupt the grieving Americans and say, 'Actually, in the UK we're going to call it "11/9".'

British troops joined the Americans in Operation Enduring Freedom (later renamed 'Operation Bogged Down in Eternal Unwinnable Conflict With No Visible Exit Strategy'). Initially it seemed that the overthrow of the repressive Taliban government had been easily accomplished and by the end of 2001 Afghan children were filmed flying kites once again (forbidden under the previous regime) and music returned to the streets of Kabul. The Taliban had been replaced by Mary Poppins. Alastair Campbell's diaries reveal the British government's frustration that there was too little focus on what would happen after the Afghan government was overthrown. The Americans were too busy trying everything they could think of to track down Bin Laden, but it turned out he was ex-directory. Campbell himself became briefly obsessed with organizing a showpiece football match in Kabul, but instead of it resulting in an easy 2–0 victory for the UK Forces XI, the game got bogged down into an eternal stalemate with everyone losing interest, thousands of injuries and still no sign of the final whistle a decade later. Because as every invading force has discovered to their cost since *Carry On Up The Khyber*, the mountains of Afghanistan do not easily lend themselves to military occupation. Just as in Iraq a few years later, Britain and America were to learn that going in and toppling a government was the easy bit.

George W. Bush had seen his father evict the invading army from Kuwait. Tony Blair's political baptism had been losing his deposit in a by-election in the middle of the Falklands War. Both of these had been relatively cut-and-dried conflicts, with a small amount of territory to be retaken and a grateful indigenous population who were not going to turn around and plant a car bomb the moment you thought you had liberated them. Perhaps the simple narrative of these untypical wars had been what convinced Tony Blair that military action could and should be used for a moral purpose.

But few could have imagined in 1997 that Tony Blair would involve Britain in more overseas conflicts than any prime minister since the Second World War. British troops would see action in Kosovo, Bosnia, Sierra Leone, Afghanistan and Iraq. But it was the latter that would cast the biggest shadow over the Blair premiership, dimming all other achievements and losing him the trust of many British voters, one or two of whom felt strongly enough to deliberately misspell Tony's surname. The police were for ever pointing out to demonstrators that the Prime Minister's name was not 'Tory B-Liar'.

Weapons of mass deception

The question of whether Tony Blair lied in the run-up to the Iraq War centred on claims that Saddam Hussein had WMD (not to be confused with WKD, the vodka-based alcopop popular with teenage girls). 'Weapons of mass destruction' was a new buzz-phrase designed to sound like it was describing nuclear weapons, even though that was one thing everyone was confident Saddam did not have. But the dictator was known to have used poison gas on his own people, and the suggestion was that he was in a position to launch such a lethal offensive against the West. The shock of 9/11 had made it seem as if anything was possible, and that a pre-emptive strike had to be made if there was even a chance of such a thing happening. Indeed the American government were more than happy to associate the Iraqi regime with the terrorists of Al Qaeda, even though it was clear there was no direct link. Basically anyone who used the letter 'q' without a 'u' was considered fair game.

In Britain, however, the public would take a little more convincing that a second war against Saddam Hussein could be justified. Tony Blair did televised question-and-answer sessions with members of the public, putting his case well and persuading many of the sincerity of his convictions. He could not have consulted more widely before doing what he always intended to do anyway. The government then produced an intelligence report claiming that 'weapons of mass destruction' could be deployed against Britain in forty-five minutes. Anxious-looking TV reporters loyally repeated the dramatic government headline, despite it all sounding rather unlikely that a bankrupt country that had struggled to get a couple of Scud missiles as far as Israel could possibly target a long-range missile on the United Kingdom. It didn't help the authority of the government's claims that much of the dossier turned out to have been cut and pasted off the web (complete with typographical errors), with a few sinister exaggerations thrown in for good measure. We had been promised a 'young government', but we didn't expect the Prime Minister to copy his homework off the internet. The so-called 'dodgy dossier' confirmed a general sense that Tony Blair was determined to support America's war against Iraq, however vague and contrived the evidence against Saddam Hussein, however damaging this course would be to European unity and whatever the political cost to his government.

Indeed Blair had resolutely stood by the White House for so long it would have been almost impossible to back out now, even if he had wanted to. His proximity to the American President had persuaded Bush to at least try to involve the United Nations, but when that failed the illegality of the war was only further underlined. In truth, Blair had little influence on the Bush administration, except that his unwavering support added legitimacy to an illegitimate course of action. It was even later argued by some government insiders that if America was to make a major international mistake, then it should not make it alone. By this logic, Richard Nixon should not have been allowed to pursue the Watergate conspiracy by himself. Ted

Heath and Harold Wilson should have burgled the Democratic headquarters while President Pompidou stood guard outside.

In February 2003, a huge march in London against the forthcoming war demonstrated the level of public opposition to the now inevitable conflict. Even the presence of Bianca Jagger was not sufficient to persuade Tony Blair to change his mind. In March the Leader of the House of Commons and former Foreign Secretary Robin Cook resigned from the government, having made a dignified and impeccably argued speech outlining the reasons why the war could not be supported. His speech was the first in the history of the House of Commons to have received a standing ovation. Cook's principled departure contrasted with the bungled resignation of Clare Short, who made lots of self-important noises about quitting the cabinet if there was a war, then voted for the war and then resigned after the capture of Baghdad.

Blair's laudable hopes of using his leverage for a wider solution in the Middle East including the Palestinian problem soon petered out. It's not clear that Bush even listened to the end of the voice-mail. In truth, the only world power capable of exerting any degree of influence over the US was the European Union, and thanks to Britain, the EU was now divided. The French made the point that the invasion was opposed by a majority of the permanent members of the UN Security Council. And the Americans made the point that the French were a load of cheese-eating surrender monkeys.* Blair's best hope as the bombing began was that Saddam would be quickly toppled, that the war would not be followed by a bloody and protracted period of occupation and that the weapons of mass destruction would quickly be found. Well, one out of three's not bad.

---

* This phrase first appeared in *The Simpsons* and was seized upon by republican commentators. In America many restaurants dropped the name 'French fries' in favour of 'freedom fries'.

Saddam statues for sale on eBay

The defining image of the speedy success of the American and British forces in Iraq was the huge bronze statue of Saddam Hussein in Baghdad that was sent toppling over to the cheers of the Iraqi crowd. Amazingly an American armoured vehicle managed to drag the statue to the ground without crushing any British soldiers underneath. The head was later removed and kept as a trophy by the US soldiers; how they got it through the metal detector at the airport on the way home remains a mystery. All over the country statues of the dictator were brought down and gleefully struck with shoes, as is the custom. The head from one statue has ended up at the Gordon Highlanders Museum in Aberdeen, although that still doesn't make it quite worth the trip.

The real Saddam, however, was proving harder to find. Although at the beginning of May a triumphalist Bush declared that the war had been won, the world's biggest game of hide and seek would go on for the rest of the year. Or maybe it was 'sardines', and Osama and Saddam would eventually be found shushing and giggling in the same wardrobe. Western journalists were shown around the inside of the dictator's palace and the world was exposed to Saddam's crimes against interior decor. Saddam's paintings resembled the cover art of 1970s heavy metal albums, and for the art critics of Radio 3 the war was finally justified. In December 2003 a bearded and dishevelled-looking Saddam Hussein was finally found hiding near his home town of Tikrit (twinned with Warrington-Runcorn). He was filmed as a torch was shone around inside his mouth, but the weapons of mass destruction weren't hiding in there either. He was later tried by an Iraqi court for crimes against humanity and hanged. His execution was recorded on a mobile phone and posted on the internet, which is not a scenario that had been envisaged when they drew up the Geneva Convention.

The end of the war had come suddenly and an orgy of looting took the occupying forces by surprise. It quickly became apparent that little thought had been given to how the country would be governed once Saddam had been toppled, and the tyranny of a brutal dictator was replaced by growing anarchy and civil war under the watch of bewildered occupying forces.

Britain had made a sizeable contribution to the military force that invaded Iraq with more than 40,000 service personnel deployed in the region. They were now charged with occupying Iraq's second city Basra, mythical location of the Garden of Eden. It had definitely gone downhill since then. Six months after the fall of Baghdad, more US and British service personnel were killed than had died in the conquest. Car bombs and seemingly random attacks on British forces took a heavy toll and four and a half years later, when the territory was finally handed over to Iraqi authorities, 84 per cent of local people said they believed that the British occupation had had a negative impact on the region.

In the UK came a growing realization that British soldiers were not seen as liberators but as an imperialist occupying army. Saddam's 'weapons of mass destruction', the very reason that British forces were there, had not turned up. Even with 300,000 American and British soldiers looking between the cushions on the sofa, checking behind the sideboard and under the bed in the spare room, there was just no sign of them. All this time, the junior ranks wondered if it might seem unhelpful to make the rather obvious point: 'Sir, if Saddam had had WMD, then surely he would have used them against an invading army that was going to depose him and see him executed.' 'Shut up, Johnson! And go and look in the garage behind the ping-pong table.'

Into this atmosphere came a renewed political storm about Downing Street's 'dodgy dossier', which had made the original claims about Iraq's ability to deploy biological weapons within forty-five minutes. By now the government might have been better off trying to claim it was a typo. 'Did we say biological *weapons*? Oh, that's supposed to say *biological washing powder*. Bloody agency typists!' A BBC journalist quoted an unknown weapons expert who said the government had misrepresented his findings. Pretty quickly the identity of this source became public and Dr David Kelly found himself at the centre of a political storm. Cross-examined by a House of Commons committee and subjected to enormous media attention, the pressure was too much for Kelly, who committed suicide the day after his appearance before MPs. The sorry tale just served to underline what an utter disaster the Iraq adventure had been from start to finish. Of course it is easy to say that with the benefit of hindsight. Except that it was completely obvious that it would be an utter disaster beforehand as well.

Thus the Iraq War has cast a pall over everything else achieved by Tony Blair. It's like Bill Clinton and Monica Lewinsky; the former president might want you to focus on all his domestic and international achievements, but your first thought is always going to be about him in the Oval Office with his trousers down. There were many in the UK who felt that Clinton's successor didn't need a Monica Lewinsky; Bush had Tony Blair for that. But it would be wrong to suggest that Britain went to war just because the American President clicked his fingers. During his first term, Blair's eagerness to put British troops on the ground in former Yugoslavia had contrasted with the reluctance of President Clinton. The idea that Tony Blair was slavishly following the American President into action against Afghanistan and Iraq does not stand up to examination. If Blair could have invaded Narnia to remove the Snow Queen he would have done so, even if the Allied forces would have underestimated the length of the Narnian winter and American friendly fire would have turned British soldiers into statues by mistake. Early in his premiership Blair looked at the massacres and human-rights abuses of recent

history and argued that the rest of the world should have intervened; that standing back and doing nothing was not an option.
But following the conflicts in Afghanistan and Iraq, Britain and
America had to relearn one of the oldest lessons of history: that
even if a war does resolve an old problem, it generally creates lots
of new ones. In the modern age of instant messaging and fast
food, Western voters somehow expect quick and easy micro-
wavable wars to go. *Conflict-Lite*™, the short, casualty-free TV
battle that you can watch over a weekend without worrying about
the cost.

The war on annoyance

The dramatic business of tackling terrorism took up much of the
time and focus of a government that still had so much to do for
the 99.999 per cent of the population who would never encounter
bombs or letters sealed with a loving dose of anthrax. For most
people in Britain, the only way their life was changed by suicide
bombers was not being allowed to carry bottled water onto the
plane or being forced to take their shoes off at airport security.
They didn't feel terror, they felt irritation; Al Qaeda weren't
terrorists, they were 'annoyists'. But it seemed that a country that
had endured three decades of bombings from the IRA now
needed a whole range of new measures to tackle twenty-first-
century terrorism.

The government proposed the introduction of identity cards,
which was delayed after human rights activists complained about
the use of embarrassing photos featuring ludicrous haircuts and
unfashionable shirts. It was made illegal to protest within one
kilometre of Parliament Square, to the outrage of Conservatives
who felt the distance should have been measured in miles. DNA
samples of anyone arrested (including those found innocent) were

kept on a police database, even if they were stuck in the wrong fridge and got mixed up with the Müller Corners. Most significant of all, the government extended the period that terror suspects could be detained without charge, as the battle to stop the terrorists taking away our freedoms involved the government chipping away at historic freedoms instead.

Separate from the creeping authoritarianism of the government, but thematically linked to it in the mind of sci-fi fans, was the loss of privacy that resulted from the advance of modern technology. By the end of the twentieth century, Britain had become the most continually observed society in the world. There were surveillance cameras in every high street, on every police car and in every major store. Middle-aged men dared not buy Phil Collins *Greatest Hits*, for fear that their musical choice would be captured on film and used to publicly humiliate them. Some people saw the proliferation of cameras as George Orwell's nightmarish totalitarian vision finally realized. But only very foolish people who had completely misunderstood *1984*. It wouldn't have been much of a novel if the hellish climax involved Winston Smith being caught by a speed camera doing 40 miles an hour in a 30mph zone. In fact, the only bit of *1984* that is worse than Orwell imagined is that instead of Big Brother watching us, we are all watching *Big Brother*.

Mobile phone technology means that our movements can theoretically be tracked and our calls monitored. Google Streetview shows the whole world your front door the day before you got round to repainting it. Another couple of clicks and anyone can see an aerial view of your back garden. How many millions of hours must have been wasted by teenage boys trying to find a topless sunbather on Google Earth? Modern technology increases the potential for a totalitarian state to monitor its populace. But Britain is not Orwell's Airstrip One, nor indeed Burma or Iran. In Western democracies, the state is generally benign. As long as you steer clear of the French riot police or Lambeth parking control, nobody is really out to get you. When Robert Peel introduced the idea of a police force in the 1820s, the same civil liberty arguments were used. Now we like the idea of a bobby on the beat looking out for villains, but if it is a modern CCTV camera watching over us, then somehow it is oppressive. Technology can be used for good or ill, or usually neither, as we can never be bothered to read the instructions properly. The real hell awaiting us in the future is not the Thought Police recording our dissenting opinions and torturing us into compliance. It is when the information on the DNA database and identity cards is accessed by the Sky TV telephone sales team. 'We see from your DNA records that you have a hereditary predisposition to Alzheimer's. Would you like additional health insurance with your Sports and Movie package?'

A diet of Brussels?

When New Labour was first elected, Britain had immediately signed up to the Social Chapter of the Maastricht Treaty, extending the human rights already enjoyed in the rest of Europe, where French children could smoke during PE and Greek dogs could be carried on mopeds without wearing a helmet. EU members looked forward to welcoming the United Kingdom into the pro-European fold, but although Tony Blair talked like a good European, the actions told a different story. After Britain split with France and Germany on the issue of Iraq, it was clear that the EU would be unable to speak with one voice in world affairs. Blair was unable to persuade his Chancellor that Britain should adopt the European single currency; instead they just watched the pound falling to the same value as the euro so at least it was easy to work out the exchange rate. Where Blair did make a difference in Europe was arguing in favour of EU expansion, and then upholding the right of citizens of the new member states to come to Britain to work if they so wished. But nobody had foreseen that they would come in such huge numbers, more than a million of them in the space of a couple of years in a huge wave of immigration that would have provoked tabloid outrage if their skins had been a different colour.

In fact, the arrival of Eastern European workers at the beginning of the twenty-first century was the single largest influx of immigrants in the history of the British Isles. Specialist shops sprang up catering for their curious tastes in spiced sausages and pickled root vegetables. In some parts of the country, road signs appeared in Polish, with councils discovering they had nowhere near enough letter Zs. The sudden influx of highly skilled but cheap labour was a huge boost for the construction industry, while ironing all the family's duvet covers suddenly seemed a possibility when next door's Czech nanny was happy to do the whole pile for a fiver. Many of the young Poles were highly educated, but seemed delighted to do manual work in the UK that earned them three times the salary they would get at home working as teachers or accountants. The result was that building sites were suddenly full of middle-class graduates, with their radios blaring out the *Moral Maze* on Radio 4, ogling the size of the library books under the arm of that passing blonde.

Shock report claims 'Children are the future'

When Tony Blair had first been elected to the Labour leadership, he wanted to find a way to stress the priorities of the next Labour government. 'I thought I might say, "Education! Education!"'

'Hmm . . . not emphatic enough, Tony, I think it needs more.'

'OK. What about "Education, education, education, education!"?'

'Now that's too much – maybe split the difference?'

Tony Blair looked at the increasingly globalized economy and saw that British manufacturing would not be able to compete against the low wages paid in places like China, India and the illegal sweatshops off Brick Lane. The only way forward for Western economies was to have a highly trained workforce that could develop new digital hardware thingys and computer programme-type stuff; he didn't really understand any of it but knew it must be important.*

Having the majority of the population earning their living from manual work was no longer viable and Labour set a target that half of all school leavers would go on to university, to make Britain a world leader in stealing traffic cones and making blobby coffee. When only 5 per cent of school leavers had gone to university, local authorities could afford to pay the tuition fees (and living costs of the poorer students). But with the ambitious targets for tertiary education, Labour finally did what no Conservative government had quite dared to do and replaced grants with student loans. It was also explained to the little ones that all that money from the tooth fairy down the years wasn't really a present and would have to be paid back eventually. The government promised that special provision would be made for those from the poorest backgrounds, because they couldn't imagine them ever applying to university anyway.

Even more controversial during Labour's second term was the government's decision to charge students 'top-up fees': an additional £3,000 towards the cost of sitting in a tutorial with a hangover, a measure which only just scraped through the House

---

* Tony Blair was unable to use computers. He had become Labour leader at just the point that the internet had taken off and despite being a champion of IT, he never found the time to learn how to use it himself.

of Commons despite Labour's huge majority. The arguments went back and forth but the government insisted it could see no other way of raising the money needed for world-class universities. 'Well, you could raise the income tax paid by the highest earners?' ventured one Labour backbencher, to the shocked gasps of all around him. And then he realized his mistake and said he was sorry, he didn't know what he was saying, but it was too late: a trapdoor opened, he fell through the floor and was never heard of again.

New Labour's first initiatives were at the other end of the age range. By 2000 the government had made available a free nursery place for every four-year-old and by Labour's second term there were enough places for every three-year-old whose parents wanted one. Class sizes were limited to thirty (as promised in one of Labour's pre-election pledges) and tens of thousands of new teachers were recruited, with special incentives for graduate teachers who would specialize in maths, science or taking Class 8C on a Friday afternoon. Teaching salaries reflected the importance the government attached to finding good leaders. A head teacher now earned considerably more than a Member of Parliament, and to the politicians' disappointment the general public did not seem particularly outraged by this statistic.

In the second term more emphasis was put on secondary education, with many failing comprehensives being turned into city academies. Often the areas of greatest need had the least effective local authorities, and it was felt that a dedicated sponsor, such as a dynamic entrepreneur or established charity, could give a school better leadership than the local council that took three hours to answer the phone when you rang for a skip permit. 'The day of the bog-standard comprehensive is over,' announced Alistair Campbell, managing to offend most of the schools in the country. It was decided that every school would have some sort of specialism, so that teenagers could spend extra time on the subjects in which they were most interested, although texting and smoking weren't on the list of options. The hope was that specialisms would also raise aspirations – pupils at an inner-city school where they specialized in business studies wouldn't turn into drug addicts but might become the drug dealers instead.

In practice, specialisms often tended to be pretty meaningless; parents did not want 'choice', the Holy Grail Tony Blair had been convinced would raise standards in schools. They just wanted one good school nearby where their children could go with their friends. But a massive investment in buildings and staff did see a huge improvement in the British education system. The proportion of a growing gross domestic product spent on education rose from 4.8 per cent when Blair came to office to 5.7 per cent by the time he left. GCSE results improved for every year of the Blair decade, so that for ten years in a row the *Daily Telegraph* front page could feature pretty teenage girls hugging one another.

'24 hours to save the NHS'

If you asked the average voter by the end of Blair's second term what they thought of Britain's education system, they would generally say, 'Oh, it's in a terrible state! They ought to do something about it.' Question Two would then be about their own children's school: 'Oh it's wonderful! They've just built this whole new sixth-form centre, and the teachers are so dedicated, and my eldest has just got really good results and is going to university . . .' The same double-think affected judgements on the National Health Service. You just had to look at the papers to read how terrible everything was, with super-bugs and waiting lists and the number of swans in casualty dying of bird flu. However, in their own town, voters would admit that they happened to be particularly lucky as their new health centre had been refurbished and the hospital's Accident and Emergency department had been rebuilt, and the nurses had been wonderful when little Timmy had been born.

Before the 1997 election, New Labour had told the voters that they had '24 hours to save the NHS', but it seems unlikely that the Conservatives would have closed it down that quickly if they'd won power. However, the election of the Labour government in 1997 was clearly a vital turning point for an institution that had suffered years of decline. Funding increased by an average of 8–9 per cent every year, and up to 15 per cent in some deprived areas. There was some criticism that the unwieldy bureaucracy of the NHS was not well placed to manage the new investment, and Tony Blair became increasingly convinced that reform of the NHS was as important as adequate funding. Britain's National Health Service is said to be the third largest employer in the world, after the Chinese army and the Indian railways, and all such massive organizations face similar problems. 'I'm afraid the operation to invade Tibet has been postponed again. We lost the file and so we're going to need to run some more tests . . .'

A determination to meet manifesto commitments to reduce waiting lists meant that the Labour government took the un-precedented step of actually paying to send some patients into the private system for operations. Health care was still free at the point of delivery; it's just that some patients got fresher coffee and a copy of *Country Life* in the waiting room. The private patients in the exclusive hospitals were a bit alarmed at having to mix with the proles, but at least they got to learn what those extra lines of numbers when they announced the lottery results were all about.

The significant building programmes undertaken by the government in health and education were undertaken using 'private finance initiatives' which to old lefties in the Labour Party immediately aroused suspicion due to the use of the words 'private' and 'finance', not to mention 'initiative'. These controversial 'build now, pay later' schemes involved the government contracting private firms to construct and manage public buildings over a period of decades without the immediate cost being felt by the taxpayer. Except that more than once, the private contractors faced bankruptcy and had to be bailed out by the Treasury. Thus it was that the government was underwriting the private companies it was paying to lease public services to the government. This was a sort of 'Third Way Ultra' – maximum-strength radical centre politics for those who liked their public–private partnerships to be beyond satire.

Blair completes hat-trick, then retires hurt

The general election of 2005 was conducted in the style of outraged teenagers in an inner-city comprehensive. 'OMG! That is like actually racist, 'cos, showing Michael Howard as a flying pig is like saying he's Jewish? 'Cos Jews don't eat pork and stuff, so like, that actually makes Labour the same as Hitler!'

The election was dominated by Iraq, but with the leadership of both main parties having supported the war, the rights and wrongs never got satisfactorily debated. Only the Liberals had opposed the war without UN backing, and they were the election's only psychological winners, increasing their tally of MPs to sixty-two: their highest representation since the 1920s. The Liberal leader Charles Kennedy* was unable to remember his party's policies during a press conference, a lapse that was put down to having just

* Charles Kennedy was elected leader by the membership of the Liberal Democrats after a number of successful appearances on *Have I Got News For You*. With the election of all the party leaders switching from MPs to the wider party membership, doing well on popular TV shows became more important than performing well in the House of Commons. It is also unlikely that Boris Johnson would have got the Conservative nomination to be Mayor of London if *Have I Got News For You* had not made him a celebrity.

become a father. However, after months of rumour and innuendo he soon resigned the Liberal leadership when his treatment for alcoholism was made public.

The expelled Labour MP George Galloway* took an East London seat from Labour for his new anti-war party Respect, but his fellow party members respected him slightly less when he appeared in *Celebrity Big Brother* dancing in a red leotard and pre-tending to lap up milk like a pussycat. The issue of the war's legality resurfaced during the campaign, and Tony Blair said that if people thought he had lied then they shouldn't vote for him. Labour's vote dropped by over a million.

In normal circumstances Labour's majority of sixty-six would have been seen as very healthy, but coming on the back of two landslides, and with another very low turnout, it seemed as if the public were tiring of New Labour, if not Westminster politics in general. Despite making a number of gains, the Tories still won fewer than two hundred seats for the third election in a row and Michael Howard resigned soon after. One of his last acts before stepping down was to reshuffle the Conservative front bench, at which point David Cameron was brought into the shadow cabinet.

R.E.S.P.E.C.T.

Re-elected prime ministers usually emerge from general elections with a new idea and agenda – it would be too much like an admission of failure to come out on the steps of Downing Street and say, 'Well, you know that thing we were trying to sort out over eight years ago. Well, we're going to keep hammering away at that

---

* In an interview with Piers Morgan for *GQ* magazine, Galloway said that it would be morally justifiable to assassinate Tony Blair. Many members of Respect were appalled – their leader was talking to Piers Morgan.

and hope we finally get somewhere.' Blair's buzzword of 2005 was 'respect'. Not in the sense that Tony Blair was going to join George Galloway's new fringe party created to protest about Tony Blair; the Prime Minister was aware that there was a general sense that courtesy and consideration for others seemed to be becoming a thing of the past, and that maybe the government should pass a law to make it illegal to jump the bus queue and rustle your sweet packets all the way through the film.

The perceived decline in good manners had been the downside to the end of deference; ever since the war there had been a gradual breaking down of the class system, in which those who ruled over us had only to open their mouths for their accents to provoke an outburst of obsequious fawning from all those around them. Those who mourn the death of polite society should remember that the genteel minority were only ever polite to each other; they were incredibly rude to the mass of the working classes. They threw them their coats, they barked orders at them, they made them dig coal without adequate safety equipment.* And new codes of etiquette have evolved for new times. Today if the British ambassador to Berlin sent a message to the Nazi government to say that a state of war now existed between our two countries, then at least he would have put a little sad face at the end.

The change in attitudes was also related to a shift in the British from a nation of producers to a nation of consumers. A customer culture extended to expecting immediate good service from schools and hospitals where once the public had been grateful just to have such things. Post-war society was initially something that we all created, in which every adult had a stake

---

* After the war the National Trust were in discussion with some of Britain's titled families about allowing the general public access to their grand estates. One of the less progressive landowners rather embarrassed the meeting by agreeing to have the public walk in his gardens but adding, 'But not inside the house. They do smell so.'

and a responsibility. Today, as consumers of society we demand that something be done by the Prime Minister or the council or basically anyone but ourselves. I blame the government.

New Labour introduced the Anti-Social Behaviour Order, aimed at curbing the irresponsible behaviour of some youngsters, and ministers did their best to sound tough about zero-tolerance and the responsibilities of parents, though the press conferences didn't always go as well as hoped.

'Er, Home Secretary? Your son has just been caught selling cannabis to an undercover *Mirror* journalist.'

'Oh, er, Jack, why don't you go and deal with that . . . anyway, as I was saying, we will not stand idly by and watch youngsters getting drunk in public.'

'And, Prime Minister, your son has just been found flat out in Leicester Square, off his face on alcopops . . . '

Eat, drink and be paralytic

It's a shame that when Tony Blair finished his decade as Prime Minister he didn't celebrate by going on an all-night bender with his mates, ending up getting arrested after puking into the fountains of Trafalgar Square. It might have symbolized the government's failure to tackle binge drinking, which continued to grow during its time in office. The average units of alcohol consumed increased across all age groups but it was the aggressive determination of the young to get very drunk which had the government wondering about dusting down the 1751 Gin Act and seeing if it might be updated. The increase in drunkenness obviously had knock-on effects in other areas such as policing and public health; basically NHS advice was that if you were going to injure yourself at home, try to do it before the pubs close, because you really wouldn't want to find yourself in the Accident and

Emergency department once the wounded, angry drunks started staggering in.

Binge drinking increased most significantly among young women. Swiss finishing schools developed special classes for the English ladies, demonstrating the correct way to puke up your kebab on the night bus. And looking out onto this nocturnal street scene, littered with horizontal teenagers off their face on Smirnoff Ice and Bacardi Breezers, stood the poor landlord of the Red Lion, wondering why his traditional English pub was now completely empty. Drinkers had discovered that they could buy alcohol more cheaply from the supermarkets or on the booze cruise to Boulogne, and so, despite the overall increase in alcohol consumption, the village pub was hit hard by its failure to rebrand itself as a cosmopolitan city centre bar. In November 2005 pubs hoped that extending the licensing hours might halt their long-term decline, but after 2007 it was no longer legal to smoke in any public building, which pubs claimed hit them even harder.*

Another reason for the decline of the traditional British pub was the vast increase in the choice of places to sit and eat or drink. Coffee bars and fast-food restaurants offered an alternative to the traditional liquid lunch enjoyed by office workers, who at least were no longer half pissed every afternoon. Going out for a meal had once been a major event in Britain; even among middle-class families, a trip to the Berni Inn for a cremated steak and a Cona coffee was only an occasional treat. But by the beginning of the twenty-first century, eating out was just part of the 24-hour-service culture; it became normal in some parts of the country to have breakfast in Starbucks, lunch at Pret A Manger and only eat at home in the evening if you were able to locate the Curry 'n' Hurry home-delivery number. Some Indian delivery services were toying

---

* Hardest hit by the smoking ban were the bingo halls, with an estimated 600,000 players suddenly staying away. Holistic yoga therapy centres were hardly hit by the smoking ban at all.

with the idea of coming back to your door a second and third time, saying, 'Any more lagers, please, sir? Some more naan bread perhaps?'

Restaurant chains eclipsed the local greasy spoon cafés, which led to the tragic extinction of various indigenous species of the botulism virus. There's no pretending that you got a better cup of coffee in the old days when a 'coffee' meant a teaspoon of Mellow Birds into a mug with three sugars and a splash of cold milk. The quality and range of food and wine became infinitely superior to that which had been available thirty years earlier, even though the triumph of style over substance seemed to spread to menus along with everything else: 'We'll take the traditional cheese and pickle sandwich,' said the guys from marketing, 'now we add three organic crisps on the side, a couple of bits of lettuce and a cherry tomato, *we cut the bread diagonally* and hey presto! Now we can charge £6.75.'

'Ch--ch.' What's missing?*

Samuel Johnson said that the pub was the heart of England and the church was its soul. That heart recently had a triple bypass operation, and the soul has now been sold for redevelopment as open-plan office studios. Britain had become increasingly secular since the end of the Second World War, with church attendance down to a few surviving pensioners and some pushy parents hoping to get their toddlers into the local C of E primary school. Sunday shopping was legalized in 1994, and after that the Sabbath was spent in a deeply reverential search for the correct brand of

---

* This was one of a number of tricksy advertising slogans used by trendier churches to try to attract worshippers. People were supposed to drive past and think: UR. It's not known whether the craze for textspeak extended to the Bibles inside: in da bgnng Gd cr8t hvn & erth : 0

trainers. In the new cathedrals of Lakeside Thurrock and the Westfield shopping centre, the congregations flocked to be sold a different version of spiritual fulfilment, one that would be attained once shoppers had forked out for the new HD-ready flat-screen television.

The Church of England was no longer central to British life in the way it once had been. The heir to the throne even proposed that he would not call himself Defender of *the* Faith like his predecessors, but the *Defender of Faith*. Charles then looked around for a reaction to this enormous historical shift, while everyone stared blankly and said, 'Sorry, say those two again – they sounded the same to me.' Britain was now a country of many religions: Christian, Muslim, Hindu, Sikh, Buddhist, Judaism, and one bloke in Redditch who was Zoroastrian. But despite the variety, strict adherents to any faith were in the minority. The withering of formal religion did not mean that the nation was now without any set of values; a new secular moral code had evolved from the Judeo-Christian-Richard-Curtis tradition. They believed that Christ may have laid down his life at the end of the Bible, but imagine he would have done so in a self-effacing Hugh Grant kind of way, making a climactic emotional speech in front of a big crowd while a great song by The Beach Boys built in the background.

There were occasional flashpoints when Western values clashed with the religions of British ethnic minorities. In 2004 a violent protest by hundreds of Sikhs prevented the performance of a play in Birmingham that offended their religious sensibilities. The episode reopened the debate surrounding the 1989 fatwa declared on British novelist Salman Rushdie for the offence his novel *The Satanic Verses* had caused to many Muslims. In both situations British politicians were not assertive enough about the overriding and non-negotiable principle of all post-Enlightenment Western liberal democracies. To paraphrase Voltaire: 'I despise what you say, but I would die for your right to say it. Well, not die; go on a march maybe. Sign a petition, definitely.'

No one should be going around offending people's faiths for the sake of it, but if a British novelist or playwright has something to say about Islam or any other religion, they have every right to do so and should get the full protection of the state to ensure that the principle of free speech is not compromised one iota. Although it might be worth using the pen-name 'Jeffrey Archer' just in case things turn nasty.

Seven seven

But Islamic extremism still felt like something that took lives in places far away, in the Middle East or Bali, even if the events of 9/11 and the Madrid bombings of 2004 had felt it creeping closer to home. By a bizarre twist of fate, on 7 July 2005, over a thousand delegates were attending a special conference in London to learn what they would have to do in the event of a major terrorist attack on the capital's transport system. Almost immediately they had to switch from theoretical practice mode to dealing with the real thing.

Britain had woken up in a good mood that morning. The day before, London had unexpectedly beaten Paris in the bid to host the 2012 Olympics, a victory that was due in no small part to the selling of Britain as a model of a multicultural society. But during the morning rush hour, news began to come through of an 'electrical surge' causing problems on the London underground. There were confused reports about 'incidents' at several stations, but only when the news showed the image of a London bus with its roof blown off did it become clear that London had become the target of a concerted terrorist attack. The four suicide bombers responsible (two of them still in their teens) had been

British-born Muslims apparently motivated by the UK's involvement in the Iraq War. Fifty-six people were killed by the attacks and a further seven hundred injured. A couple of weeks later, similar carnage was only prevented by a number of home-made bombs failing to detonate. No one knew how wide this new terrorist network was or how many potential suicide bombers had been recruited. In this heightened atmosphere police shot dead Jean Charles de Menezes, an innocent Brazilian electrician, at Stockwell underground station, thinking him to be a terrorist. Police accounts of their 'pursuit' and 'warnings' proved to be false, though no prosecutions were ever brought.

The investigation into the bombings concluded that the young men who had carried out the attacks had not been recruited and trained by any international terror network, and although Al Qaeda claimed the bombers as their own, it seemed that the terrorists had just taken it upon themselves to come to London to kill random commuters of all nationalities and religions.*

Senior politicians were keen to give the security services everything they wanted to prevent such a thing happening again, but for the first time since becoming Prime Minister, Tony Blair suffered a defeat in the House of Commons, when a bill to extend the period for detaining terror suspects to ninety days was thrown out.

The problem with granting the police and security services everything on their shopping list is that the rest of us have to be able to trust them totally with such excessive powers. But the summary execution of Jean Charles de Menezes, and the barrage of lies that followed from the police about what happened, had just confirmed that power and responsibility do not automatically go together.

---

* Among the dead were European Muslims as well as a Turk, an Iranian and an Afghan national.

Make poverty history (if only to shut up Bono)

The events of 7/7 had overshadowed the national elation that followed Britain winning the bid to host the 2012 Olympic Games, an achievement that had shown Tony Blair at his persuasive best. While the French President had flown in for the final presentation, made one pompous speech and flown out again, Blair spent three days in Singapore, charming delegates and winning them over on their individual concerns. Rather wonderfully, after the Olympic decision came through, Blair was with Chirac and all the other major world leaders for the G8 summit. Whether he kept putting an extended thumb and index finger to his head and saying 'Loser' to the French President is not recorded.

Which country hosts the spectacle of the Americans winning all the gold medals is not particularly important in global terms, but Tony Blair used the same diplomatic skills at the Gleneagles summit to persuade his colleagues to commit to a $50 billion increase in Third World aid, and a doubling of the aid to Africa. With their colourful chugger vest-tops and clipboards, Blair and Brown cheerfully bounced up to the other world leaders who were hoping to hurry past without making eye contact. It was just a question of getting them to take a leaflet, then persuading them there and then to commit to a direct debit.

In the run-up to the summit, Bob Geldof organized Live8, a chain of concerts around the world two decades on from Live Aid that would focus attention on the momentous decisions being taken. Kofi Annan and Bill Gates appeared on the stage in London, but sadly did not team up to sing their own version of 'Islands In The Stream'.

Across the country hundreds of thousands of campaigners demanded that world leaders 'Drop the debt!', and the government rather took the wind out of their sails by saying, 'OK then.' The entire $40 billion owed by the eighteen most indebted countries was written off following intensive preparation by Gordon Brown, who early in Labour's first term had taken a lead in cancelling Third World debt. It was a small price to pay not to have to be lobbied by Bono any more. By 2006 Britain spent more on overseas aid than any country except the United States. In Tony Blair's final year, he even appeared in a Comic Relief sketch and reminded everyone what a good actor he was,* which was rather disconcerting for everyone thinking back over the years when he had seemed so sincere about everything.

The momentous achievements of Blair and Brown in the area of international development and debt cancellation never received the acknowledgement they deserved, perhaps because the effects are so difficult to measure, and because good deeds never sustain an extended news narrative in the same way as a controversy.

For all the accusations about 'spin', the government failed to control the news agenda as effectively as they might have done with a little more effort. To drag out the positive news stories as long as possible, the Labour Party should have faked huge internal battles, with resignations, sackings and last-minute deals, until an exhausted Tony Blair came out of Downing Street at midnight, his shirt-sleeves rolled up, to announce that, yes, they had finally got a deal on parental leave for new fathers. While in the background could be heard a barrage of boos and catcalls from a small group of hostile dads who were desperate to get back to the office as soon as possible.

The long goodbye

A leaked memo revealed that Downing Street had wanted some

---

* Tony Blair had previously done the voice for his own appearance on *The Simpsons*, when Homer had recognized him as 'Mr Bean'.

eye-catching media highlights for Tony Blair's final year. None of the suggestions included him becoming the first Prime Minister to be questioned by the police during the course of an investigation. Detectives were responding to claims that the main political parties had accepted large loans from donors who were subsequently recommended for political honours. Fortunately the old bill did not kick in the door to 10 Downing Street at five o'clock in the morning and drag the suspect out of bed in his grubby boxer shorts while his Scouse wife swore at them, sobbing that 'my Tony never done nothing'. Despite a long investigation, no charges were ever brought, but rather disappointingly the chief investigating officer was not given a peerage, a knighthood and an OBE immediately afterwards.

The protracted scandal contributed to the general sense that Tony Blair was a tainted brand and that Labour's poll rating might improve under a new leader. There is also an immutable rule of politics that once a party has been in power for so long that it cannot remember life in opposition, then it conjures up an internal opposition of its own. The damaged egos of ex-ministers and the frustrated ambitions of overlooked talents will eventually accumulate to drown out the people in charge.

As the tenth anniversary of New Labour's election approached, Tony Blair risked losing control of the timetable for his own departure. Labour had fared badly in the 2006 local elections, and a brutal reshuffle saw demotions for a number of the big beasts in the cabinet. The Brown* camp felt that their man had been sitting in the waiting room at 10 Downing Street for quite long enough and in September 2006 there were a number of resignations

---

* The simmering hostility between the Brown and Blair camps broke through the surface at the Labour Party conference. In his speech Brown declared that he was proud to have served under Tony Blair and Cherie Blair was overheard saying, 'Well that's a lie.' In his own speech Blair said, 'Well at least I don't have to worry about her running off with the bloke next door.'

among junior ministers demanding that Blair name the date for his resignation (although the *Sun* had already helpfully announced it as 31 May 2007). Blair apologized to voters for the apparent warfare within the Labour Party and announced that he would not be Prime Minister by roughly the same time the following year.

The extended departure of Tony Blair then turned into a show-business farewell that would have put a James Brown finale to shame. Time and again, the Godfather of Social Democracy looked as if he was leaving the stage, his minders draping his cloak around him as he reluctantly shuffled off to the wings . . . but no! He had to do one more encore. He threw off his cloak and was back at the mic doing that old classic 'For The Many Not The Few'. Then he segued into a string of his all-time hits: 'New Labour; New Life For Britain', 'Britain Forward Not Back' and an extended remix of 'A Lot Done, A Lot More To Do' before heading for the wings and then coming back and doing it all over again.

There was a last conference speech, a last cabinet meeting, a last appearance in the House of Commons* and a final farewell staged in the Labour club in his constituency, where his political adventure had begun in the year when it had seemed like Labour would never hold office again. Before he became leader, Labour had lost four elections in a row. But Tony Blair led them to three victories on the trot, something never before achieved by the People's Party. Precisely which people's party it had become was open to debate; at least the Militant infiltrators had the honesty to sell their Trotskyist paper outside Labour Party meetings. The social democrat entryists had been more coy. By rights the Millbank Tendency should have clearly signalled their centrist

---

* At his final Prime Minister's Question Time, Tony Blair listed his engagements and appointments, as is traditional, saying, 'This morning I had meetings with ministerial colleagues and others, in addition to my duties in the House. I will have no such further meetings today – or any other day.'

middle-class agenda by standing outside meetings selling the Boden catalogue and shouting, 'Support the campaign for residents' parking!' 'Join Saturday's march to the garden centre!'

Although the living standards of the poorest had been raised during the Blair era, the gap between rich and poor had continued to grow. All the evidence is that this does not make for a happy and well-adjusted society. Crime, depression and debt are all fuelled by a pervading sense that we are failing unless we can match the material wealth of the richest people around us. Although the Bible clearly states that thou shalt not covet thy neighbour's ox, it didn't say anything about his BMW convertible and villa in Tuscany.

Blair's government did many great things, from the New Deal to Northern Ireland, from gay rights to cancelling Third World debt. And although it will probably go down as one of Britain's most effective post-war governments, some will look back and wonder whether as much was achieved as might have been possible, given New Labour's huge majority, the enormous well of political goodwill and the booming economy Tony Blair had the good luck to oversee. But on 27 June 2007, he had a quick look at the economic forecasts, discovered that 'credit crunch' was not a type of breakfast cereal and said, 'OK, Gordon, why don't you take it from here . . .'

Capitalism collapses; bank bosses rush to return bonuses

Between 2004 and 2006, US interest rates had risen from 1 per cent to 5.3 per cent, leaving many families in the poorer parts of America struggling to pay for the bare essentials, such as food, heating and an array of automatic rifles. Millions of low-income Americans who could barely afford the rent in their trailer park had been persuaded to sign up for mortgages on which the print saying 'your home may be at risk if you cannot keep up payments' was nowhere near as eye-catching as that picture of the proud and happy home-owner, mowing his front lawn as his laughing kids played with the Golden Retriever. The phrase 'sub-prime mortgage' entered the vocabulary as it became clear that a lot of greedy banks had given loans to millions of people whose credit rating was so poor they'd already been denied a card from Blockbuster Video.

Loans had been packaged together and sold on to other banks, who then bundled them in with other loans and sold them on again. Maybe if they could keep all these debts moving around indefinitely, nobody would notice that they weren't actually being repaid any more?

The first sign in Britain that something had gone badly wrong was when the Northern Rock bank asked the Bank of England for emergency financial support. The next day depositors withdrew £1 billion in what was the biggest run on a British bank for over a century. There were long queues outside every branch, which were mainly in the north, much to the annoyance of all the London financial correspondents who had to go all the way to Lancashire to report on them. Money continued to drain from the bank until the government stepped in to guarantee their savings. Before long Northern Rock would be nationalized along with a number of larger, more famous high street banks as the new Prime Minister took state control of a sector that even the post-war Attlee Labour government had thought was a nationalization too far. British socialists celebrated that the capitalist banks finally belonged to the people. It was a shame there was no actual money in them.

'No time for a novice'

Gordon Brown experienced a brief honeymoon as Prime Minister. In June 2007 the Queen had asked him if he would form a government and he thought about it for a minute and decided he might as well. He had been effectively unchallenged for the Labour leadership and enjoyed a summer of popularity as the electorate found his low-profile business-like manner a refreshing change to the spin-obsessed Prime Minister they believed had gone before. However, you only get credit for not trying to control the news agenda for a very short time. Soon after that, the news agenda is dominated by lots of negative stories in place of all those positive ones that used to pour from the Downing Street press office.

Brown's popularity was already fading by the time the depth of the financial crisis became apparent, and given that he had been at the Treasury for the previous ten years it was a bit difficult to find someone else to blame it all on. Soon the credit crunch had escalated into a full-scale international fiscal meltdown, followed by a parliamentary expenses scandal that left politicians lower in public esteem than at any time in living memory, followed by a European election that saw Labour's worst result since the Second World War. 'Prime Minister? Tony Blair's on the phone to ask how it's all going. Shall I tell him you're busy?'

It will be many years before we can gauge the long-term effects of the financial crisis that began in 2007 or make a judgement about the interventionist response of Gordon Brown that was followed by most other Western economies. No one will be able to criticize the government for standing by and doing nothing. Brown spent £500 trillion, billion, gazillion, marillion to prevent a full-scale 1930s-style depression. We as taxpayers lent the banks £550 billion, and are now entitled to send them rude letters and call them in for a patronizing telling off, in revenge for how mean they were to us when we were students.

We've been here before . . .

And so a story that began with Britain almost crippled by war loans in 1945 ends with the country even deeper in debt six decades later. The first massive overdraft was the result of a heroic fight against the most evil tyranny of modern times, during which everyone in society made enormous personal sacrifices. The second was the result of decades of greed and short-sighted materialism, the relentless pursuit of a lavish lifestyle far beyond our means. Our grandparents feared for a world in which totalitarianism might push civilization back into the new dark ages. Our fear is that we might be denied the opportunity to do quite as much shopping.

Britain is a transformed society from the exhausted and bombed-out nation of 1945. In the decades since the British Empire's 'finest hour', the Empire has disappeared and Britain and its people have changed perhaps more rapidly than at any time in its history. That titanic struggle guaranteed the British freedom from foreign tyranny, but there were other more subtle freedoms still waiting to be won.

Freedom of choice existed in law but not in practice. One half of the population was constrained in a society that was still deeply conservative in its attitude to women and the home. Women were patronized and stereotyped in a way that would be unacceptable today. Granted, some women had done essential services like driving trains on the London underground, but it didn't really work out because they kept edging forwards really slowly to make sure the train fitted through the gap. Today, such ridiculous stereotypes would not even be aired in public. The position of women has been transformed, although the battle for gender equality, like the struggle for racial equality, is still a work-in-progress. Just having Zeinab Badawi read the news doesn't mean we can tick off both boxes.

The population that celebrated the end of the Second World War was almost uniformly white. This was a people that had defeated fascism and racism but unthinkingly believed in the innate superiority of the white man. Despite the odd riot in places like Notting Hill in the 1950s and 1970s (and again in the 2000s when they realized David Cameron was moving there), the transformation of Britain into a multicultural society happened without the 'rivers of blood' predicted by Enoch Powell. Racism exists (and is getting worse in some parts of the country) but it is at nothing like the levels that have been experienced by French Arabs or the black population of the southern states of America.

There is a mobility within British society that was almost non-existent sixty years ago; now it is possible to be born poor and through your own talents and efforts, ~~steal all the gold at the Brinks Mat warehouse~~ diligently work your way up from the shop floor to the boardroom. An oppressively rigid class system has also been broken down, even if it has given way to a new aristocracy based on celebrity and wealth. New Labour's reform of the House of Lords seemed to miss this crucial point. Instead of replacing the old dukes and hereditary lordships with elected nobodies and worthy party nominees, the Upper House should have been packed out with the new aristocrats, such as his noble famousness David Beckham and Lady Posh of Spice. Parliamentary legislation could then have been scrutinized by the wise and respected counsel of Lady Winehouse of Oddbins or the Right Reverend Jeremy Kyle of Daytime.

There has been the technological and material transformation that has given us instant communication and unlimited information on everything except how to activate that free printer from

PC World. There has been the steady accumulation of labour-saving devices like washing machines and microwave ovens and a few labour-creating devices like the eco-briquette paper log maker. Most families own a car, can take a holiday abroad and are gradually paying for their own home complete with central heating, computers and a telly in every room so they don't have to actually talk to one another.

And of course, as any dinner-party bore will happily tell you, the entire country has been completely ruined by crass Americanization. There are so many ways that the culture and influence of the United States has invaded our lives, it is almost impossible even to begin to list them all. Bloody McDonalds, bloody shopping malls, bloody muzak, bloody stretch limos, bloody graffiti art, bloody traffic lights, bloody light bulbs, bloody personal computers, bloody air travel, bloody dishwashers, bloody transistor radios, mobile phones, credit cards, laser technology, smoke detectors, satellite navigation, rock and roll, decent coffee, fantastic films, brilliant novelists, bloody *choice*. I mean, there we were, perfectly happy with our 1949 polio epidemic and then the Yanks have to come over here with their fancy bloody vaccine.

Much of the lazy anti-Americanization in Britain is just grumpy old anti-*modernization*; changes that would have happened here anyway occurred in America first. It also provides a way for people who purport to be left wing actually to be reactionary and xenophobic. From Genghis Khan to the Spanish conquistadors, the world's most dominant powers in history have generally been brutal, immoral, murderous and corrupt. We are lucky to be living in an age dominated by a super-power that has an enlightened constitution, a belief in democracy and a generally observed belief in human rights. Those who moan about American values and interests dominating the globe should do their best to stick around a bit longer and see how much they like it when it's the Chinese government calling the shots.

Welcome to Britain

But despite a rapidly shrinking globe and American mono-culture seemingly enveloping the entire planet, Great Britain remains a unique and highly influential country, with an enduring national character and deeply embedded values that have survived the loss of empire, rapid industrial decline and thirty series of *Last of the Summer Wine*. Among the least corrupt countries in the world, the UK remains one of the most tolerant, fair-minded and safest places you could ever want to live. As long as you're not too friendly to your neighbour for the first five years, and you don't spill the pint of that big bloke with the spider's web tattoo on his neck, you should be fine.

It would be hard to explain to a new arrival exactly what to expect when they arrive in twenty-first-century Britain. But after thousands of years of confused immigrants putting too much Marmite on their toast or serving pints of beer almost two-thirds full, the government finally got round to producing a booklet outlining a few basics. *Life in the UK* is the official guide to British idiosyncrasies for those trying to make some sense of the cold, wet country they hope to make their home. Or you can get it on audio tape, which, on realizing you are foreign, shouts at you in slow, over-simplified English.

Since 2005, immigrants who have successfully applied to become British citizens get a formal ceremony to mark this enormous step in their life. In waiting rooms in town halls across the country sit a number of hopefuls, perhaps a refugee from war-torn Congo or a Ukrainian student who is marrying someone she met while studying here. Opposite them is a newly qualified Indian doctor and maybe an Australian bar worker who was just fed up with all that sunshine back home. They have all read the booklet and passed the multiple-choice test and are now feeling a little excited and nervous, about to make the formal oath that will admit them into their new extended family. All right, so the first application form got sent to the wrong office and the stroppy woman in reception couldn't find their file. That's all part of the assimilation process.

'I was a bit confused by that first question,' says the Ukrainian. 'You are in a train crash and other passengers are hurled across the carriage onto where you are sitting. Do you a) check that no one is seriously injured and then call the emergency services? Or b) say, "Oh, I'm terribly sorry, my fault completely"?'

'I was expecting a question about cricket,' says the Indian. 'I love cricket! I wanted to come to England. I wanted to see great cricket!'

'Well, make your mind up,' says the Australian.

'I just wanted somewhere safe for me and my family,' says the refugee. 'A friendly place where there is no civil war and there is food and shelter and proper medical care and we are safe from murder or torture.'

'But, er, no other reasons apart from that?'

And soon afterwards, each of them steps into the wood-panelled council chamber where a slightly outdated picture of the Queen looks down at them and the Union flag is propped up in the corner. In turn they pledge to fulfil their duties and obligations under the law and uphold the democratic values of Great Britain. 'Congratulations! You are now a British citizen!' says the council official conducting the ceremony and they smile as the room bursts into applause. And then they walk out into the streets of Britain to help create the next chapter in the history of the United Kingdom.

'After you,' says the person holding the door for them.

'No, please. After you . . .'

Bibliography

There are thousands of facts in this book that have been sifted from dozens of books and old newspapers, and about three very minor details that are original exclusives I have gleaned from talking to people who were close to the action at the time. I apologize now for any mistakes that may have slipped through the process of checking and re-checking, but in my defence, the errors are nowhere near as glaring as that left-wing 1983 manifesto that began, 'The next Labour government will . . .'

There were a number of websites that were incredibly useful, particularly when the history reached the point at which the events were reported at the time on the web. So a hat tip is due to the BBC's wonderful news website and its history site, as well as www.british-history.ac.uk and Wikipedia, where some of the more significant entries are now locked off, to prevent John Major going in and writing about how effective he was. The following list is not comprehensive, as I didn't want to admit to using my kids' GCSE textbooks.

Anderson, Bruce, *John Major: The Making of the Prime Minister* (London: Fourth Estate, 1991)

Bartlett, C. J., *A History of Postwar Britain 1945–1974* (London: Longman, 1977)

Benn, Tony, *Office Without Power: Diaries 1968–72* (London: Hutchinson, 1988)

Benn, Tony, *Against the Tide: Diaries 1973–76* (London: Hutchinson, 1989)

Benn, Tony, *Conflicts of Interest: Diaries 1977–80* (London: Hutchinson, 1990)

Benn, Tony, *Years of Hope: Diaries, Papers and Letters 1940–62* (London: Hutchinson, 1994)

Bernstein, George L., *The Myth of Decline: The Rise of Britain Since 1945* (London: Pimlico, 2004)

Boulton, Adam, *Memories of the Blair Administration: Tony's Ten Years* (London: Simon and Schuster, 2008)

Burk, Kathleen (ed), *The British Isles since 1945* (Oxford: Oxford University Press, 2003)

Campbell, Alastair, *The Blair Years: The Alastair Campbell Diaries* (London: Hutchinson, 2007)

Campbell, John, *Edward Heath: A Biography* (London: Cape, 1993)

Clarke, Peter, *Hope and Glory: Britain 1900–2000*, 2nd edition (London: Penguin, 2004)

Coopey, R., S. Fielding, N. Tiratsoo (eds), *The Wilson Governments, 1964–1970* (London: Pinter, 1993)

Cosgrave, Patrick, *The Strange Death of Socialist Britain: Post-war British Politics* (London: Constable, 1992)

Davies, Christie, *Permissive Britain: Social Change in the Sixties and Seventies* (London: Pitman, 1975)

Eatwell, Roger, *The 1945–1951 Labour Governments* (London: Batsford Academic, 1979)

Hattersley, Roy, *Fifty Years On: A Prejudiced History of Britain Since the War* (London: Little, Brown, 1997)

Healey, Denis, *The Time of My Life* (London: Michael Joseph, 1989)

Hennessy, Peter, *Never Again: Britain 1945–51* (London: Cape, 1992)

Hennessy, Peter, *Having It So Good: Britain in the Fifties* (London: Allen Lane, 2006)

Hernon, Ian, *The Blair Decade* (London: Politico's, 2007)

Hobsbawm, E. J., *Age of Extremes: The Short Twentieth Century, 1914–1991* (London: Michael Joseph, 1994)

Kynaston, David, *Austerity Britain 1945–51* (London: Bloomsbury, 2007)

Major, John, *John Major: The Autobiography* (London: HarperCollins, 1999)

Marr, Andrew, *A History of Modern Britain* (London: Macmillan, 2007)

Masters, Brian, *The Swinging Sixties* (London: Constable, 1985)

McKie, David and Chris Cook (eds), *The Decade of Disillusion: British Politics in the Sixties* (London: Macmillan, 1972)

Mercer, Derrik (ed), *Chronicle of the 20th Century* (London: Longman, 1988)

Morgan, Kenneth O., *Labour in Power, 1945–1951* (London: Clarendon Press, 1984)

Morgan, Kenneth O., *The People's Peace: British History 1945–1989* (Oxford: Oxford University Press, 1990)

Pelling, Henry, *The Labour Governments 1945–51* (London: Macmillan, 1984)

Pimlott, Ben, *Harold Wilson* (London: HarperCollins, 1992)

Sandbrook, Dominic, *Never Had It So Good: A History of Britain from Suez to The Beatles* (London: Little, Brown, 2005)

Sandbrook, Dominic, *White Heat: A History of Britain in the Swinging Sixties* (London: Little, Brown, 2006)

Seldon, Anthony (ed), *Blair's Britain 1997–2007* (Cambridge: Cambridge University Press, 2007)

Sked, Alan and Chris Cook, *Post-War Britain: A Political History 1945–1992* (London: Penguin, 1993)

Toynbee, Polly and David Walker, *Did Things Get Better?* (London: Penguin, 2001)

Turner, Alwyn W., *Crisis? What Crisis? Britain in the 1970s* (London: Aurum Press, 2008)

Vinen, Richard, *Thatcher's Britain* (London: Simon and Schuster, 2009)

Wall, Stephen, *A Stranger in Europe: Britain and the EU from Thatcher to Blair* (Oxford: Oxford University Press, 2008)

Wheatcroft, Geoffrey, *The Strange Death of Tory England* (London: Penguin, 2005)

Williams, Charles, *Harold Macmillan* (London: Weidenfeld and Nicolson, 2009)

Williams, Hywel, *Guilty Men: Conservative Decline and Fall, 1992–1997* (London: Aurum Press, 1998)

Williamson, Bill, *The Temper of the Times: British Society Since World War II* (Oxford: Blackwell, 1990)

Wilson, Harold, *Memoirs: The Making of a Prime Minister 1916–64* (London: Weidenfeld and Nicolson and Michael Joseph, 1986)

Young, Hugo, *One of Us* (London: Macmillan, 1989)

Acknowledgements

I would like to thank the wonderful staff of the London Library where much of this book was researched and written. I would also very much like to thank Bill Scott-Kerr, Georgia Garrett, Pete Sinclair, Sarah Whitfield, Mari Roberts, Tim Goffe and the late Laurie Rowley. But most of all Jackie, Freddie and Lily O'Farrell for putting up with me disappearing to work during holidays and weekends, and for the way that the dates of the Cod Wars seemed to displace any memory of the dates of family arrangements I had been told a couple of hours earlier.

Index